ENGLAND IN 1815

ENGLAND IN 1815
A CRITICAL EDITION OF
THE JOURNAL OF JOSEPH BALLARD

Edited by Alan Rauch

ENGLAND IN 1815
Copyright © Alan Rauch, 2009.

All rights reserved.

First published in 2009 by PALGRAVE MACMILLAN® in the United States—a division of St. Martin's Press LLC, 175 Fifth Avenue, New York, NY 10010.

Where this book is distributed in the UK, Europe and the rest of the world, this is by Palgrave Macmillan, a division of Macmillan Publishers Limited, registered in England, company number 785998, of Houndmills, Basingstoke, Hampshire RG21 6XS.

Palgrave Macmillan is the global academic imprint of the above companies and has companies and representatives throughout the world.

Palgrave® and Macmillan® are registered trademarks in the United States, the United Kingdom, Europe and other countries.

ISBN-10: 0-230-60148-0
ISBN-13: 978-0-230-60148-2

Library of Congress Cataloging-in-Publication Data

Ballard, Joseph, 1789–1877.
 [England in 1815 as seen by a young Boston merchant]
 England in 1815 : a critical edition of The journal of Joseph Ballard / edited by Alan Rauch.
   p. cm.
 Originally published: Boston : Houghton Mifflin, 1913 as: England in 815 as seen by a young Boston merchant.
 Includes bibliographical references and index.
 ISBN 0-230-60148-0
 1. England—Social life and customs—19th century. 2. Americans—England—History—19th century. 3. Ballard, Joseph, 1789–1877—Travel. 4. England—Description and travel. I. Rauch, Alan. II. Title.

DA625.B2 2008
942.07'3—dc22   2008024443

A catalogue record of the book is available from the British Library.

Design by Scribe Inc.

First edition: January 2009

10 9 8 7 6 5 4 3 2 1

Printed in the United States of America.

Contents

Preface		vii
General Chronology of Ballard's Voyage to England		xiii
Introduction to *England in 1815*		1
The Journal of Joseph Ballard		25
Appendix A	The Treaty of Ghent	111
Appendix B	Vauxhall	115
Appendix C	Labor Conditions	121
Appendix D	Monarchy, Regency, and Politics	127
Appendix E	Cab Fares and Street Life	133
Appendix F	Celebrating the Defeat of Napoleon ["Boney"]	137
Appendix G	British Currency	139
Notes		141
Bibliography		201
Index		209

Sites visited, or referred to, by Ballard during his travels in England and Wales.

Preface

One of the most serious counterbalances to the pleasure of travelling is that after having formed an acquaintance with those whom you would esteem through life you are obliged to part, and this without a hope of ever again meeting them!

—Joseph Ballard

Although Joseph Ballard's reflections about the pleasures of travel are familiar to anyone who has undertaken a journey of substance, his wistful observations about parting with friends has particular resonance to his memoir, which has itself travelled a very irregular path. Just as many of Ballard's acquaintances in England were never renewed or refreshed, his memoir describing those acquaintances has twice disappeared, leaving very little hope of readers meeting them again. Ballard's journal, never published in his lifetime, languished forty years after his death until his family, working with the Boston publisher Houghton Mifflin in 1913, arranged to have them printed in a limited edition of 525. Since then, in spite of its estimable qualities, Ballard's book has been all but forgotten.[1]

Whether the first publication of the book was intended for consumers in general or for the extended descendants of the Ballard family is not clear, nor is there any evidence, if they were sold generally in local bookstores, how well the book fared. Even with such a small printing, Ballard's narrative managed to find its ways to a variety of libraries and used bookstores in both the United States and England. It was in one such bookstore, in Cambridge, England, that I came across the neatly slip cased volume with a "tipped in" label on the spine that simply read "England in 1815/Ballard." It was a good day as book buying goes because what I found was a wonderfully lucid and engaging narrative told by an unpretentious and energetic young American merchant, someone who almost seemed like a friend.

Here, in this relatively brief but richly detailed book, was a fresh look at England, written not by an established author and not by someone who, after having received classical training at Harvard or Yale, was eager to flaunt his erudition. Instead, Ballard was simply traveling to restore business relationships that surely declined during the War of 1812, which had ended only months earlier and, for whatever reason, he left a journal of that voyage. He is clearly excited at the prospect of traveling and is deeply curious about England, the country from which the United States had only revolted less than forty years earlier. For Bostonians, like Ballard, and more specifically for many Federalists (from whom Ballard distances himself), the renewal of hostilities with Britain, however complicated the reasons, seemed not only unnecessary but an impediment to economic growth.

Interestingly enough, although Ballard is certainly engaged by economic issues while in England, he mentions business only rarely. Though economic historians might regret the absence of what could have been an interesting mercantile adventure, the very fact that the memoir owes its existence to trade is engaging in its own right. It is also interesting how distanced Ballard seems to feel from England, which some readers, and I confess to having been one of them, might have expected to have been framed as the "mother country," a term Ballard clearly considers suspect and uses only once, late in the book. Ballard thus demonstrates an American sensibility that is free from any nostalgia or sentimentality and is certainly free of any regrets about the past or any awkwardness about being American.[2] Rather, Ballard consumes the English experience wholesale, if you will, and distills it for his readers in a detailed manner that reflects genuine learning, curiosity, and excitement.

It struck me that this view of England, at a critical point in British history, would be a wonderful resource to make available to *anyone* interested in what is generally called the late Georgian period, which comprehended everything from Napoleon to Jane Austen to the War of 1812. The Georgian period takes its name from the succession of Georges who served as English monarchs, concluding with George IV who, in 1815, ruled as "Prince Regent" while his father, King George III, a victim of porphyria, was slipping ever more seriously into madness and eventually death. The significance of this era—known for Romanticism, for Regency style and politics, for Dandyism, for scandal and moral decline, and for the quiet emergence of the young Queen Victoria—cannot be underestimated.

My objective in bringing Ballard's memoir back into print is to provide students, scholars, and simply interested readers with a firsthand account of life in England, particularly London, in the early nineteenth century. I hope that all readers will be excited by the fact that this is a work that will be new to virtually everyone who comes across it. I also hope that they will agree that this narrative was lost to posterity, not for lack of merit, but because it fell outside the traditional canon of high literary texts. Now, almost one hundred years later, Ballard's memoir will resonate, I believe, with modern critical interests in material culture, social ethnography, and noncanonical historical perspectives. Ballard gives us a feel for daily life in an era we typically try to understand through the remarkable literary contributions of the Romantic era or the complicated political history of the Regency. That's not to say that both conventional approaches to the literature and history of the time are not critical to this work, but rather that both will be made clearer and more accessible by having read Ballard.

To that end, I have tried to complement Ballard's original text (at least as it appears in the 1913 Houghton Mifflin edition) with materials that, rather than distract from Ballard's writing, will help the reader make sense of the context and background of Ballard's work. In addition to the ensuing introduction, which provides a necessarily compressed discussion of historical, literary, and cultural background of 1815, the text is annotated throughout. Original footnotes (now moved to the endnotes) from the 1913 edition are identified by enclosure in brackets. Restraint, when annotating a text, does not come easy, and while the endnotes that I have provided cover a lot of ground, they try to help a wide range of readers (of varying expertise) negotiate the world of 1815. The reader who chooses to ignore them entirely can easily enjoy Ballard's memoir in spite of them. However, if the reader chooses to consult the notes, my hope is that the annotations will successfully introduce interesting and useful dimensions to the text.

Throughout the body of the text, I adhered to the conventions and spelling in the 1913 Houghton Mifflin publication of Ballard's journal. The inconsistencies in that text, which sometimes use English spelling and sometimes American and, at times, capitalizes words that are later in lowercase, may or may not be exactly transcribed from the original Ballard manuscript, but rather than modernize the text, it seemed appropriate to defer to the only text that is available. A number of early reviewers did express concern, however, that the original journal entry dates in the text were difficult to follow. To remedy that problem, I have complemented Ballard's references to individual dates by adding, in brackets, the day of the week and the month.

I have also tried to provide helpful illustrations from sources roughly contemporary with Ballard's visit, and the reader will also find a map at the outset, depicting the places Ballard visited in England. It was impossible to map out Ballard's itinerary, which, on occasions, seemed a little haphazard, so I have provided a chronology of his visit instead. Finally, the reader will find appendices that may have items that are either helpful or interesting, including a review of British currency and an extract from the Treaty of Ghent.

The process that led to this reprint of Ballard's work has been challenging at times but always very exciting. First and foremost, I owe a debt of thanks to Palgrave Macmillan, which agreed to undertake this project, and to Christopher Chappell in particular. I have imposed on Chris's patience and understanding far too many times, and on each occasion, he has responded in a way that indicated his remarkably even temperament as well as his unflagging confidence in this book.

I have also imposed on many readers to look at the original manuscript as well as the manuscript in progress. In particular, I'd like to thank William Galperin for his insights and comments, all of which helped improve this book. On many occasions, his quick and sharp wit was more important to me than I can express. Frances Ferguson has been very supportive in this and other projects dealing with the early nineteenth century. I feel very fortunate to be able to count on her friendship and her encouragement. My friend and former colleague, Greg Nobles, deserves more thanks than I can offer here. He was instrumental in helping me understand the American historical perspective in the early nineteenth century and did so gracefully, without ever mocking my Canadian roots and, thus, my woeful lack of American history. I have also relied heavily on the genuine kindness and support of other colleagues, including George Levine, William Keach, Kirk Melnikoff, Jennifer Munroe, Richard Grusin, Alice Jenkins, and, on details about the British navy, H. J. K. Jenkins.

I would be remiss if I didn't acknowledge the important encouragement I received from family and friends, including Jared and Audrey Rorrer, Shannon Randall, Helen Hull, Riva Rauch, Joyce Rauch, Carol and Amos Dykeman, Diane Leaghty, Wayne Kirschbaum, Itzik Pripstein, Deborah Childers, Patricia O'Hara, Anna Olswanger, and Pamela Paris. Coren O'Hara, whose interest in the book has been very helpful and heartening, warrants special appreciation.

While working on this project, I have drawn on the comments and feedback of many extraordinary students at the University of North Carolina (UNC) at Charlotte, including the graduate students in my "Regency England" seminar, all of whom read and commented on Ballard's memoir. These include Khaled Alkoor, Jennifer Armour,

Matthew Brown, Michael Avery, Rachel Brown, Sarah Blackwell, Antara Das, Scott Faile, Ashley Mattei, Amanda McGuire, and Amy Puckett.

A number of other students who were willing to take time to read and comment on the Ballard text were Sam Nicolosi, Elizabeth Caruso, and Kalie Hairston.

Among the students, I have to single out Rachel Brown, who brought a keen intellect, informed curiosity, and a precise eye to this project. I owe her a debt of gratitude for voluntarily taking on the challenges of looking at a manuscript in various unfinished states. The book has benefited greatly because of Rachel's tenacity, engagement, and honesty.

Kristy Lilas at Palgrave MacMillan helped keep this project on track and negotiated everyone involved through the heavy traffic of e-mail correspondence dealing with text, notes, illustrations, and every other element that went into this book. It has been a delight working with Jenn Kepler at Scribe who served as the project manager for this book. Jenn's keen eye for detail as well as her patience, humor, and intelligence have contributed to improving the book in ways that the reader may not see but will certainly appreciate.

I am grateful to Patrick Jones of UNC Charlotte's Department of Geography and Earth Sciences who prepared the map of England for this book and who patiently worked through countless drafts. Elizabeth Falsey, reader services librarian at Harvard's Houghton Library, remained patient throughout all of my inquiries about documents related to either Ballard or Crocker in the Houghton Mifflin archives. At UNC Charlotte, the interlibrary loan service, coordinated by Ann Davis, was remarkably helpful, as were additional resources pursued assiduously by Chuck Hamaker, associate university librarian for Collections and Technical Services.

I owe many thanks to Professor Robert Leitz, curator of the impressive James Smith Noel Collection at Louisiana State University in Shreveport. Some of the images in this book have been taken from that collection, and several were specifically photographed by Robert himself, who generously volunteered both time and effort. The resources at the UNC Chapel Hill Library, the Guildhall Library, the New York Public Library, and Charlotte's Mint Museum of Fine Arts were very important to my engagement with Ballard's text and some of the selected images from these collections will, I hope, be useful to the reader as well.

The Graduate School at UNC Charlotte, headed by Dean Thomas Reynolds, provided a very generous subvention grant for illustrations used in this book. I was also very fortunate to have been awarded a fellowship from the Gilder Lehrman Center for American History, which afforded me the opportunity to examine American and British documents related to the transatlantic history of 1815. I was also fortunate to receive a timely fellowship from the Boston Athenæum, which not only allowed me to peruse the history of private subscription libraries but to also augment my ongoing research for this book. The library of the Athenæum is truly an American treasure, and I must thank Richard Wendorf, Stanford Calderwood director and librarian of the Boston Athenæum, and the staff of the library for their support and for the opportunity to explore the collection.

Over the last twenty years, Amy Dykeman has been responsible for much of my education about American history and culture and has patiently shared my interest in British literature and culture. More important, her intelligence, warmth, and constant support have enriched my life in every way, and so I am delighted to dedicate this book to her.

Finally, I am grateful to Joseph Ballard who left to posterity a warm and engaging document that enriches our understanding of early nineteenth century England, of the early American Republic, and, to some extent, of Ballard himself. It is a privilege to be able to reintroduce him to readers on both sides of the Atlantic, who will, I hope, enjoy making his acquaintance as they share the pleasure of his travels.

General Chronology of Ballard's Voyage to England

Date	Location	Page
March 12	Boston	27
April 4	Encounter the *Musquito*	28
April 7	Arrive at Liverpool	29
April 8	Warrington	32
April 16	Sheffield	36
April 20	London, Covent Garden	39
April 22	London, Astley's Amphitheatre	44
April 23	London, Whitehall Chapel	45
April 24	London, Drury Lane	46
April 25	London, St. Paul's	46
April 28	Greenwich	47
April 29	London, Drury Lane	51
April 30	London, Chelsea Hospital	51
May 1	London, May Day, Westminster Abbey	52
May 4	London, Queen's levee	54
May 7	London Andrew's & Foundling's Hospital	55
May 8	London, British Museum	56
May 14	London, St. Catherine's Church	59
May 16–17	Travel North to Leeds	59
May 19	Outside of Leeds, Kirkstall Abbey	61
May 20	Leeds, Cloth Hall	62
May 21	Leeds, Church (Trinity Sunday)	62
May 22	Trip to Manchester via Rochdale	63
May 24	Manchester to Liverpool, Liverpool Theatre	64
May 25	Liverpool, Botanic Gardens	66
May 27	Liverpool, Herculaneum Pottery	67
May 28	Church and Servant's Hovel	68
May 30	Northwick, Salt Mines	69

General Chronology of Ballard's Voyage to England

Date	Location	Page
May 31	Chester	70
June 2	Warrington-Manchester via Peak District	71
June 11	Presbyterian Church	74
June 15	Departure for London via Stafforshire	75
June 17	London, Opera	76
June 20	London, Carlton House	78
June 22	London, Celebration of Victory at Waterloo	79
June 23–24	London, Waterloo Celebrations Continue	80
June 26	London, British Institution & Bullock's	80
June 27	London, Vauxhall	82
July 1	London, Drury Lane	84
July 2	Camberwell Grove	85
July 4	London, Dolly's Chop-House	85
July 7	London, Covent Garden	86
July 8	London, Synagogue	86
July 9	Camberwell Grove, Dr. Dodd's nephew	87
July 10	London, Smithfield & Strand Bridge	87
July 12	London, Prince Regent prorogues Parliament	87
July 13	London, Barker's Panorama & Lackington's Bookstore	88
July 16	London, St. Andrew's Church	89
July 17	Richmond Hill	89
July 18	London, Westminster Abbey	90
July 22	London, Haymarket Theatre	91
July 23	London, Highgate	91
July 30	Camberwell Grove, Church	93
July 31	London, East India House	93
August 6	Trip to Oxford via Kew & Windsor	95
August 7 (?)	Blenheim	97
August 8	Stratford	98
August 9	Liverpool	99
August 14	Winwick	101
August 16	Eaton House	102
August 17	Liverpool	104
September 8	Liverpool on Board	106
September 12	Weigh Anchor at Liverpool	107
November 9	Arrival in Boston	109

Introduction to *England in 1815*

In the waning days of March 1815, news arrived in England that could only have shocked Londoners and provincials alike: Napoleon Bonaparte had escaped from Elba and, as the *Times of London* reported, onlookers could only watch in "horror the reestablishment of that Monster in human shape, on his blood-stained throne."[1] Napoleon's return, which took place less than a year after his abdication on April 6, 1814, threatened to reignite a war that had already lasted eleven years (1803–1814) and reinforced British anxiety about the stability of France since the violent days of the French Revolution in 1789.

Almost at the same moment as Napoleon was making his way back to Paris, a confident, young Bostonian merchant named Joseph Ballard was taking advantage of the recent Treaty of Ghent, ending the conflict between England and the United States that we now call the War of 1812.[2] Eager to reinvigorate his business in rugs and carpeting, Ballard boarded the *Liverpool Packet*[3] along with several other New England merchants, completely unaware of Napoleon's resurgence. In fact, news traveled so slowly in those days that as the *Liverpool Packet* was crossing the Atlantic, it was detained by *The Musquito*, a British man-of-war whose captain was so behind in terms of recent events that he could only take it on faith that the war was actually over. To be on the safe side, lest he was still dealing with the enemy, he made certain the *Packet* was escorted by a flotilla until it reached its ultimate destination, the active port of Liverpool.

Although Ballard and his American shipmates were "cheerfully" received in Liverpool, concern about Napoleon's latest movements had to be brewing among both the citizens of Liverpool and members of the Royal Navy. It is difficult for contemporary readers to comprehend the sense of fear, anxiety, and simple astonishment that the British must have felt upon hearing of Napoleon's return to power. Ballard himself could not believe that Napoleon had actually escaped from Elba and thought that the British captain must have been testing his gullibility with a "a hoax which he was playing off on us Yankees." However, Napoleon was indeed on the run, and Ballard was in the fortunate position of being in Britain throughout "Napoleon's 100 Days," culminating on June 18, 1815, with the Battle of Waterloo, which historian Boyd Hilton characterizes as "the most publicly celebrated battle in English History" since Agincourt.[4]

Adding to the historical significance of 1815 was the fact that England was only four years into its Regency, a period that lasted until 1820, when George III finally died and the Prince Regent could assume the throne as of King George IV. Parliament reluctantly declared the Regency, which allowed the Prince of Wales (later George IV) to serve in place of his father, in 1811 when George III's fits of madness (the consequence of porphyria, a disorder with neurological consequences) rendered him unfit to rule. Even though George III had earlier bouts of illness, Parliament was slow to implement a regency because it meant that Prince George, his profligate and extravagant son, would assume power. At age fifty, Prince George (or "Prinny" as his critics called him) was hardly a dignified, never mind respected, individual, and he was typically caricatured as an overweight and self-indulgent buffoon more at ease with his mistresses than with Parliament or his people.

It was into this world that the young Joseph Ballard sailed. Though anything but naïve, he was still only twenty-six years old, and while hardly devoid of education, he was not, like so many other transatlantic travelers, college educated. Interestingly, Joseph Ballard Crocker, who undertook the first printing of the narrative in 1912, apologizes for his ancestor's lack of education. He wonders, if Ballard "had the advantage of modern educational methods," might he have "acquired a greater ability to express his thoughts"?[5] Whatever truth there is to this, Ballard's narrative is nothing if not thoughtful, observant, and articulate. In fact, there is reason to be grateful that this narrative was not written by someone who had to justify its value by freighting it with classical references and erudite musings produced by the educational system of the time. Instead, we have a very plainspoken memoir that traces Ballard's aesthetic, emotional, and intellectual responses to a culture that, despite ostensible familiarity, is clearly new to him. He brings both gravity and humor[6] into his narrative when needed and never dwells on either for the sake of effect. "Mr. Ballard tells his story well," wrote F. H. Allen[7] in his report on the manuscript, "in a plain gentlemanly style without flourishes."[8]

The history of Ballard's manuscript is uncertain. Ballard's descendant, George Uriel Crocker, secured a contract with Houghton Mifflin in 1912 for the publication of Ballard's memoir, probably with an eye to having it published on, or close to, its one hundredth anniversary. It is not clear whether Crocker, or even Houghton Mifflin, had an audience in mind beyond the community of Ballard descendants, but it was published "on commission," and so only 525 books were printed.[9] Joseph Ballard Crocker (1867–1955?), who wrote the introduction, may well have annotated the manuscript (indicated by the use of brackets in the endnotes of this edition). Some of the correspondence related to the contractual agreement with Houghton Mifflin is housed in the Harvard University Library, but nothing appears to remain of the manuscript itself. Thus it is impossible to tell how much, if any, editing of the original manuscript took place, but given Crocker's attentiveness to annotating the work and his comments about its style, it would appear that the text is faithful to the original manuscript. Though not widely reviewed after its publication, some periodicals did take note of its publication.[10]

The title of Ballard's work, *England in 1815*, may elicit a tiny bit of confusion for those familiar with this period because of the work of the great French historian Élie Halévy (1870–1937), whose magisterial four volume work, *A History of the English Peoples in the Nineteenth Century* (1913–1947), begins with *England in 1815*. Curiously enough, Halévy's book was published in France in 1913 (as *L'Angleterre en 1815*) exactly at the same time that Houghton Mifflin published Ballard's memoir. Beyond the coincidence of title and publication date, the two books could never be mistaken for each other, but it is worth mentioning if only to remind readers of this text of Halévy's valuable and detailed "case study" of this momentous year in English history. Halévy's study can be dated at times, but it is still remarkably readable and has remained influential as one of the great early examples of cultural history. Other books have followed, including most recently Boyd Hilton's impressive *A Mad, Bad, and Dangerous People?: England 1783–1846* and James Chandler's *England in 1819*, and we can anticipate many more books on the era. What they all speak to is the compelling fascination of the

Regency era, which transformed Great Britain[11] and even America, as Ballard himself surely felt and understood, in ways that we are still trying to grasp.

The "Regency"

Historical periods, which often owe more to convenience than logic, always have a number of confusing and often overlapping names, and it may be worth taking a moment to sort them out. The broadest designation for the period between 1714 and 1830 is the "Georgian Period" because it encompasses the reigns of George I, George II, George III, George IV.[12] The Georges are associated with the House of Hanover in Germany from which the fifty-four-year-old George I was plucked,[13] so to speak, to ensure a continuous reign of Protestant monarchs. Ballard's visit takes place in the latter part of that period, which literary historians designate the "Romantic Period." In Britain, that period is said to begin in 1798 with the publication of William Wordsworth's and Samuel Taylor Coleridge's collection of poems called *Lyrical Ballads*. The period represents a transition from the pure rationalism of the eighteenth century "enlightenment" to an era that engaged more abstract ideas about nature, matter, and human identity. Of course, the Industrial Revolution[14] was also taking place at this time, so it would be absurd to consider Romanticism without thinking about the rapid advances in technology and science. It is well worth noting that many scientists had little problem reconciling their research with the Romantic "spirit." The German writer, scientist, and philosopher Johann von Wolfgang Goethe (1749–1832) might be said to be a significant force behind this reconciliation, which in England included the celebrated chemist Humphry Davy (1778–1829); the discoverer of oxygen, Joseph Priestley (1733–1804); and the renowned physician and poet (and grandfather of Charles) Erasmus Darwin (1731–1802).[15]

The final term applied to this period is "The Regency," so called because of the need to replace King George III, who had been designated as mentally unfit to rule as monarch in 1811 (the fifty-first year of his reign). His son, the Prince of Wales, also named George, served in his father's place from 1811 to 1820, but as the actual king was still alive, George the son was designated the Prince Regent. In 1820, when George III died, the younger George could become monarch rather than regent and thus ruled as George IV until his own death in 1830. If we go strictly by numbers, the official Regency only lasted nine years, but the term has come to represent a cultural ethos in early nineteenth century England, which might be said to date as far back as 1788, when George III had a bout of madness significant enough for English politicians to consider implementing a regency.[16]

Regency Style

In spite of the fact that the Regency was distinctive for self-indulgence, dandyism, and reckless spending, the term itself has come to represent—even to this day—the notion of elegance and style that were a by-product of lives led in extravagance. This contradiction, if it is one, though prevalent was epitomized in a single person, and that was Beau Brummell (1778–1840).[17] Born in reasonably affluent circumstances, Brummell attended both Eton and Oxford, where he apparently cut an admirable figure and developed his penchant for "high style." With an inheritance of £20,000 at merely sixteen years old (in 1794, when his father died), Brummell had the financial wherewithal to support an elegant lifestyle in the company of the Prince Regent. Notwithstanding some of the more outrageous outfits worn by other men of fashion, such as Lord Alvanley (1789–1849), Frederick Gerald "Poodle" Byng (1784–1871), and, particularly, Sir Lumley Skeffington (1771–1850), Brummell's style was understated, consisting of beautifully tailored fabrics in relatively muted tones. It is said that Brummell was responsible for what has become the conventional men's suit and simple black for evening wear, what we now call "white tie and tails." Still, Brummell's excesses, including the claim that it took him five hours to dress and that he polished his boots with champagne, set him apart even among "fashionable" men.

Perhaps the best place to find dandies in London was at Almack's, an elegant club in the affluent St. James district, which also admitted women. It was here that other vices, such as gaming (gambling) were indulged, and controversial pastimes (such as the waltz) were explored. Other clubs existed in London, and much of London's culture was emulated in Bath, where, as Jane Austen's novels reveal, a shabbier—or perhaps a faux—set of dandies and ladies of fashion might be found. In *Northanger Abbey*,[18] for example, John Thorpe—a thorough imposter—attempts desperately to impress

Catherine Moreland with his horsemanship, his vehicle (a used gig), his cavalier attitude toward wealth and station, and, finally, his generous use of "cant"[19] in everyday speech.

Fashion among women included muslin[20] dresses that ranged from demure to risqué, depending on how diaphanous the material was allowed to be and how much of the bust was revealed. Even in the plainest of clothing, dresses were marked by a very high waistline and contours that offered a natural, if not revealing, silhouette. Fashion, and design in general, also reflected Egyptian influences stemming from the occupation of Egypt by the French and, subsequently, the English.[21]

One of George IV's lasting legacies is the architectural impact of the projects he arranged, most significantly, in London. George had many ambitious plans for London, and he relied heavily on the architect John Nash (1752–1835), who had a modest reputation for designing country houses with the great landscape architect Humphry Repton (1752–1818). Nash was eager to design structures that brought a neoclassical elegance to London's hodgepodge of architectural style; the elegantly curved and still fashionable Regent Street, with its uniform façade, is perhaps the best example of Nash's vision. Nash's work was complemented by major contemporary projects including Sir John Soane's (1753–1837) Bank of England and Robert Smirke's (1781–1876) British Museum.

Travelers in England and Their Narratives

Among the prominent early American tourists to England was the scientist Benjamin Silliman (1779–1884), a chemist from Yale who visited England (1805–1806).[22] Another interesting narrative is by Louis Simond[23] (1767–1831) who, though born in France, emigrated to the United States and established a business in New York. In 1809, he traveled to England and published his memoirs two years later. Simond's observations often anticipate those of Ballard, yet Simond's visit takes place at the height of financial, social, and political instability, as the Napoleonic Wars continued to escalate. In the final analysis, Simond reads the English social political landscape through a French lens, speculating whether the kind of revolutionary unrest that has turned France into the tool of Napoleon's ambitions could ever exist in England. Simond concludes that he does not "conceive it possible for some of the horrible scenes of the French Revolution to be acted [in England]," where the people are "more disposed to be just," yet English extravagance, especially during these hard times, is hard for Simond to understand. "The propensity to luxury and ostentation is so strong," he observes, "as well as so general here, as to expose this same sense of justice to hard trials" (168).

There are a number of later American narratives, including James Fenimore Cooper's *Gleanings in Europe*[24] (1837), Calvin Colton's *A Voice from America to England* (1839)[25], D. W. Bartlett's *What I Saw in London Or, Men and Things in the Great Metropolis* (1852),[26] and Andrew Bigelow's (1795–1877) *Leaves from a journal; or, Sketches of rambles in North Britain and Ireland* (1824).[27] Each of these subsequent memoirs sheds fascinating insights on early nineteenth century England, to say nothing of Ballard's own experiences, yet they are distant enough from 1815, the year of Ballard's writing, to warrant caution in making direct comparisons. Historians have also found *A Residence at the Court of London*, the memoirs of Richard Rush (1780–1859)—the attorney who, in 1817, replaced John Quincy Adams[28] as minister to Britain. Rush's observations are fascinating, but as a diplomat, he is more than circumspect. In his first meeting with the Prince Regent, then fifty-six years old, he signals his impressions of the Regent but refrains from risking even the slightest political faux pas. "It would be out of place in me," Rush comments dryly, "to portray the exterior qualities of this monarch."[29]

One of the most unusual touristic memoirs of England was that of Robert Southey (1774–1843), the Romantic poet (later poet laureate) who, under the guise of the pseudonym Don Manuel Alvarez Espriella, offered a description and critique of early nineteenth century England from the perspective of a visitor from Spain.[30] In what is a fairly lengthy work, Southey ostensibly uses his disguise to offer a distanced view of his own culture, although the narrative is equally telling about his own views of Catholic Spain. Even more striking is Southey's irrepressible (if often ambivalent) pride in his own country, which emerges throughout his narrative. After meditating upon the penchant among the English for plum pies at Christmas time, he digresses easily on the virtues of his native country:

> Perhaps no kingdom ever experienced so great a change in so short a course of years, without some violent state convulsion, as England has done during the present reign. I wish I could procure materials to show the whole contrast:—A metropolis doubled in extent; taxes quintupled; the value of money depreciated as rapidly as if new mines had been discovered; canals cut from one end of the island to the other; travelling made so expeditious that the internal communication is

tenfold what it was; the invention of the steam-engine, almost as great an epocha as the invention of printing; the manufacturing system carried to its utmost point; the spirit of commerce extended to every thing; an empire lost in America, and another gained in the East.[31]

Having made his point, he slips back into character in the following chapter, offering a critical view of the taxation on cards and dice "avowedly for the purpose of discouraging card-playing," when, in fact, "the lottery is one of the Ways and Means of the Government." Although Southey would eventually be criticized, after his appointment as poet laureate, for being a pawn of the establishment, his *Letters* reflect the ability to reconcile an indomitable pride for England while simultaneously expressing contempt for many of its social and political practices.

Another early native traveler was the antiquarian Sir Richard Colt Hoare (1759–1838),[32] whose journals outline travels through Wales and England from 1793 to 1810. Hoare, in his effort to take in as many historical sites and picturesque sites in England (including "Tinterne" [*sic*] Abbey, whose interior "is unique" and "not to be equaled in this kingdom"[33]), also captures the rise of industrialism in many English and Welsh towns.[34] Even before Hoare and Southey, Daniel Defoe (1659–1731) wrote his *Tour Through the Whole Island of Great Britain* (1724–1726), in which he offered a view of the newly formed Great Britain (produced by the Act of Union in 1707 by unifying England with Scotland). Although hints of an industrialized Briton, in cities such as Leeds, appear in Defoe's work, his narrative captures a country that retains a more bucolic feel. It's also worth noting the work of Defoe's contemporary, Celia Fiennes (1662-1741), whose diary *Through England on a Side Saddle*, though not published until 1888, describes her travels in northern England and Scotland.

The desire to visit England in the early nineteenth century and to see London in particular was widespread. London, after all, was the largest city in Europe at the time and served as a major center for commerce.[35] It is not surprising, therefore, to find guidebooks to help tourists negotiate their way through the London metropolis and the more noteworthy sights of the countryside. The enterprising John Feltham, for example, published on an annual basis (and ostensibly updated each year) *The Picture of London, Being a Correct Guide to All the Curiosities, Amusements, Exhibitions, Public Establishments, and Remarkable Objects, in and Near London*.[36] Feltham's guide, replete with maps and illustrations, was eventually taken over by John Britton (1771–1857), and it went through twenty-seven editions from its initial appearance in 1802 until 1833.[37] Feltham also covered a variety of other popular locations in England with his *Guide to all the Watering and Sea-Bathing Places: with a Description of the Lakes; a Sketch of a Tour in Wales; and Itineraries*, which remained in print from 1802 to 1824.[38]

Guidebooks are only a fraction of the poems, plays, and illustrated memoirs that provide valuable insights into early nineteenth century England. Pierce Egan (1772–1849), a journalist of boxing and sporting life, turned his attention to a world of fops and dandies in his very popular *Life in London, or The Day and Night Scenes of Jerry Hawthorn Esq. and his Elegant Friend Corinthian Tom* (1821). Though hardly a literary masterpiece, it remains an important chronicle of Regency attitudes and culture.[39] Two other significant books, valuable both for both text and illustrations, are *The Microcosm of London*—published in 1808 by Rudolf Ackermann (1764–1834)[40] and illustrated by Thomas Rowlandson (1756–1827) and Augustus Pugin (1762–1832)—and Thomas Shepherd's (1792–1864) *Metropolitan Improvements*[41] (1827), which depicts the impact of Regency architecture on the city.[42] Baron D'Haussez (Charles Lemercker de Longpré), who served as Minister of Marine (Secretary of the Navy) under Charles X, offers a detailed and quite candid view of the United Kingdom in his *Great Britain in 1833*.[43] It may also be worth noting the journals of two later German visitors, Prince Hermann Pückler-Muskau (1775–1881), who visited from 1826–1828,[44] and Freidrich Raumer, who wrote *England in 1835, A Series of Letters Written to Friends in Germany during a Residence in London and Excursions to the Provinces*. The two authors would eventually be lampooned by Charles Dickens in the figure of Pickwick Papers's Count Smorltork, "The famous foreigner—gathering materials for his great work on England."[45] Smorltork, whose comprehension of English is sketchy at best, plans his "great work" on experiences, as Pickwick discovers, drawn from little more than two weeks in the country.

American Identity and England in Nineteenth Century

Ballard's departure for England occurred almost forty years after the American Revolution and, needless to say, even by 1776, many families had been well established in the American colonies for decades.

Thus while there is a temptation to retain a perspective of England as the old "mother country," as many scholars were wont to do, it seems clear, even amongst the Federalists, that any sense of longing for England was essentially replaced by the assertion of American self-will in the early nineteenth century. Thus it is not surprising that Royall Tyler's *The Contrast* (1787), which is considered the first original American dramatic production, is a study of the differences in British and American social conventions. Tyler, a Harvard educated Bostonian who fought with the Continental Army, makes it clear in his play that America has emerged as a distinctive society and exorts, through the central character Colonel Manly, to recognize that "probity, virtue, honour, though they should not have received the polish of Europe, will secure an honest American the good graces of his fair countrywomen, and . . . the applause of the public."[46]

Of course, the War of 1812, which saw a renewal of tensions between England and America, was a pivotal time in the formation of American identity because it represented the final major hostility with England and established America's steadfastness and immovability on issues concerning trade and self-determination. The very fact of the war itself was divisive with the United States. It became a pivotal issue between the Republican movement of the South, headed by Thomas Jefferson and James Madison who asserted American independence and believed it needed to be defended and asserted at all costs. On the other side was the Federalist movement, centered in the northern states, but particularly in Massachusetts and Connecticut, where commercial trade with England was critical to the livelihoods of so many merchants.

The Federalists were not merely concerned about their own financial future; they were disturbed by the possibility that the Republican aggression and obstinacy would land them in a prolonged conflict with potentially disastrous economic consequences. To that end, local leaders began to generate politically driven groups that ultimately led to the Hartford Convention, which, simply put, explored possibilities of secession with the United States. Representatives of the convention were on their way to Washington to attempt to renegotiate the status of the northern states within the union when news of the Treaty of Ghent emerged, obviating the purpose of their mission.

Though often forgotten in general American history and not touched upon directly by Ballard, the Hartford Convention underscored the intensity of feelings in the United States. Those feelings were not necessarily constructed on a love for Great Britain, but rather in the recognition that Britain was inevitably America's primary trading partner and the key to American financial growth and prosperity. Ballard himself, though undoubtedly descended from English stock, expresses curiosity about England but, notwithstanding that his family could only be several generations removed from England, he shows little or no emotional attachment. For him it is essentially a foreign country—familiar in many ways, yet strange and removed in others.

Entertainment

Of all of London's attractions, it is not surprising that theatre was most appealing to Ballard. Theatrical performances offered wonderful entertainment especially for a youthful tourist, but the quality of the dramatic productions themselves were often marginal at best. The Regency is not an era remembered for great dramatists, but it was known for its great performers. Sarah Siddons (1755–1831), who officially retired in 1812, still cast a long shadow in the theatre world. Edmund Kean (1787–1833) was often considered as the greatest male dramatic performer since David Garrick (1717–1779), especially after his scintillating performance as Shylock at Drury Lane in 1814. This was also the heyday for the comic actors, and while history may not have been kind to individuals like John Liston, Joseph Munden, or Charles Matthews, they were wildly admired in their time. Perhaps the most revered comic actor was Joseph Grimaldi (1778–1837). Born in England to an Italian immigrant performer, Grimaldi acted in pantomimes and was wonderfully acrobatic. He created a persona on stage: a clown who, covered in greasepaint and dressed in outrageous costumes, astonished audiences with extravagant acts of humor. Indeed the figure of Grimaldi captivated Charles Dickens, who not only loved the theatre but who, in his own right, created dozens of remarkable, though literary, clowns. Devoted to preserving the memory of Grimaldi, Dickens took up his life and compiled his memoirs.[47]

The major theatres in London were Covent Garden, Drury Lane, and the Haymarket. These all held royal charters, which meant that they could mount fully dramatic production like the plays of Shakespeare. Other theatres could not produce dramas but instead looked to opera and pantomimes. The Haymarket's charter allowed it to host drama only during the summer when both Drury Lane and Covent Garden were dark. Theatrical performances, which generally consisted of a serious production in five acts, were typically followed by a pantomime or musical entertainment in two acts. The theatres opened their doors again after the third act of the drama and admitted customers at reduced rates. Among the late arrivals were prostitutes obviously confident of finding a ready clientele in the audience. Thus plays typically began in the early evening and lasted for two or more hours before patrons moved on to dinner and other entertainment, such as the dances and festivities at Vauxhall Gardens.[48]

COMMERCE

England, in the early nineteenth century, was a compelling place, particularly for commercial tourists. New technologies and factory production were emerging in a variety of industries ranging from the production of steel in Birmingham to the manufacture of wool and cotton in Leeds and Manchester. The introduction of steam power in general, particularly power looms, increased English productivity dramatically and also led to dissatisfaction among laborers, who saw technology stealing away their jobs. As a consequence, many laborers would try to destroy power looms and became known as frame breakers or—drawing on the so-called leader of the group, Ned Ludd—"luddites."[49] Although there was no dearth of malevolent factory owners who warranted serious opposition, there were few individuals who tried to ease the burden for workers. Foremost among these was Robert Owen, who, as one of the principle owners of the mills in New Lanark, attempted to create a "socialist" factory community in which children would be educated and workers receive health care. New Lanark was successful for decades, although when Owen tried to export his utopian ideas to the United States in the community of New Harmony, Indiana, he found a great deal of resistance.

While the royal family was living the "high" life, Britons in general were struggling with military conflict, unemployment, and the rising cost of food. Even British currency was a subject of tension.[50] Paper currency did not yet exist, but individual banks were permitted to issue "notes," which, like contemporary paper currency, were meant to represent a sum of money ostensibly held by the bank itself in gold bullion. The prevailing question was, however, whether banks did, in fact, need to have enough gold bullion to back up every note they issued. The so-called bullionists, lead by the great British economic theorist David Ricardo, argued that they should, whereas the anti-bullionists (perhaps looking to growth and expansion) argued that such measures were not necessary. What brought the question to a head was a 1797 scare that Napoleon had landed in England, causing holders of banknotes to demand the value of their note in gold, which, unlike paper, would retain value under any subsequent political turmoil. It is fascinating that one of Ballard's first observations is of Jewish merchants, who—uncertain not merely of the times but of their own status in English culture—inquired almost immediately whether he and his American shipmates had any gold to trade.

Visual Culture

The decades between 1790 and 1830 saw the success of some of the best-known satirical cartoonists in British history or, at least, some of the best known after William Hogarth (1697–1764). A strong social critic, the London-born Thomas Rowlandson (1756–1827) offered amusing vignettes of everyday life with images that were often crammed with figures displaying both the best and the worst aspects of British life. However exaggerated his images were,[51] they inevitably had a feel for the familiar. James Gillray (1757–1815), an early friend of Rowlandson, established himself as a master of political satire, and his caricatures and cartoons spared no individual, no movement, and no national interest. His prints are among the best and most telling images of the temper of the times, and Londoners flocked to New Bond Street, where the shop window of Hannah Humphrey (his partner and his print seller) was crammed with Gillray's latest drawings. George Cruikshank (1792–1878), who was deeply influenced by Gillray and continued in that tradition of satire and critique, was only emerging as a caricaturist around 1815, but it was in that year that he began a close relationship with the social activist and pamphleteer William Hone (1780–1842). Together they produced scathing indictments of the Prince Regent and his circle as well as pamphlets that upheld the right to free speech and an open press.

The need for new forms of visual culture was as compelling in the early nineteenth century as it is now. Among the new forms of attraction was the panorama, a large painting that enveloped the viewer in a well-illuminated circular space. Richard Barker (1739–1806), an artist for whom the word "panorama" was coined, had a structure built in London's Leicester Square to show the panoramas off to best advantage. By the time Ballard arrived in London, Barker's patent had expired, and several other panoramas had sprung up.

Elsewhere in London, Ballard was able to see Miss Linwood's remarkably successful gallery where she displayed her needlework renditions of famous paintings. Ballard also visited the galleries of the Royal Institution, a popular destination for well-heeled tourists. He takes particular note of the paintings by American born artists, most notably Benjamin West, who by this time had been a central fixture of the English art community for decades. Ballard also compliments the work of Washington Allston and Charles Robert Leslie (1794–1859) but, oddly enough, is particularly critical of the paintings of his friend Samuel Morse.

Among the many industries that flourished in the early nineteenth century was the production of earthenware pottery, particularly in Staffordshire where potters such as Thomas Minton (1765–1836), Josiah Spode (1733–1797), and Josiah Wedgwood (1730–1795), made significant contributions to the decorative arts. Although we tend to think of pottery and porcelain as items that were restricted to affluent homes, Staffordshire figurines were mass produced and thus could be found on the mantelpieces of many middle-class homes.[52] In an era when the tax on paper made prints very costly, mass produced figurines were available and, more important, affordable to a broad spectrum of customers.

Literary Culture

Ballard's visit to England coincides with the height of the Romantic Period in literature and, as William St. Clair has observed, a rapid increase in the reading ability and habits of "men, women, and children" (10).[53] William Wordsworth (1770–1850) and Samuel Taylor Coleridge (1772–1834) published their conceptually important collection, *Lyrical Ballads*, only seventeen years earlier, but even by 1815, poems such as "Tintern Abbey" by Wordsworth and "The Rime of the Ancient Mariner" by Coleridge were influencing poets and writers alike. George Gordon, Lord Byron (1788–1824), had gained some notoriety with his *English Bards* and *Scotch Reviewers* in 1808, but it was the publication of *Cantos I and II of Childe Harold's Pilgrimage* in 1812 that established him as a poetic force to be reckoned with. After the first printing of five hundred sold out in two days, Byron had indeed woken up to find himself famous. Elsewhere, perhaps the best known poet in the United Kingdom at the time, Sir Walter Scott (1771–1832), who had published the Lay of the Last Minstrelsy (1805) and Marmion (1808), recognized the turning tide in poetry and devoted himself to fiction, where once again he had enormous success with novels like *Waverly* (1814). Echoes of the turning political tides both in the United States and in the early days of the French Revolution were clear in British writing. Thomas Paine (1737–1809), the British-born Quaker, was a central figure in voicing the spirit of the American Revolution in his pamphlet *Common Sense* (1776), which he published while in America. His subsequent book, *The Rights of Man* (1791), released while Paine was in France, advocated substantial reform in Great Britain, where he was accused of sedition *in absentia*. While many Britons felt some empathy with the American colonists and their decision to throw off the British yoke, the "republican" impulses of the French Revolution were greeted much more seriously and skeptically. Edmund Burke's *Reflections on the Revolution in France* (1790) offers a highly critical response to the overthrow of the French monarchy, which he interpreted less as a progressive move to self-authority than a mob-driven overthrow of historical tradition. Burke's fear of the power of the mob in an unstable and self-indulgent regime undoubtedly was due to the angst of so many Britons facing difficult Corn Laws as well as a future under either mad King George or the somewhat reckless Prince Regent. As if to negotiate a path between the radicalism of Paine and Burke, William Godwin (1756–1836) wrote *An Enquiry concerning Political Justice, and its Influence on General Virtue and Happiness* (1793), which argues against monarchy and privately held property but holds out the hope that people are capable of improvement and self-governance. Godwin's popular novel *Things as They Are; or The Adventures of Caleb Williams* (1794) was an effort to repackage these ideas in a popular format that would reach a broader audience.

Notwithstanding the fact that Godwin, at least theoretically, opposed the institution of marriage, he did eventually marry the great feminist writer Mary Wollstonecraft (1759–1797). Wollstonecraft had achieved political fame first with her pamphlet *A Vindication of the Rights of Man* (1790) and subsequently with *A Vindication of the Rights of Woman: with Strictures on Political and Moral Subjects* (1792), which remains both a central and a powerful text in the history of feminism. Unfortunately, Wollstonecraft died of septicemia in 1797 after giving birth to Mary Wollstonecraft Godwin (1797–1851), who, as Mary Shelley, wrote the novel *Frankenstein* (1818).

The Romantic era is also known for the proliferation of educational texts that recognized the significance of the child as an individual with a capable mind. Books such as *Practical Education* (1798) by Maria Edgeworth (1767–1849) and her father, Richard Lovell Edgeworth (1744–1817), extended the idea of intellectual "improvement" to the world of children, as Priscilla Wakefield's (1751–1832) aptly titled *Mental Improvement* (1799) indicates. Anna Lætitia Barbauld (1743–1825), who was also responsible for a number of important works for children, was a significant poet and radical essayist in her own right. Her poetry addressed the rights of women, republican sentiments, and opposition to the wars with France and America. Her poem "Eighteen Hundred and Eleven" takes a hard look at a Britain whose soil has been untouched by the wars it has initiated and whose population seems smug and self-satisfied about Britain's dominant position in world culture and politics:

> And think'st thou, Britain, still to sit at ease,
> An island Queen amidst thy subject seas,
> While the vext billows, in their distant roar,
> But soothe thy slumbers, and but kiss thy shore?
> To sport in wars, while danger keeps aloof,
> Thy grassy turf unbruised by hostile hoof?
> So sing thy flatterers; but, Britain, know,
> Thou who hast shared the guilt must share the woe.
> Nor distant is the hour; low murmurs spread,
> And whispered fears, creating what they dread;
> Ruin, as with an earthquake shock, is here.[54]

The critical nature of Barbauld's poem did not escape readers and reviewers who responded harshly and often with anger to her critique of British policies. Later poets, especially Percy Shelley, whose poem "England in 1819" evokes Barbauld's title, would find poetry a convenient medium to attack the government when they saw fit. Shelley responded to the massacre of innocent protesters in St. Peter's Fields Manchester, later called "Peterloo," with the poem the "Masque of Anarchy" (1819). Although both poems appeared well after Ballard left England, Shelley's "England in 1819" expresses sentiments of contempt for English governance, which Ballard himself observes in his journal. Shelley's famous poem, stinging and blunt, opens with an attack on the royal family:

> An old, mad, blind, despised, and dying king,
> Princes, the dregs of their dull race, who flow

Through public scorn, mud from a muddy spring,
Rulers who neither see, nor feel, nor know,
But leech-like to their fainting country cling.[55]

Not all poets, to say nothing of other writers, expressed so harsh a view of British governance, but it is doubtful that any artist—and we need only look at later writers such as Dickens, Thackeray, and Thomas Carlyle—could look back upon the Regency without regret or perhaps even wonder about its excesses and irregularities. The emotional and intellectual impact of the Regency left an indelible impression on British writers, artists, and intellectuals for decades.

It only makes sense to conclude this section with a consideration of Jane Austen (1775–1817), whose work has almost come to epitomize the Regency. By 1815, Austen already achieved a degree of critical and popular success with her novels *Sense and Sensibility* (1811), *Pride and Prejudice* (1813), and *Mansfield Park* (1814). One of Austen's admirers, much to her chagrin, was the Prince Regent himself who was interested in having her next novel dedicated to him. It was a request that she could not refuse, and even though his own lifestyle made a mockery of the values Austen held most dear, *Emma* (1815) was "most respectfully dedicated" to him. In general, Austen's novels tried to stem what she perceived to be a rapid moral decline in society, a concern that preoccupied other novelists including Fanny Burney (1752–1840), whose novels—particularly *Evelina* (1778)—influenced Austen. However, Austen's novels stand apart from those of any writer of the time, whether Burney or Maria Edgeworth, because of her astonishing ability to capture the nuances of dialogue and the subtlety of manners that are at the heart of human social complexity. Moreover, Austen is significant, as William Galperin has observed, because of her insight as "a chronicler of the everyday," who captures "'the ordinary business of life' without also being merely ordinary."[56] Whether Ballard had ever heard of Austen is something we will never know, but his very presence in England—to take advantage of a rising and unprecedented capitalism—speaks to another dimension of her concerns about society. Austen understood that as England was being transformed by what historian F. M. L. Thompson calls "an instinct for commercial survival,"[57] the opportunities for social advancement were undergoing a radical (and, for Austen, a not entirely desirable) transformation. "The English are forever upon the alert," Ballard comments perhaps in unwitting empathy with Austen, "to make money out of everything."

English Politics

The level of political tension and uncertainty in early nineteenth century England is difficult to appreciate. It might be best to begin by recalling that the Battle of Yorktown, which signaled the ultimate defeat of the British, took place in 1781. The early loss of such an important colony was a devastating loss for Britain, and the later revival of hostility, resulting in the War of 1812, was a painful reminder to the British of their complete loss of control of their longheld colony. In 1789, the French Revolution seemed to indicate the strength of republicanism once again, and even more significantly, in a country less then a few dozen miles away by ship. Many Britons admired the initial spirit of the revolution in France only to become disappointed by the subsequent reign of terror that seemed to equate republicanism with mob rule. The subsequent rise of Napoleon not only crystallized the long-held belief that the inevitable outcome of revolution was tyranny but, in more practical terms, it also represented a direct threat to the security of England as a nation.

In 1801, facing the fear that Ireland, which in the Rebellion of 1798 had already tried to overthrow English rule, might become a strong ally of the French, parliament passed the Act of Union, which officially merged Ireland into Great Britain. The union resulted in the abolition of the Irish Parliament and consequently the suppression of Irish power and authority. The "Union Flag" (the "Union Jack") that emerged from the 1801 act is still the flag we associate with Great Britain.

I have already touched on a number of causes for political instability, including the declining health of George III, the war in France, and domestic economic troubles. Still, given that Ballard's visit occurs at the midpoint of the Regency, it is worth appreciating how extreme the behavior of the younger George, then Regent, (and his brothers) could be. As a young prince of only twenty-one years of age, George had disgraced the crown by marrying in 1785—without permission[58]—the much older Mrs. Fitzherbert who had at least three strikes against her. First, she was Catholic, which was unthinkable for a future king who would also serve as the head of the Anglican Church. Second, she was a commoner with no royal blood to justify so steep a rise through marriage, and third, although no fault of her own, she was already twice widowed at age twenty-nine. Although the marriage was declared invalid, their romance continued openly well after George married Princess Caroline of Brunswick in 1795.

As husband and wife, George and Caroline, his first cousin, must certainly rank as one of the most incompatible royal couples in British history. It was said that they were disgusted by each other at their very first meeting, never again sharing a bedroom after the second night of their marriage. Still, the marriage—however disastrous—did result in a daughter, Princess Charlotte Augusta (1796–1817). Within a year, estranged from her husband and her daughter (who was kept away from her), Caroline embarked on a series of scandalous affairs of her own.[59] She left England for the continent in 1814 and began accumulating greater debts and more lovers, including the notorious Bartolomeo Pergami.[60] Although she had been encouraged, both verbally and monetarily, to stay away, Caroline returned in 1820 when the Prince Regent was to accede to the throne, making her Queen Caroline. Though efforts were made to deny her the crown in a kind of parliamentary trial, ostensibly on the grounds of adultery (a vice for which George himself was renowned), she remained very popular with the British public. Nevertheless, she was barred from George IV's lavish coronation and, after taking ill a few days later on July 19, 1821, she died on August 7, 1821.

The incredible debts and scandals that pursued George, his brothers, and his consort Princess Caroline were astonishing for any period of time. What's more, illegitimate children abounded amongst them. The Duke of Clarence (1765–1837), who later became William IV, took the lead by having ten children (the so-called FitzClarences) with the famous actress Dorothy Jordan.[61] After the tragic death in childbirth of George IV's only legitimate daughter, Princess Charlotte, in 1817, the fifty-three-year-old William saw fit to make a legitimate match and thereby lay claim, if he could, to succession of the crown. His marriage to the then twenty-five-year-old Princess Adelaide of Saxe-Meiningen, though not an unhappy one, produced no children who survived beyond a year. Two of George's other brothers scrambled to marry legitimately now that succession was, so to speak, up for grabs. Prince Adolphus, Duke of Cambridge (1774–1850), the youngest of George IV's brothers, made it to the altar just weeks before his elder sibling, the Duke of Kent (1767–1820), married Princess Victoria of Saxe-Coburg, and it was their daughter who eventually succeeded to the throne as Queen Victoria.

Two other major scandals are worth noting, if only to round out an account George IV's brothers. Frederick, Duke of York and Albany (1763–1827), who was commander in chief of the army, found himself in difficulty when, in 1809, it was revealed that his then mistress

Mary Anne Clarke (1776–1852) had been selling army commissions. The uproar was considerable and Frederick resigned his position, while Mary Anne, after serving time in prison, retired to France. Finally, we have Ernest Augustus I (1771–1851), who acquired the epithet "Wicked Ernest" primarily because of his vitriolic temperament and his resistance to social change, but the label surely stuck because of the rumors that he had murdered his valet, to say nothing of the suggestions (perhaps politically motivated) of incest with his sister Sophia and other incidents of sexual assault.

If all of this is somewhat breathtaking to the modern reader, keep in mind, as Ballard surely did, that all of this was taking place against the more pressing backdrop of the wars with France and America. Yet the Royals, the aristocracy, and the well-to-do gentry seemed comfortable indulging their own whims, even as war continued, as basic prices (for grain) rose, as working conditions degraded, and as poverty increased. It was in 1815, for example, that the Prince Regent actually began construction on the Brighton Pavilion, a lavish seaside residence designed by John Nash, George's favorite architect, to resemble an Indian palace.[62]

The difficult financial times, exacerbated by the wars being fought, were never far from the politics of the times. The severe hardships of many sectors of English society could be seen in a variety of ways, but perhaps the most frightening example of its intensity was evident in the assassination of Prime Minister Spencer Perceval, who was formerly Chancellor of the Exchequer (the highest post in the cabinet for financial affairs). No English prime minister then or since had ever been assassinated, but in 1812 a former merchant named John Bellingham, who blamed Perceval for his complicated financial reverses, shot the Prime Minister in the House of Commons.

Tellingly, Perceval was assassinated while on his way to an inquiry about the Orders in Council against trade. As Prime Minister, he implemented the orders—which were ultimately meant to allow the British navy to block trade with France—in 1807, but the Navy applied the orders indiscriminately and ultimately interrupted the flow of trade not merely between the United States and France but with cargo intended for England as well. This, of course, was one of the major concerns of the United States, who felt that England was overstepping their bounds, and one of the prime causes of the War of 1812.

Perceval's successor was Robert Banks Jenkinson, second Earl of Liverpool (1770–1820), who had been serving as the Secretary of State for War and the Colonies. Liverpool, who remained Prime Minster for fifteen eventful years (until 1827). He lacked charisma but was able to use his diplomatic talents to negotiate his government through the closing years of the Napoleonic Wars, the Congress of Vienna (which restructured the map of Europe), and the first half of George IV's reign as monarch. Liverpool relied on fellow Tories such as Castlereagh, who led the House of Commons, and later Canning, who eventually succeeded Liverpool as Prime Minister. Nevertheless, Liverpool's government was consistently nothing if not controversial. Canning and Castlereagh, who opposed each other over military strategies, already fought a duel in 1809 (wounding Canning in the leg), and so when Liverpool formed his government with Castlereagh as the new Secretary of State for War and the Colonies, Canning refused to join. The restrictive Corn Laws of 1815, as Ballard notes in his entry for May 24, were extremely unpopular.[63] In London, writes Ballard, "the populace were so much exasperated at this bill that they attempted to tear down a member of Parliament's house for voting for it." Ultimately, the populace would continue to be unhappy as taxes would have to increase to cover the national debt,[64] which, strained by the expenses of the war itself as well as the cost of pensions for returning soldiers, almost seemed insurmountable.

SCIENCE AND TECHNOLOGY

If the Regency period saw a flourishing of Romantic poetry, it also witnessed a remarkable transition in both science and technology. Medicine had taken remarkable steps forward with the research of Robert Hunter (1728–1793), who advanced the understanding of human physiology and diseases. Edward Jenner's (1749–1823) investigations on using a strain of cowpox to immunize people against the virulent smallpox virus was, by the time of the Regency, well-known and being widely implemented. Other notable physicians of the time included John Abernethy (1764–1831), an expert on diseases, and the more controversial William Lawrence (1783–1867), whose *Lectures on Physiology, Zoology, and the Natural History of Man* (1819) anticipated evolutionary thought. Perhaps one of the most influential works in natural history was William Paley's (1743–1805) *Natural Theology; or Evidences of the Existence and Attributes of the Deity* (1802), which argued that a divine "intelligence" was responsible for the design of every living organism. Ironically, Paley's best-known disciple was the young Charles Darwin who, fascinated by the zoological analogies in *Natural Theology*, developed the theory of evolution, which set aside the need for a superintending deity. I have already mentioned the remarkable polymath Joseph Priestley (1733–1804), but we must not forget figures like the chemist John Dalton (1766–1844), whose work on atomic principles laid the groundwork for all modern chemistry. Humphry Davy (1778–1829), also mentioned earlier, was among the first celebrity scientists. His lectures at the Royal Society in London, which were always filled to capacity, reflected not only Davy's charisma but also a genuine interest in how the world worked on a material level, that is, according to science. Audiences saw no conflict between the practical and the theoretical aspects of science or even any divide between science and technological innovation. Thus Davy's work on the chemistry of chlorine (a central ingredient in bleach), his inquiries into the potential effects of nitrous oxide (laughing gas, which Priestley discovered), and his 1815 modifications to the "Safety Lamp," which was designed to prevent explosions in mines, made him a public hero in virtually every walk of life.

The coal mining industry was significant throughout England and the need for coal and iron increased with the demand for steam-powered machinery. The Soho Metalworks in Birmingham, which saw the pairing of Matthew Boulton (1728–1809) and James Watt (1736–1819), became the foremost foundry for steam engines in England. As the demand for coal grew, whether for domestic or industrial uses, it seemed necessary to survey Great Britain in general to determine the distribution of mineral resources. The first great geological map of England was produced by William Smith (1769–1839) in 1815, and while it received little acclaim when it first appeared, it was subsequently recognized as a founding document for Britain's outstanding accomplishments in geology and paleontology.[65]

Transportation, in general, was difficult in early nineteenth-century England. Although steam engines were abundant by 1815, it was not until 1827 that George Stephenson developed a commercial steam engine that could propel itself while also pulling additional cars along a set of rails. The late eighteenth century witnessed a remarkable expansion of the system of canals, which, though unsuitable for individual travel, were ideal for the transportation of coal, agricultural products, and manufactured goods. In the meantime, individuals who needed to travel had to rely on a system of roads, which, though much better than American roads, were poorly regulated and were maintained either by individual Parishes or by notoriously unreliable private ventures called Turnpike Trusts.[66] The two major figures behind the systematic improvement of English roads were Thomas Telford (1757–1834) and John Loudon McAdam (1756–1836). Each had developed similar techniques in road making that would allow a new era in stagecoach travel and thereby bring the more remote corners closer and more accessible to each other and to London. In 1810, based on the extensive improvements that Telford had made to the roads in his native Scotland, he was commissioned by parliament to develop a plan for the improvement of roads in England. After several delays, work finally began in 1815 on considerable improvements to the London-Holyhead road, allowing for faster journeys to Holyhead in Wales, the primary point of departure for Ireland.

Conclusion

The improvement of roads and their impact on transportation is probably as appropriate a topic as any with which to close this brief survey of England in 1815. Ballard's journey to England, though not comprehensive, included visits to what might be considered several out-of-the-way places and in a sense, the impediments of travel benefit us as readers. Like Pickwick and his entourage in Dickens's *Pickwick Papers* (1836–1837), Ballard must negotiate the English countryside in fits and start, thus observing haphazard sights, when the coaches stopped to change horses or to allow the passengers to dine or rest overnight. What Ballard sees and experiences in 1815 would not have been possible in a matter of thirty years, as the railroad developed, bringing individuals more rapidly from one destination to the next without experiencing much in between. Ballard's experience would not have been the same only a decade or two earlier, before the commercial pressures of industrialism really necessitated connections among provincial towns and cities as well as London. As the *Penny Magazine for the Diffusion of Useful Knowledge* observed in 1832, "Roads are the veins and arteries by means of which the circulation of the social body is carried on. Where they do not exist there can hardly be said to be a community. The people have nothing in common. They are not one people in anything but the name. No commerce, nor intercourse of any kind, mixes them up together into one mass."[67]

Thus the tone and temper of Ballard's memoir were shaped by a way of life that lasted not much longer than the Regency itself. Ballard occasionally lets the reader know that getting around was not all that easy, but ultimately, he seems to have enjoyed the circumstances of his relatively brief tour. From the reader's perspective, the conditions faced by the young commercial traveler were ideal, having given him a nuanced and detailed sense of England's people, places, and customs. As a merchant who surely dealt with a wide variety of customers in his native Boston, he also brought an affable demeanor clearly well suited to engaging individuals in almost every rank and class. The very existence of his memoir, calculated in Romantic terms to "instruct and amuse," seems to suggest that Ballard saw himself as something of a scholar-citizen who, in the emerging republic of the United States, newly at peace with Great Britain, had worthwhile insights to offer future generations both at home and abroad.

THE JOURNAL OF JOSEPH BALLARD

ENGLAND IN 1815

AS SEEN BY A YOUNG BOSTON MERCHANT BEING THE REFLECTIONS AND COMMENTS OF JOSEPH BALLARD ON A TRIP THROUGH GREAT BRITAIN IN THE YEAR OF WATERLOO

INTRODUCTION

This journal has a personal interest to Mr. Ballard's descendants as being the work of their ancestor, but they have published it in the hope that it may be found to be of interest to others as a picture of the life and times in England in the year of the Battle of Waterloo, as seen through the eyes of a patriotic young American.

Joseph Ballard was born on June 2, 1789, on Bromfield's Lane, formerly Rawson's Lane, now Bromfield Street,[1] in Boston where his father conducted a livery and hack business,[2] having established the first hackney carriage in Boston. In 1795, the family moved to West Street, which was then considered far uptown, and in 1824, Mr. Ballard purchased a house on Washington Street, near Hollis Street, where he continued to live for fifty-three years until his death in 1877.

Mr. Ballard's school education ended when he was fourteen years old at which time he received a Franklin Medal[3] at the hands of President John Adams in Faneuil Hall.[4] In 1803, he became an apprentice to Standfast Smith,[5] an Englishman who was a dealer in carpets, cutlery, upholstery goods, and other household wares on Franklin Street. At the end of his apprenticeship, Mr. Ballard and his brother

John became partners of Mr. Smith. Later, the firm was J. and J. Ballard, and afterward, Ballard and Prince. The firm was located at 168 Washington Street from 1822 to 1846, and then it moved to 11 Bromfield Street.

One of Mr. Ballard's boyhood friends and fellow apprentices was S. F. B. Morse, who later became noted as a portrait painter in England and afterward became famous as the inventor of the Morse telegraph system and alphabet.

Mr. Ballard retired from the active management of his business at middle age and devoted the remainder of his long life to his family, his books, and his farm in Hampton, New Hampshire, where he spent more than six months of every year. He was twice married. He was left a widower with three young children in 1822. He married again in 1824 and lived for fifty-three years with his second wife, who survived him.

A century ago, opportunity for education was limited. Books were scarce and libraries few. Mr. Ballard, however, after leaving school, found the opportunity to educate himself by reading *The Spectator*, *The Gentleman's Magazine*, Cook's *Voyages*, and similar books, and, at the same time, he attended to the arduous duties of an apprentice with fidelity.

It is interesting to conjecture whether at twenty-six years of age, when this journal was written, he would have acquired a greater ability to express his thoughts; a more considerable knowledge of social, political, and economic conditions; and a keener power of observation if he had had the advantage of modern educational methods.

JOSEPH BALLARD CROCKER.
December, 1912.

Journal of Joseph Ballard
March 12–November 9, 1815

On Sunday the twelfth day of March One Thousand Eight Hundred and Fifteen,[6] I sailed from Boston on board the Ship Liverpool Packet, Samuel Nickels commander, bound for Liverpool, England. My fellow passengers were Messrs. Barnett, Bangs, Blanchard, Webster,[7] Wheelock, Plumer, Wright, White, and Nielson.[8] The weather was remarkably fine and appeared likely to continue so, but early in the afternoon there came on a gale of wind with bad weather which lasted with very little interruption until we arrived in the mouth of the Channel. For twenty days scarcely a day passed without snow, hail or rain, and none without a gale of wind. The cold was exceedingly unpleasant to the passengers as the wind prevented our having a, fire in the cabin, blowing down the funnel in such a manner as to fill the cabin full of smoke. I suffered more than any other from seasickness, the horrid disagreeable sensations of which I think I shall ever remember. In four days however I was perfectly hearty and well, which I attribute to fasting as many of the rest suffered longer from having eaten while the sickness was upon them.

A few days out we discovered a large island of ice computed to be two miles long and eighty or ninety feet out of water. This alarmed us very much for although we were gratified by the singular beauty of its appearance, yet much was subtracted from that gratification by our sense of danger. We were obliged to be extremely cautious in keeping a good lookout as our commander was apprehensive of running upon it in the night.

[Wednesday, March 29] On the 29th we experienced a tremendous gale of wind. The waves ran mountain high, and presented a scene so terribly grand as to surpass all description: then I would have gladly exchanged our gilded palace of a cabin for the meanest hovel in creation. I do not know a scene in which a man can be placed wherein he appears in one view more insignificant and at the same time in another more powerful,—To view the wide expanse of waters furiously agitated by the storm, and to contrast his best efforts with the power of the elements, shows his insignificance;—when we see him by his nautical skill baffling the force of these elements we are astonished at his power![9]

At night the gale still continuing we were gratified by a most magnificent and sublime sight. Hundreds of black fish[10] from eighteen to twenty feet in length were sporting amid the "mountain waves." Their appearance when first seen very much resembled a drove of hogs, their bellies being of a dirty white color. During the storm the fears of us fresh water sailors was not a little augmented by the solicitude expressed in the countenance of one of our fellow passengers who on a former voyage was upset in a vessel and after remaining upon the wreck for ten days was providentially rescued from death by a vessel passing that way. One of his fellow seamen was torn in pieces by a huge shark before his eyes, and he suffered everything that human nature could bear and yet exist.

We passed our time very pleasantly when it did not blow a tempest. Books, conversation and cards served to fill up the vacuity of time. Once in a while we held a court of justice where offences against the dignity of the ship were tried, and the culprits fined in sundry bottles of wine to be paid at Liverpool: they being obliged to find security for the liberty of the ship until their arrival at that place. These and other pleasantries served to amuse us.

[Tuesday] April 4th we fell in with sixty sail of English of the Musquito,[11]—brig of war[12] from whom we were boarded. They had heard a rumor of peace and the officer appeared highly rejoiced at our confirming it. Our mate went on board with the ship's papers and the captain's compliments offering to furnish their commander with refreshment. After a short detention he returned with the British captain's steward to whom we gave some fowls and newspapers. I gave the boarding officer some of my papers as he observed he should not get a peep at the "old man's."[13] The next morning we were chased by a frigate[14] who compelled us to heave to after firing her bow guns at us several times. It was vexatious in the extreme to be thus detained with a fair wind, but as "might gave right" we were forced to comply.[15]

When she came up with us she proved to be the La Pique[16] of 36 guns mounting 45. We had a full view of her as she passed directly under our stern. She appeared to be a very beautiful vessel. The British lieutenant soon made his appearance upon our quarter deck, and was invited by our captain down into the cabin. He first asked if peace was certain, and was pleased with our answering in the affirmative. Speaking of the treaty he asked "what had become of the southern states" (presuming, I suppose, that the northern ones had made a separate treaty).[17] In the reply something was said respecting the New Orleans affair, when he changed the conversation by a remark upon the weather. The convoy of ships they had with them were from

St. Thomas and consisted of one hundred sail, forty of which they parted with in the violent gale of the 29th. After overhauling our papers he returned on board the ship and most graciously permitted us to proceed. From the time we were boarded from the Musquito until our arrival at Liverpool we were surrounded by this fleet. The pilot whom we took on board informed us of Bonaparte's return to Paris, but this we considered so improbable an event as to pay no serious attention to it, but thought it a hoax which he was playing off on us Yankees.[18]

On our arrival in the harbour we were boarded by an officer of a 74-gun ship brig[19] at anchor there, who requested Captain Nickels to furnish him with a list of his crew, that in the event of any of them being impressed[20] they might be known and liberated. These orders were from the government, and certainly they indicated a disposition to make the peace of lasting duration as far as regarded this cause of complaint.

At our landing on the wharf at Liverpool[21] we were surrounded by a tribe of girls of the town who welcomed us most cheerfully.

These and innumerable others whom we met in going to our lodgings, together with the sombre appearance of the buildings, first by lamplight made visible, gave me no favorable opinion of the place. After a long walk which (owing to inactivity on board ship) fatigued me exceedingly I arrived at the Liverpool Arms[22] (the Inn where Silliman[23] lodged and whose waiter Louis he had most unjustly accused of practising by his politeness upon the purses of the customers). The appearance of the attendants at an inn with hair bepowdered and dressed in an appropriate style was to me so new that it was some time before I could make up resolution to call in a consequential tone to the waiter to bring me anything wanted. The next day we were much pestered by Jews who wished to purchase our gold which at this time was at a great advance above paper money.[24] It was extremely amusing to hear these fellows talk of their American connections. They all positively declared that they did all the trade that was done in their line with America. They also asked very many curious questions—"Were Charlestown S. C., Baltimore and Norfolk near Boston" &c. &c.[25]

Liverpool possesses an Athenæum[26] which contains a very large collection of books in every department of literature. There was one book I saw which I thought a great curiosity. It was for teaching the blind, the letters being raised so as to be felt by them.[27] I could not distinguish them by feeling, but suppose a blind person could, as the

Figure 1 Illustration of a blind beggar from John Thomas Smith's *Etchings of Remarkable Beggars, Itinerant Tradesman, and Other Persons of Notoriety* (1815). Author's collection.

sense of feeling is with them more acute. I was extremely fortunate in my visit to the blind asylum[28] as I found the objects of its charity were engaged in singing. It was extremely solemn. I had never witnessed a scene more so. Twenty five blind men, women, girls and boys composed the choir. They were singing anthems. The female voices were uncommonly fine-toned. There were many spectators present among whom I observed a man with a small blind lad (I presumed his son) whom he had brought for the purpose of being admitted. During the singing the father appeared to be very much affected and "the big tears chased each other down his cheeks." In the hall are tablets whereon are inscribed the donors to this establishment and in every room is a money box with "pray remember the poor blind" written upon it. I was witness to one blind person's walking alone the yard, going up stairs, and seating himself to work at a loom. This he did as readily as if he were blessed with sight. One of the rooms is appropriated as a sales-room where baskets, rugs, &c. are shewn. This admirable institution is certainly an honor to humanity'![29]

The Exchange and the Town Hall are superb buildings. In the former are contained a reading room and an insurance office similar to Lloyd's at London: in the area is an elegant monument to the memory of Lord Nelson.[30] The expense of erecting it was defrayed by voluntary subscription, and the cost 45,000 dollars.

[April 8] I took my passage on Saturday in the coach for Warrington eighteen miles distant from Liverpool. The gardens and fields looked delightful being in quite as forward a state of vegetation as ours in June. I was much amused at the activity of the tumbling boys who turned head over heels at the side of the coach and with such swiftness as to even keep up with it for some time, which is done in expectation that the passengers will throw them a penny, their parents being so miserably poor that this is resorted to as a means of subsistence.

There were six passengers inside and twelve outside the coach besides the coachman and an abundance of luggage.[31] This added to the weight of the vehicle (which generally is two tons or more), makes it almost incredible that they should be able to go at the rate of seven and eight miles per hour. There is not the least derogation from respectability in riding upon the outside.[32] I should certainly myself give it the preference in fine weather as you enabled to have a much better view of the through which you pass than when in the coach. The danger is however greater in the event of an accident happening to the Coach, but as they are made so very strong they are in a degree guarded. We passed the seat of the Earl of Derby.[33] The park is very large. Earl Derby married the celebrated actress Miss Farren. He is much addicted to horse racing and gambling. Warrington[34] is a manufacturing town. The manufactures consist of glass-houses, iron foundries, cotton works, breweries, &c. It has a gloomy dirty appearance in consequence of these works and the quantity of coal used in them. A large part of its inhabitants subsist by their daily labor in these manufactories. It was late in the evening when I arrived. Opposite the inn were assembled a vast crowd of these workmen having (as it was Saturday night) received their weekly wages. This they were spending in ale which soon intoxicated a greater part and such a scene of riot ensued as I shall not attempt to describe. These men are generally intemperate: were it not for this habit they might live quite comfortably on their wages. As it is, their families are starving for food while they are spending all they can in drink. Saturday night does not satisfy them. Sunday and Monday which is called "blue" or "St. Monday"[35] is kept the same, nor can any emergency of business whatever call them to resume their work if their last week's wages are not all spent. The old women seen in the streets are the most shocking looking creatures I ever beheld. I have seen them clothed in a man's hat and a short jacket over their gowns driving a little jackass through the town shewing such a countenance as to bring immediately to one's mind Shakespeare's scene of the witches in Macbeth. There is also an incredible number of children from two to four years of age swarming the street in such a state of nudity and uncleanliness as is quite disgusting. These wretched little beings are at quite an early age buried in the manufactories.[36] I saw some in one who were not seven years of age. They had scarcely a rag to cover them. These poor little wretches earn sixty-seven cents a week! Could but the advocates of the manufactures of our country but witness the misery attached to those in Warrington, Sheffield, & Leeds, I am sure they would not so strenuously argue that it is for our national welfare that they should be established in America. I went through an extensive glass work, the proprietors of which pay £600 per week duty to government and £150 wages to the Workmen. They were making a service of glass for the Prince Regent of Portugal,[37] a very superb thing; tumblers were $15.00 each, wine-glasses $5.00. The whole would cost $15,000. It will take one year to finish it. I was here introduced to a Swiss gentleman, whom I found an intelligent person. Being a fine day we rambled into the country. The fields bore a charming appearance surrounded by hedges cut in a most regular manner and blown out in flowers resembling the barberry when in blossom. We stopped at the country house of Mr. A. (with whom we went) and partook of a luncheon of bread, cheese, and ale, and returned to W. to dine. There is but a slight difference between their etiquette at this meal and ours, consequently I have nothing to remark about it except the introduction of apples from France, at the dessert. A conversation took place after dinner respecting the English Clergy, when many sad instances of their misbehaviour were mentioned.[38] This, it was observed, would oft be the case as long as they were independent of their hearers. The Earl of Derby has a living[39] in his gift the income of which is £10,000 a year.[40] This is now in the possession of his lordship's nephew, until his son becomes of age to take it. The occupant of course is making the most of it and the poor tenants are ground to the dust with his exactions. The dissenting clergy, being chosen by their congregations, are an exception to this and are an honor to their profession.

During a walk after dinner we came to a monument erected in commemoration of the defeat of the Scottish rebels in 1775.[41] It is over the spot where the person who erected it concealed his money and plate. These rebels were stopped at Warrington and prevented from crossing the river by the destruction of the bridge. At the glass works I witnessed a most singular operation in the removal of a broken pot from a furnace "seven times heated," and a perfect pot taken from another furnace equally heated and put in the place of the injured one. These large vessels weighed six to seven Cwt.[42] and were so hot that I was obliged to stand at several yards distance from them. A large iron bar was inserted in the month of the pot, while another crossed it. The men, clothed in wet sacks, bore it along until it was fixed, in its proper situation. A few years ago a workman slipped and fell into the furnace but was not injured, the sack preventing his being burned.

At Warrington I became acquainted with Mrs. I. and daughter, with whom I was much pleased. When I entered the house I found Miss I. occupied in the old-fashioned Yankee employment of darning stockings. I was delighted with the ease with which I was received. The young lady continued her work until I inquired for a direction to a place, when she offered to accompany me as a guide. So away we trudged, arm in arm, like old acquaintances. We had a deal of chat and I found her a very pleasant companion.

I took leave of my Warrington friends after many kind invitations to return and pass a few days with them, then went to the Inn and after paying my bill, "boots,"[43] waiter and chambermaid, departed in the coach for Manchester. In passing some farmhouses I observed a way they have of fastening fruit trees in the manner of a vine to the side of the house, which answers both for ornament and use, as the reflection of the sun ripens the fruit, while the vine hides the dismal looks of the wall, which is solid in consequence of the window tax.[44]

Manchester at its entrance has an agreeable appearance, as there are many fine houses in the suburbs, which serves only to render the disappointment more extreme when you enter the town. It is a very irregularly built place; a stranger may think himself fortunate if he does not lose himself twenty times a day. The warehouses are in courts, the entrances to which are obscure and difficult. The rooms in which they show the goods are so darkened by the window squares being painted that a person must be a perfect judge of the effect of light and shade or he may be greatly deceived with regard to their fineness.

There is an athenæum and a reading-room here, supported by subscription.[45] I was highly gratified in viewing the old church, an ancient Gothic building, the tower of which is of a great height: in the interior is some curious carved work, and over the altar a large tapestry picture, the subject of which I could not make out, as it was so defaced by the hand of time.[46] Over it was a painted window, the colors, in the highest perfection, although ages have elapsed since the work was executed. The whole interior has a cold, damp and gloomy aspect, as the whole floor is composed of gravestones, it being used as a cemetery. Some part of the outside was undergoing a repair.

In the evening I attended the theatre.[47] The performances were "The Battle of Hexham"[48] and "The Miller and his Men."[49] The acting was tolerably good, but the scenery and decorations not so handsome as at Boston. There were many ladies in the pit, which is customary here. John Bull[50] in the gallery was quite noisy. Encores were persisted in until every song was repeated, and when a player who had danced a hornpipe did not make his reappearance John became extremely outrageous and kicked up a row which only subsided by the performer's coming forward, stating that he had lamed himself and offering the customary apology beginning with Ladies and Gentlemen, etc.

Manchester is quite a smoky place. Upon my walking a little way out of town I found it was quite fine weather, and what I supposed a foggy day was only an accumulation of coal smoke from their manufactories.

The next day I took the coach for Leeds and after passing rapidly through several small places came to one of the most barren, desolate spots of earth I ever beheld. It was very extensive and covered with a brown heath. In other parts of England I have seen similar tracts of land, some of which was not so sterile, and considering the immense population I think might be made to produce something either for man or beast. At the top of a mountain we passed a reservoir of water for supplying a canal in a dry time, the whole a work of art, and from its size it must contain an amazing quantity of water. After passing the wastes mentioned I saw many farms, the land appearing to be in the highest state of cultivation. The farmers all over the county employ old women and children to pick up dung in the streets and roads, and they gain (I am informed) one shilling per day by this miserable employment. The passengers in the coach were a democratic Scotsman[51] and a most loyal English colonel. The Scot was a warm friend to Bonaparte and asserted that the ministers had broken every treaty they had made with him. This was sharply resented by the colonel, and there is no telling where the dispute might have ended had not the conversation turned upon American affairs. The colonel complimented the American troops in a curious manner by observing that they were brave and it was not to be wondered at since they "were descendants of Englishmen." It required all my gravity to make an acknowledging bow for this compliment! I frequently found that the bravery displayed by the Americans in the last war was accounted for from this source.

Leeds is a town of considerable consequence. It is not as gloomy and dull in appearance as most of the manufacturing places. The bricks of which the houses are built are of a lighter color, and more resembling ours. There is a reading room here to which I was introduced by a friend.[52] It was well supplied with newspapers, and served me to pass a leisure hour away. This place is famous for its woolen [*sic*] manufactures. On market days a vast quantity of woolens [*sic*] of every description is exposed for sale in a large building called the cloth-hall. The dealers in the respective cloths here purchase them and have them dyed and finished to suit themselves. I took a short ride to a village in the vicinity of Leeds, called Heckmondwick.[53] My friend and I dined at a small ale-house, just such a one as Fielding[54] describes in his novel of *Tom Jones*, and *Joseph Andrews*. The description was so forcibly brought to my mind by the place that I almost expected Jones or Parson Adams[55] would make his appearance. There was a kind of bread made of oatmeal hanging in large sheets from the ceiling,[56] and pork suspended from the wall, this being the way they cure it, as they seldom pickle it in the manner we do. On our way back to Leeds we met many little children driving jackasses with paniers [*sic*][57] of coals on their backs. They were carrying them into a neighboring village for sale. We passed near to a large coal pit. The entrance to it was so forbidding that I did not venture down. At Leeds there is a steam engine which draws twenty eight loaded wagons several miles.[58] On Sunday I attended divine service in the morning and in the afternoon took the coach for Sheffield. On the road there, passed some ruins, and a pyramid erected by Lord———[59] at a vast expense as the boundary to a view from Wentworth Castle.

[Sunday, April 15] At dusk arrived at Sheffield and sat myself down a solitary being in the travellers' room. I should have preferred the society of a favorite dog or cat to have passed away the "lagging moments" which were to me almost unsupportable. The next day visited some manufactories of cutlery, &c. &c.[60] The manufactories of steel are brought to wonderful perfection. I saw twenty pairs of scissors so small that they were kept in a quill of the common size. The town is surrounded by hills, and were it not for its almost infernal smoke and fire, it would be quite pleasant. The inhabitants of this place partake of the misery resulting from manufactures. The poorer classes are worse off for the articles which they immediately manufacture than the inhabitants of the American back settlements are. Many children not eight years of age are at work in these cursed holes, deprived of education; they consequently grow up in ignorance and all the comfort or pleasure they have is in drunkenness and sensuality. Many of these little wretches are sent from London workhouses[61] to these manufacturing towns. Often has my heart bled to see a poor little sickly being hard at work, deprived of liberty and fresh air, when its situation demanded the indulgent care of a tender nurse. In the evening I met at the inn the printer of a newspaper, who remarked that Gales[62] who edits the Intelligencer was obliged to fly the town for fear of justice, and that his sisters still carry on a book-shop formerly his. Montgomery[63] the poet is the printer of a newspaper here. He bears a most excellent character, and is much esteemed.

Left Sheffield for London; passed through many fine towns. The country was throughout the whole route highly cultivated. There were three buxom damsels in the coach. After having travelled through the night one of these pulled out a small bottle of rum from her "indispensable" and most kindly asked me to partake with her and her companions. At Woburn passed the seat of the Duke of Bedford. The park wall continued about two miles along the road until it terminated by an elegant gateway,—the entrance to the Abbey (as the house is called). Near here the road was cut through a mountain of chalk. It lay in large heaps on each side.

[April 19] As we approached London the country became thicker settled and more highly cultivated. At St. Albans, twenty-one miles this side, saw the famous abbey which bears that name.[64] The edifice is of stone and is very large. At Islington the houses were pretty and neat, but when I entered the great city I was a little disappointed at the narrow streets and lanes, and its appearance generally, which struck me as being dirty and gloomy. I took lodgings at the New England Coffee House, the general resort of Yankees.[65] After I had dined with the assistance of Mr. Porter found out Mr. Webster and with him, in the evening, attended Drury Lane Theatre.[66] The building is a most noble structure and is furnished with elegant scenery and decorations. The play was "The Unknown Guest,"[67] the concluding scene of which was the storming and blowing up a castle. It was admirably represented. There were soldiers drawing cannon, bomb shells flying and bursting upon the ramparts, &c. &c., the whole forming I should suppose, a perfect resemblance of a battle. The after-piece was "The Woodman's Hut";[68] one scene of which represents a cottage struck by lightning and consumed, another a wood which took fire and spread until it consumed a row of cottages. One of the actresses much resembles Mrs. Darley.[69] Munden[70] is much like Bernard.[71]

On visiting the Bank of England[72] I was astonished at its magnitude and the number of clerks employed. Many of the rooms in this great paper-mill of England resembled an extensive school, where the clerks like boys were each set down to his task. The entrances are guarded by the porters dressed in scarlet coats with badges on their arms denoting their employment, and by Beadles with a curious uniform and huge gold-laced hats.[73] Guildhall[74] is a very large building but, with the exception of a few monuments, is not handsome. These monuments are quite elegant and are erected in memory of Chatham,[75] Pitt,[76] Nelson[77] & Beckford,[78] the last representing Beckford in his Mayor's robes holding in his hand the famous speech which he made to the King in 1770. This was erected by the city as a testimony of their approbation of his sentiments. There are also two mighty images here painted as fine as puppets called Gog and Magog.[79] The Royal Exchange[80] is a capacious building, but has been robbed of a deal of its elegance by the hand of time. The statues

Figure 2 Illustration of a parish beadle from George Cruikshank's *London Characters*. Beadles wore elaborate uniforms that signaled their prominence (if not their authority) as heralds and keepers of the local peace. Courtesy University of North Carolina at Chapel Hill.

in the niches are very much decayed, which altogether renders it less interesting as a fine building than I expected. All the public buildings in the city are injured in their appearance by the smoke of coal (which is here burnt altogether for fuel) and which adheres to the stones.

In the area of the Exchange, merchants from all parts of the earth meet to transact business. It is hung around with advertisements; one I remarked as being very singular:—a dentist had formed his of the decayed teeth which he had extracted from the jaws of his patients. These were arranged in such a manner as to give a much prettier effect than one would suppose rotten bones were capable of doing. The Mansion House, the residence of the Mayor of London, has a very heavy and gloomy appearance, more befitting a prison than for the purpose it is intended.

[Thursday, April] 20th. This evening attended Covent Garden Theatre.[81] The outside, as well as that of Drury Lane and the Opera, is guarded by soldiers to keep proper order. The play was Shakespeare's "Romeo & Juliet." Miss O'Neil[82] sustained the character of Juliet in a style which as far surpassed our actresses as the celebrated Cooke[83] did our actors. The funeral scene was extremely solemn; the friars and attendants were over sixty persons who chanted the service in the manner of the Romish church. The music and singing was very fine.

Figure 3 The Guildhall courtyard as depicted in Thomas Allen's *Panorama of London* (1830). Author's collection.

Figure 4 The Royal Exchange on Threadneedle Street near the Bank of England as depicted in Thomas Allen's *Panorama of London* (1830). Author's collection.

Figure 5 A view of the Thames and St. Paul's Cathedral from Thomas Shepherd's *Metropolitan Improvements* (1827). The bridge crossing the Thames here is Blackfriars. Author's collection.

The after-piece[84] was Lembucca,[85] a modern melodrama resembling Tekeli.[86] The scenery and dresses to this were very handsome. There were frequently one hundred performers on the stage at once. The decorations of this house on the auditors' parts (in the auditorium) are not so elegant as those of Drury Lane, yet I think the scenery more elegant. There is always attending these theatres an immense number of women of the town. With the exception of the first boxes which are designated as dress boxes they go into all parts of the house and seat themselves where they please. I have often seen many of them in boxes with ladies and gentlemen apparently respectable. The streets are also thronged with these miserable wretches who accost every person who passes along. Many of them have not where to lay their heads, and pass the night in the streets in any corner which will afford them a shelter. At Covent Garden Theatre, Liston,[87] one of the performers, is endued with such comical powers of countenance that one must have a perfect command of the risible powers to prevent himself from laughing before he utters a word. There are also some fine dancers at this house, but these ladies are so thinly clad and throw themselves into such indecent postures that I think a New England audience would not have tolerated them. At night a good many of the streets and stores are lighted up with gas.[88] The brilliancy of light thrown out this way is astonishing; compared with it the oil lamps look like a "dim candle at noon." It is prepared in some building

Figure 6 The interior of Covent Garden Theatre from Rudolph Ackermann's *Microcosm of London* (1830). Courtesy of the James Smith Noel Collection, Louisiana State University in Shreveport.

erected for the purpose and conducted through the streets in pipes like an aqueduct, consequently all the proprietors have to do is to turn a cock and apply a candle and the house or street is lighted.

Within these last few days there has been posted upon the walls and distributed about the city a handbill offering a reward of £1000 to any person who will apprehend and bring to the old Bailey[89] for trial, Seignor Napoleon Buonaparte, accused with the murder of Captain Wright[90] "contrary to the statutes of Geo. &c. &c. in that case made and provided." One of the public papers remarks that Government should look to this handbill, but as it appears so much like catching the devil it is pretty well understood to be a hoax.

The Tower of London[91] is a large pile of buildings surrounded by a deep moat. At my entering within the walls I was joined by one of the yeomen of the guards[92] as a conductor. He was habited in the uniform worn by that corps ever since the reign of Henry the 7th which is grotesque enough! In the first place he conducted me to the Spanish armory where there is an immense collection of the arms used by the Spaniards in their attempts to invade England with the Armada.

Queen Elizabeth's effigy dressed in the identical clothes worn by her at that time is in this room, standing by the side of her horse. The horse armoury, where are the seventeen kings from William to George the 2nd on horseback, is next shown. This room also contains a great many suits of very ancient armor preserved in the highest perfection. The attendant generally gabbles through the history of these curiosities in a dull monotonous tone, and should you unfortunately ask him a question in the middle of his story, you must have the patience to hear it all over again, as they never can tell where they stopped. One of the effigies of a king whose armor had been taken off to be repaired had a dirty old bed blanket thrown over his head and shoulders. He of course made a most laughable appearance sitting on horseback among his brother kings in polished armor. My guide, not noticing the circumstance, when he came to him went on with countenance unmoved in his story— "this is King &c., with his polished armor of steel, &c &c." Upon my laughing out at his description of the poor blanketed king, he looked up and exclaimed "Oh dear! I've forgotten; his armor's gone to be mended!" The Volunteer Armoury is the most beautiful of the whole, containing more than thirty thousand stands of arms, most fancifully arranged into pillars and other devices. The next is the Sea Armoury, containing arms sufficient for 50,000 sailors and marines. In the royal train of artillery are many curious cannon and mortars, the trophies of victories. Last is shown the Jewel Office, where the Regalia are kept. This is shown through iron bars to prevent theft. A few weeks ago an insane woman made an attempt to snatch some of the jewels from the crown, but did not succeed in getting any of them, although she considerably injured it.[93] The value of these jewels and plate is two millions of pounds sterling. They are shown to you by a woman who repeats parrot-like her story. At coming out you write your name and place of residence in a book kept for the purpose. The yeoman points out the rooms occupied by Sir Francis Burdett[94] during his imprisonment here, also the room where the young princes were smothered by order of Richard the Third,[95] and the staircase under which they were buried. Tower Hill, so famed for the executions performed upon it, is near the Tower, and takes its name from that circumstance.

In my visits to Mr. Webster I have had occasion to notice the celebrated Hospitals where so many of our physicians have received a part of their education. Guy's Hospital is a spacious building designed for the reception of patients afflicted with any disease. In front is a large court-yard wherein stands the statue of Sir Thos Guy its founder.[96]

Opposite the building is St. Thomas' Hospital, a similar institution. In one of its courts is the statue of Edwd 3rd[97] and in another of Rob[t] Clayton,[98] both its benefactors. There are also several other statues in niches. The number of patients received yearly into these institutions is immense.

They have a wonderful way in this great city of showing off to advantage everything they have to sell. One has at his windows roasting jacks,[99] with shapes of birds, mutton, beef, &c. cut out of wood turning upon them, another a patent hat which (to show that it is water proof) is floating in a vessel of water; another water filtering through a stone, another men's eyes, legs, arms, &c, to supply the loss of those members; in short, there is such an endless variety of objects at the shop windows that it would take a volume to describe them. The draper's and jeweller's shops are set out in such an enticing manner that it is absolutely dangerous to the purse of a stranger. A one-pound note goes here just about as far as two dollars. Many articles (not excluding those manufactured here) are retailed at but a little lower price than in Boston. This is caused by the excessive taxes and the high price that all articles of living bear. Beef is one shilling;[100] veal 10^d; butter 2^s 4^d, and everything in proportion.

[Saturday, April] 22nd. This evening went to Astley's amphitheatre[101] near Westminster Bridge. The interior is very pretty, lighted by a splendid chandelier, which descends through the ceiling and when coming down makes a beautiful appearance. The performances were of the pantomime and equestrian kind, the subject being the Life and death of the high-mettled racer. During this piece there was a correct representation of a horse race. The pit was railed through the centre, and the horses started from the back of the stage at a long distance from the audience, and passed through the pit. A fox chase was also admirably done, from the starting of the fox until his death, the dogs and horses in full speed after the little animal. This was so illusive that the audience heartily joined in the tally-ho of the huntsmen, etc. In the course of the harlequinade a curious transformation set the house in a roar. A barber was carrying a wig box whereupon was written "Judge Wisdom's wig." The clown desiring to see it, he set it down and opened it, when a large wig (such as the judges in this country wear upon the bench) appeared.[102] Harlequin[103] struck it with his sword and out marched a venerable owl who majestically stalked across the stage and made his exit. Such success had this piece met with that tonight was the one hundredth night[104] of its representation.

[Sunday, April,] 23rd Being Sunday I attended divine service at Whitehall chapel.[105] Before this place Charles the I was beheaded.[106] It was formerly designed as a banqueting house. The inside is handsome; at one end is a splendid canopy, composed of crimson and gold, erected for the allied sovereigns when upon their visit to this country the last summer. Here are also suspended the banners captured from the enemies of England at different periods, among them some French eagles, and four or five American standards taken at Detroit and Queenstown. The galleries were filled with officers and soldiers, being the church that the military attend. The preacher was a very good one; the subject of his discourse being the comfort derived from a religious life, particularly under the loss of friends. The music was admirably performed by the Duke of York's band. The introduction of the trumpet particularly gave it a grand and sublime effect. I was not a little distracted from my devotions in looking at the ceiling, which is finely painted; the subject (being designed for the banqueting room) presented a curious contrast to the solemnity of the service. Very near this place are the King's mews,[107] which I went through. There are some fine horses here, particularly six cream-colored ones, whose skins were so sleek that they resembled satin. They are scarcely ever used except when the Prince goes to Parliament. The expense of keeping these beasts amounts to more than President Madison's salary,[108] yet they are quite useless a great part of the time. I asked my friend who accompanied me if he did not feel a pride in showing a plain republican all this grandeur (for the building was like a palace). He replied in the affirmative, but his self satisfaction was not a little dissipated on my reminding him that he by taxes, &c. dearly had to pay for it. Seeing all this unnecessary expense to a country groaning beneath its weight of taxes, must make an American more dearly appreciate the simplicity of the establishment of his own government, which has excluded this useless waste of money.

I took dinner at Kentish Town, a small village three miles from London.[109] The hospitality with which I was treated was highly gratifying to me, a stranger. In the evening I attended divine service and was pleased with the church, a small neat building, the sides of which were full of monuments, many of them handsomely sculptured. The service was devoutly performed. There is something so inexpressibly solemn in beholding old and young, rich and poor, upon their knees supplicating the Supreme Being to hear their prayers, that I wish it were adopted into our form of worship. *Gloria Patri*[110] sung by a choir of small children had a charming effect. The subject of the discourse was our duty to love God with all our might and strength. The preacher was a good one and seemed to feel impressed with the importance of his subject.

On Monday morning I went to London and at night attended Drury Lane to see Kean111 in Richard the Third. He is quite a favorite of the town. His conception of the character is just, and in many scenes falls not short of Cooke, but his voice is so bad that when he attempts to raise it above a certain pitch it destroys the effect of his acting. The after piece was a modern production of the kind where sense is banished to please the eye with fine scenery, &c.[112]

[Tuesday, April] 25th This day went through St. Paul's Cathedral.[113] The particular description of this wonderful building is so well known to all that to attempt it would be unnecessary. It is a source of great regret that it is in so crowded a situation. There should be a large space unencumbered with buildings, around it, to show it to advantage. In the court of the building are many fine marble monuments. These are daily augmenting, as it is appropriated for that purpose, in the manner of Westminster Abbey which is now quite full. From the galleries are suspended many tattered flags. Some of these were taken by the Duke of Marlborough at Blenheim. The model of St. Paul's in one of the towers is a great curiosity.[114] It was made by Sir Christopher Wren, and it was intended to have this church built like it. The floor of the Library is also very curious, being composed of a vast number of pieces put together without nails. From the whispering gallery you can look down into the court or area below, and such is the amazing distance that a man walking there looks no larger than a mite. Passing up the great number of stairs through one of the small towers is apt to bring to mind scenes described in romances. When I descended from the dome, I found that the service had just begun in the chapel. Curiosity led me in and I found eight or ten men and boys dressed in dirty surplices chanting prayers in such a lazy, ridiculous manner that had I not been disgusted with the impropriety of it I should have laughed outright. I thought that they had not only "erred and strayed" but sung like "lost sheep." It rather resembled the braying of an ass. If this is the way the Deity is to be petitioned, I should like to know what idea the chapter of St. Paul's has of Him. There were not more than twenty auditors present for such mockery was more calculated to drive them hence than to invite more. In almost every room in the building is a person who demands two-pence for showing it. This is a great disgrace to a nation possessed of the taste to erect such a magnificent pile. It is the fashion, however, in this country to demand a fee for showing all curiosities, either public or private.

In walking the streets in the city a person must always keep upon the right-hand side or he will receive many a knock. The carriage, always drive the reverse. There is always an immense number in the street, extending as far as the eye can reach, one line coming and another going, the side paths so full at the same time of foot passengers, that if one makes full stop he stops fifty behind. As I came from the church I met a funeral. It was preceded by two mutes,[115] with black staffs and bands, then a man bearing a board full of black ostrich feathers upon his head, after this the plumed hearse "came nodding on"[116] followed by mourning coaches and mutes in bands and cloaks. There is always enough to attract a stranger's attention in the streets of London; persons with large labels pasted upon boards to inform you where are the best eating houses, or who always sells the highest prize, or some wonderful medicine that cures every disease. These fellows thrust small papers into your hands as you pass by. Any tradesman who has served the royal family, even in the minutest articles, immediately becomes pastry-cook, &c. to his loyal highness the prince regent, and by raising the royal arms elegantly carved and gilded over his door takes special care that none shall remain ignorant of his honor. I happened to meet in the street the Lord Mayor and sheriffs returning in state from Guildhall. The coach is carved and gilt all over. The picture of it is in almost every child's picture book. This, as well as the liveries of the servants, is in the same style which has been in use for years. The whole equipage is most plentifully bedaubed with gold. The mace bearer was in the carriage with the mayor, and the sheriffs in their carriages followed,—the whole escorted by a mob of boys huzzaing!

[Friday, April] 28th. Today went to Greenwich. The road is over London Bridge. This bridge is esteemed to be quite unsafe and is to be pulled down and another erected in its stead. Near the bridge the Monument[117] "like a tall bully lifts its head and lies!"[118] This is all accounted in a ruinous condition and is considerably out of the perpendicular, so much so that the workmen apprehend considerable trouble whenever it is removed, as the upper stones act as a binder or balance and when taken off will cause the bottom part to fall. From London Bridge there is a fine view of the shipping and boats on the river. On the road I observed an inn-keeper's sign with this inscription:

Figure 7 View of the Monument on St. Botolph's Lane from Allen's *Panorama of London* (1830). Author's collection.

"Thomas Smith, formerly coachman to the honorable Alexander Hope."

This man, it seems, is not ashamed to tell who he was! I found Greenwich hospital[119] to be indeed a "royal institution." Its appearance bespeaks more the magnificence of a palace than a receptacle for the infirm and aged. I saw many old seamen reclining at their ease beneath the piazza. They were clothed in blue clothes and cocked hats. Many of these hardy veterans had lost an arm or leg, and almost all were scarred. Each one has a little cabin fitted up like the stateroom of a ship. These are kept perfectly clean and neat, and many of them are ornamented with little pictures, &c. according to the fancy of the occupant. One who had been in the Battle of the Nile[120] had Nelson's portrait and a picture of the action to adorn his cabin. These little luxuries are at their private expense, as they have a shilling a week tobacco money allowed them by the institution. This and similar establishments for the comfort of aged and infirm warriors have conduced in a great manner to make England "invincible in arms," as the sailor has the comfortable assurance that his country will not neglect him in his old age, who has devoted his younger days to its service. The hall of the hospital is a most beautiful place. The ceiling was painted by Sir James Thornhill.[121] There are many ingenious deceptions in the painting of the sides also, such as pillars, doors, &c. A gentleman who was present with some ladies in company, had a key handed to him by the guide who told him to go through a door in the wall and show the ladies the garden. He readily took the key but was not a little mortified at finding that what he and all the spectators present had taken for a door was only a deception of painting. In this hall is a superb car whereon Lord Nelson's remains were carried to St. Paul's for interment, also a splendid vase and furniture for the hall to the amount of £10,000, presented by a widow lady. The chapel opposite is very elegant. The floor is of checquered marble. Over the altar is a picture of the shipwreck of St. Paul, by West. The observatory, (so celebrated) is situated in a park of great extent, from which there is a noble view of London and the river Thames.

A stranger finds no difficulty in getting a conveyance at any hour in the day to any of the adjoining villages, as there are coaches which ply to and from the different places, the fares of which are quite moderate, being from London to Greenwich (six miles) one shilling. In every noted street in the city coaches stand at all hours of the day

Figure 8 Illustration of a Greenwich pensioner from George Cruikshank's *London Characters*. After serving in the navy, Greenwich pensioners lived out their days at the Greenwich Hospital, which was intended for the relief and support of retirees. Many, though infirm, were capable of work and could earn tobacco money to supplement their pensions. Pensioners wore blue frock coats with brass buttons and a tricorn hat. Courtesy University of North Carolina at Chapel Hill.

and night. They are not so elegant as ours, yet are decent. The drivers are kept in order by the severity of the laws. They are obliged to give you a ticket of their number if you demand it, which is evidence as to the carriage in case they take improper fees, or otherwise impose upon you. The magistrates always severely punish these fellows when found guilty.

[Saturday, April] 29th This evening went to Drury Lane and saw Kean perform Penruddock in "The Wheel of Fortune."[122] I think I never saw finer acting. He particularly excels in characters where the voice is not to be raised very high. Mr. Bartley[123] performed in the farce Sir David Dunder.[124] This he did in his admirable style. He is famous in the character of Sir John Falstaff.

[Sunday, April] 30th This day walked out to Chelsea to view the hospital.[125] It is a similar establishment to Greenwich, being for the comfort of decayed soldiers. The edifice is not so elegant as that of Greenwich, but the situation is airy and pleasant. I found the soldiers in the chapel, a plain room ornamented with a picture over the altar of the resurrection of Christ with the soldiers around the tomb. The hardy looking veterans were all kneeling at their prayers. There were a great many strangers present. Passing from the chapel I entered the dining-hall and found the dinner-table spread in a neat and clean manner. Each soldier is allowed for his Sunday dinner a pound of meat, a loaf of bread, a quarter of a pound of cheese and a quart of beer. At one end of this room is a fine picture representing Charles the Second trampling Rebellion under foot. In the background is the hospital, to which he was a benefactor. Viewing the ease with which these old soldiers pass the remnant of their days makes me feel not a little ashamed of my native land, nor could I help contrasting the comfort of their lives with many of our old Revolutionary patriots, who bled for the independence of that country which leaves them in old age to indigence and want.

Returning I passed through St. James[126] and Hyde Parks.[127] These are delightful promenades. Over the canal is a gingerbread looking bridge of the Chinese fashion,[128] which was erected when the grand jubilee took place.[129] St. James' and Queen's palaces are quite inferior looking buildings. There are many handsome squares and streets in the west part of the town, which [is] the residence of the nobility and gentry. In the evening attended divine service at the Magdalen hospital, a receptacle for penitent prostitutes.[130] The Duke of Gloucester and the Princess Sophia were present. They are children of the king's brother.[131] They came in the carriage with servants and attendants in abundance. The church was very much crowded. The "magdalens" were in a gallery, screened from the view of the audience. The subject of the sermon was the resurrection of our Saviour, at the close of which an affecting appeal was made to the penitents. The music was very fine. The choir was composed of the unfortunate girls, whose leader was a woman who formerly received the benefit of this institution, is now reputably married, and is hired for that purpose. When I reflected how many females were rescued from perdition by this admirable institution I could not withhold my prayers in the words of the anthem "that these walls might be with gladness crowned,"[132] nor could I help regretting how few of our sex there are

"who scorn
To plant within the female breast a lasting thorn."

When I arrived at my friend's door, a gentleman who was in company took his handkerchief out to wipe his face, and in returning it to his pocket a person behind received it into his hand and made off.[133] This afforded us much mirth, as a person here never gets his pocket picked but he is laughed at for complaining about it.

[Monday] 1st May.134 This day the chimney sweeps have a grand jubilee. These sons of soot parade the streets fantastically dressed out in gilt paper jackets with gaudy wreaths around their heads, their faces besmeared with soot, and their hair powdered. They go from house to house begging money. Lady Montague,[135] who had lost her son, and after a very long search found him apprenticed to a sweep, left by will a sum of money to purchase annually a dinner at Paddington for as many of these sable sons as choose to attend.[136] The hackney coachmen also have abundance of ribbons on their hats in honor of the season.

It being a charming morning I went to Westminster Abbey.[137] My way was over Westminster Bridge[138] which is much the handsomest structure of the kind which is finished. Being rather heated with walking I took a turn in Westminster Hall to cool myself, as the dampness of the Abbey renders it dangerous to go into in that state. The Hall is quite large. There were many lawyers, dressed in their gowns and wigs, promenading it. At one end is the Court of Chancery, a small, dirty, dark room, 30 feet square. The judge, Sir Thomas Plomer,[139] sat upon a bench at one end, and the lawyers in a pit in the middle of the room. As the pleadings were quite uninteresting to me I soon left the place. The Abbey is an ancient and noble building. I entered at the Poets' Corner;[140] found divine service performing. The effect of the organ through the long arched aisles was inexpressibly sublime and grand, and the appearance of the painted windows through the same truly beautiful. Time has crumbled to dust many of the ancient monuments, but the great beauty of some of the modern ones deserves notice, particularly one to the memory of Lady Nightingale.[141] It represents Death bursting from the tomb and aiming his dart at the bosom of the wife, who is looking up with confidence expressed in her countenance for protection from her husband, whose agony is extreme at beholding her implore that assistance which is unavailing. The work is so well done as to raise doubts at first of its being marble. The monuments of Wolfe, Chatham, Pitt and André are fine pieces of sculpture. You are also shown, to the disgrace of the nation, some wax figures in cases. I hardly need observe that after viewing these fine pieces of workmanship, such baby-works are peculiarly disgusting and insipid.[142] The Coronation chairs are here. In the seat of one of them is the stone brought from Scone in Scotland and on which the Scottish kings were crowned.[143] I could not resist among the rest of the visitors the desire to sit in the chairs which have been successively occupied by a "line of kings." In one of the chapels are hung the banners of the Knights of the Garter,[144] with the crests and armorial bearings, beneath which are seats for their use on state occasions. The workmen were repairing one end of the Abbey which was damaged some years ago by age.

In the afternoon went to the House of Commons. The room in which the members sit is 40 feet by 80 feet, and not much more elegant than our old court-house at Boston. Over the Speaker's chair are the royal arms, carved and gilded. The Speaker (Mr. Abbott[145]) seemed to be quite an active man. His head was covered with a large wig similar to those the judges wear. The Commons were debating upon the propriety of accepting a most impudent petition from the city against going to war with Bonaparte. In this petition they called the Parliament a corrupt one, and the ministry wicked, weak and dangerous men. Lord Castlereagh[146] made no reply. The speakers were Whitbread,[147] Best,[148] Ponsonby,[149] Vansittart,[150] Sumner,[151] Curtis, Burdett, Baring,[152] Tierney,[153] and Peele.[154] Whitbread resembles Otis[155] in fluency and Ponsonby, Dexter[156] in solidity of arguing. The rest were not above mediocrity. Sir Francis Burdett[157] was a miserably bad orator, I think, but it is hazarding perhaps a hasty opinion that the talents of our State Legislature would not lose much by a comparison with that of the House of Commons.

[Thursday] May 4th. This day it is the custom for the priests and parish[158] officers to take a number of boys of the parish to the boundaries of it for the purpose of perpetuating in their memories the recollection of it. I chanced to be in a warehouse which stood in two parishes, and was a witness to the novelty. The boys, headed by the officers, entered without ceremony into the place, and with wands which they had, struck a plate of brass affixed to the wall. Sometimes they meet with the boys of another parish, and not infrequently does a combat ensue.[159]

The Queen[160] held a levee[161] this morning. The park was crowded with spectators to see the company go into the palace. The equipages were extremely brilliant. Many of the carriages had behind three great fellows with splendid liveries[162] and gold-headed canes in their hands. The gentlemen wore powdered hair and bags; the ladies were elegantly dressed with three ostrich plumes on their heads, in the manner of the Prince Regent's plume.[163] Many of these fair dames had them of such immoderate length that they were obliged to sit stooping for fear the top of the carriage would discompose their head-dress. The most singular spectacle was some ladies in sedan-chairs,[164] dressed with hoop petticoats, preceded by two and three footmen. The Prince Regent[165] and Duke of Kent[166] surrounded with a body of fine horse-guards passed along in their carriages with great rapidity. Guards were also stationed along the park where they drove. The Prince Regent is not very fond of showing himself to the people, as they take a disagreeable liberty of speaking very frankly to him. He endured much mortification when the Emperor of Russia was here last year, for when he made his appearance with him, the mob would cry out aloud, "You d——d rascal, where's your wife?"

At night attended Covent Garden Theatre to see Mr. Kemble[167] and Miss O'Neil[168] in the play of "The Stranger."[169] The performances this evening were never, in my opinion, surpassed for excellence. Kemble has a very singular voice, and I think is a little too formal and precise, yet his acting is elegant. When I speak of Miss O'Neil I cannot find words to express sufficiently my admiration of her acting. It is said she excels Mrs. Siddons when she first appeared upon the London boards. Her person is most beautiful. She possesses a fine tonic voice and a very expressive countenance.

I observed at a print shop a paper headed "British Valor." It was a proposal to publish two prints representing the victory of his Majesty's ship Endymion over the American frigate "President" with a comparison of the respective weights of metal and number of men, whereby is shown the vast superiority of the latter over the former —the whole designed by a relative of Captain Hope of the "Endymion."[170] John Bull swallows all this nor would disbelieve it if Admiral Hotham's letter was in the next window, for he has always been taught that "Britannia rules the waves."

[Sunday, May] 7th. Attended divine service at St. Andrew's church.[171] The subject of the discourse was the ascension of Jesus Christ. I was not much pleased with the preacher. He seemed to be quite insensible to the importance of his subject. The church is adorned with a painted window representing in one compartment Christ's Last Supper, and in another the Ascension. These paintings are more than two hundred years of age, yet the colors remain perfect and brilliant. At each side of the organ are paintings; one representing our Saviour healing the blind ("and after that He put His hands again upon his eyes and made him look up and he was restored and saw every man clearly" Matt. 8:25); the other His delivering His Sermon on the Mount. "He went up into a mountain and when He was set His disciples came unto him."[172] I think the fine paintings illustrating the events of our Saviour's life with which the English churches abound are calculated—

> "To raise at once our reverence and delight,
> To elevate the mind, and charm the sight,
> To pour religion through th' attentive eye,
> And waft the soul on wings of ecstasy
> For this the numic Art with Nature vies,
> And bids the visionary form arise
> Who views with sober awe, in thought aspires,
> Catches pure zeal, and as he gazes, fires,
> Feels a new ardor to his soul convey'd,
> Submissive bows, and venerates the shade"
> Louth[173]

There were present about two hundred charity children who are supported and educated by the parish. They were dressed in a neat blue uniform appropriate to their condition. In the evening went to the Foundling Hospital,[174] an institution for the reception of deserted infants. Here they are maintained and educated until of proper age to be apprenticed out. I was fortunate enough to arrive at an interesting period. Sixteen young men and women who had been apprenticed out this evening returned thanks to Almighty God for bringing them to this charity when they were deserted by their natural parents. The text of the discourse was "Jesus wept."[175] It was a very finished composition and particularly adapted to the occasion. The preacher in an elegant and argumentative manner pointed out the advantages of Christian sensibility and inferred that from that source the support of this institution flowed. The singing was very beautiful. Several eminent musical performers assisted the choir. There were upwards of five hundred of the children present, their ages from three to eleven years. At the end of the chapel is a picture by West of Christ receiving little children. "Suffer little children to come unto Me and forbid them not, for of such is the kingdom of heaven."[176] It is impossible to see the countenance of our Saviour as expressed by the pencil of West without the heart acknowledging that this was "the Man of Sorrows and acquainted with grief."[177] At the door a person stands to receive the charity of the visitors, which (as it is always crowded) amounts to a very considerable sum, and as it is understood that it is strictly applied to the purpose of the establishment, the liberality of the donors is conspicuous.

[Monday, May] 8th. This morning I spent four hours in the British Museum.[178] The building is capacious and contains curiosities to a vast amount, being the collection of years. Here is a grand collection of Roman and Grecian household utensils, coins, statues, &c. &c.; with this department I was particularly pleased, as it was very interesting to behold relics which brought us home, as it were, to their very households. Several students were busied in drawing from the statutes. The other part of the building contains a large library, manuscripts, minerals, and other curios, a particular account of which is given in the catalogue. This institution is shown with some regard to national honor, as no money is allowed to be given to the attendants, who are quite as civil as those paupers who show other places. Every visitor is obliged to write his name and place of residence in a book, upon entrance.

Miss Linwood's gallery of needlework[179] is perhaps the most extraordinary exhibition in the world; there are fifty-three large pictures done by her own hands with the needle, in worsted.[180] The execution of them is so admirable that it requires a nice eye to discriminate between them and paintings.[181] Jeptha sacrificing his daughter and a head of our Saviour are particularly fine. In one room fitted up to resemble a Gothic abbey are apartments wherein are many interesting pieces executed in the most natural manner.

At night went to Sadler's Wells, a little theatre at Islington.[182] The house was crowded with spectators; the performances were of the lowest kind of buffoonery and harlequinade. Grimaldi the celebrated clown performed. His fame has certainly not been over-rated, as he is one of the drollest dogs I ever beheld. The amusement of the evening concluded with a representation of the Battle of the Nile, on real water. The battle ships maneuvered about in a dashing style. The whole concluded with blowing up of the French ship L'Orient.

This month the exhibition of paintings at Somerset House[183] is open for the reception of visitors. The building is magnificent and has beside the apartment for the exhibition many rooms for public offices. The pictures exhibited here above one thousand, and consisted of the choicest works of the artists. With pleasure I observed two pieces done by Americans, one by Allston representing the Lady Mencia in *Gil Blas*[184] recovering from a swoon in the cave of the robbers.[185] It was finely executed but it appeared to great disadvantage, being placed in a bad light. Morse's[186] picture did not so warmly meet my approbation, as his subject, young Payne in the character of Zaphna, was not calculated to display much taste. The pictures which most pleased me were the "Distraining for Rent"[187] [and] the "Departure for London." In the first the terror and grief which the poor cottagers are thrown into by the sheriff's officer and their nonchalance in the midst of it, with all the minutiae of the furniture of an humble cot are so well delineated that the illusion is complete, and you are placed in the midst of the scene. In the "Departure for London" an old man has a young one by the hand while the rest of the family are busied in packing his trunk for the journey. In the background a domestic is tying his dog to prevent his following him. The anxiety of the old man's countenance was forcibly expressed. He seems to be saying "Take care that the temptations of the great city do not undermine those good principles which it has been my greatest pleasure to inculcate." There were many fine specimens of sculpture [in Somerset House]; in particular one designed as a monument to General Brock[188] who was killed in Upper Canada.

In the afternoon curiosity led me and two friends to the far-famed King's Bench Prison.[189] It is in the Burrough over London Bridge. The walls around it are very high and capacious. Within, it resembles a small town. There is a market, coffee-house, post-office, bake-house, shops, etc. etc. There were confined here 500 prisoners, a great many of whom were enjoying a game of racket.[190] Some were smoking and drinking and others were promenading the yard. The guide pointed

Figure 9 Paintings on exhibit at Somerset House from Ackermann's *Microcosm of London* (1830). Courtesy of the James Smith Noel Collection, Louisiana State University in Shreveport.

out to us de Berenger[191] the person who personated the Frenchman in Lord Cochrane's hoax. Lord Cochrane[192] is closely confined in a room for making his escape from his imprisonment here. After he had done so he took his seat in the House of Commons, where he was arrested. We were shown the room where the celebrated Mrs. Clark[193] was confined. It was a small place and formed I should presume quite a contrast to the apartments of the royal Duke. There were many genteel looking persons in confinement. The keeper observed that some lived at the rate of ten or twelve pounds a week expense ($50) and that very few who came with money ever departed with any, and that this was not caused by the high prices of articles, (for they are at liberty to send without the walls for them) but to an extravagance which all become habituated to. On our walk home we passed by a building newly erected for the purposes of a Bedlam.[194] Its exterior is perfectly elegant, more resembling a palace than a madhouse. We were not permitted to view the interior of the building. In the evening went to the Surrey Theatre, a small house devoted to dramatic and equestrian performances.[195] I was not pleased with the acting, but the scenery was quite as elegant as at the larger houses. The audience was of the citizen order, the nobility never making their appearance at such common places!

Sunday, [May] 14th. Attended St. Catherine's church[196] this morning. Like most churches in which I have been, it has marble monuments in memory of the dead. One of them is a recumbent figure; I thought it handsome. The prayers were read remarkably well, and the music consisting of a choir of charity boys and girls was good. The sermon was designed as preparatory to a collection, to be taken on the ensuing Sabbath, for the purpose of aiding missions and Bible societies; the text was Acts 10th, 34th verse.[197] The preacher observed in the course of it that the ancestors of those present once sacrificed to idols, and were it not for the exertions of missionaries sent to them by the pious Christians in the earlier ages they might now be groping in "heathen darkness" and that those places where now stands the altar of Christ but for this might now be the places of sacrifice to idols. He aroused the feelings of many a pious mother by recounting the number of infants sacrificed in India and the manner in which it was done;[198] and he finally concluded with the observation "that if religion did not command their aid, the common principles of humanity required it." At night I went to the Foundling Hospital but was not so much gratified with the preacher as on the last Sabbath. The subject was the example of the apostles; he said that their perseverance in establishing the gospel should be a, guide to us in the practice of its precepts. The music was fine, being anthems and hymns set to music by the first masters.

[Tuesday, May] 16th. I left London for the country. There were three passengers in the coach, a gentleman and his lady and a young lady, all of whom I found quite agreeable persons. The country was beautiful, as the trees were in bloom, and the pure air was grateful to me who had breathed nothing but coal smoke for so long a time. We passed many residences of the nobility. Near Stamford is Burleigh House, the seat of the marquis of Exeter. At the entrance of the park is a most noble gateway in the Gothic order. At Stamford are many churches one of them apparently very antique. The steeple to it is of immense height.[199] While [we] were here changing horses we were almost stunned with the music of a peal of bells which some amateur in that science was playing upon. At Newark we saw the ruins of the castle of that name, which was destroyed by Oliver Cromwell in the civil war. The battlements were many of them entire, and the moon shining span them added very much to their romantic appearance. At

Ferrybridge we crossed the river Aire over a remarkably handsome stone bridge.[200] During the journey I was frequently regaled with refreshments which the gentleman had brought and which he was so polite as to offer me. We travelled all night. At dusk I was not a little surprised at beholding my fair fellow traveller, who was quite a pretty girl, take off her bonnet, tie on her night cap, and leisurely compose herself to sleep in one corner of the coach, where she made quite an interesting appearance. After going with almost incredible swiftness, we arrived at Leeds, at 6 o'clock in the morning, being at the rate of eight miles and one-third each hour (including stoppages for refreshments, changing horses, etc.)—a velocity with which I desire never to travel again.

At Leeds[201] in the evening I saw the Indian Jugglers, three natives of India.[202] Their performances were wonderful. They were so out of the common sphere of exhibitions of this kind that I was perfectly astonished. The last feat was the swallowing of a sword, the blade of it twenty inches in length. This was not sleight-of-hand, but the practice of doing it from a child had rendered it familiar. The amazing power of mechanism compared to manual labor is demonstrated at Leeds in a variety of ways. At a warehouse I saw a packing press having thirty two tons power, arising from the pressure of a pail of water pumped up to the ceiling through a small pipe, and which in returning forces the press down with this amazing weight. It is so easy in its operation that a lad of eight years has sufficient strength for the purpose. There are also in Leeds eighteen wagons for carrying coal, the weight of which when loaded cannot be estimated at less than one hundred tons. These are propelled altogether by steam. They run upon a perfect plane with irons which fit into grooves on the wheels. These wagons deliver an immense quantity of coal at Leeds. The price of them is about seven shillings a chaldron [32 bushel]. At a manufactory I saw the different operations from the beginning to the finishing of a piece of cloth. The whole machinery was put in force by a steam engine which cost the proprietor one thousand guineas. Here also were imprisoned about fifty wretched boys and girls, the eldest not over ten years of age. They were all besmeared with dirt and grease arising from the wool. The proprietor observed in reply to my asking him if they never went to play, that they were there at six in the morning and never left off work, except for dinner, until seven at night. Thus these poor little wretches are confined in these hells—for I cannot find a more appropriate name—deprived of education and buried in these dark, noisy and unwholesome dens.

They either pass a quick but miserable existence or furnish turbulent, ignorant and vicious members of society.

[Friday, May] 19th. I dined this day at the seat of a gentleman a few miles out of town. The situation, surrounded with pleasure grounds and gardens, was pleasant. Among the shrubs in the garden was a barberry bush, which is here esteemed as a great curiosity. At dinner there was a number of handsome and agreeable ladies present. This meal was served up in a most splendid style. The excessive attention of the servants was to me quite disagreeable. Lady F., one of those present, was very sociable and asked me many questions respecting America. Speaking of our navy she remarked that all our ships were manned by Englishmen, and proved the remark by saying "Otherwise, how could they fight so?" I was not astonished at the manner of her reasoning as I have often heard the same opinion expressed by many persons when speaking of our navy. After dinner the whole party took a walk through many fine gardens and fields until we came to the brow of a hill when all at once a most beautiful landscape presented itself. At a short distance was a wood near the banks of the river Aire, over which was thrown a pretty stone bridge. On the left were the ruins of Kirkstall Abbey,[203] once a most magnificent building. The grandeur of the turret is still visible on a nearer approach. I was highly gratified. We entered the cemetery under the abbey. Here were several stone coffins which once contained the ashes of some nun or monk. The roof of the dining hall is quite entire, the gothic arches which support it being very beautiful. The southern window is very fine, and quite perfect.

Beyond the grand gateway is the hall or chapel. The galleries to it are supported by immense stone pillars, all in high perfection. Some of the towers are whole; one of them had a circular flight of stone steps which led to the top. From vestiges of the walls around the ruins which still remain, it is presumed the lands belonging to this institution were of large extent. In one part of this land is a large cistern hewn out of solid stone. The venerable walls and towers overgrown with ivy and tinged with the last rays of the setting sun, together with the delightful landscape around, rendered the scene truly charming; so much was I gratified that I determined to pay this place another visit before my departure. During conversation in the evening a lady observed, after one of the young ladies had been singing and playing, that it was quite shocking now to behold every vulgar, ill-born wretch attain an accomplished education, and that she understood that every tradesman's daughter was taught music, etc. Most unfortunately she directed her remarks to me, and by the manner in which they were delivered she seemed to require my assent to her observations. This she did not have, and, I suppose, for my republican notions, forfeited the lady's good opinion of my politeness.

[Saturday, May] 20th. This being market day here,[204] I went at nine o'clock into the Cloth Hall. This is quite large, being four halls of three hundred and fifty feet in length. Each person has an allotted space, marked with his name and town, whereon he exhibits his cloths for sale. At the ringing of a bell the sales begin and continue one hour. Except at that time no one is allowed to buy or sell in the building. There were on this day exposed for sale above one thousand pieces of cloth. The owners of them spoke such a curious dialect that I could not understand one word in ten they uttered. Part of the Prince Regent's own regiment is stationed at Leeds.[205] They are the finest looking men I ever beheld. There are also other soldiers here, whose recruiting parties parade the street, with a noble band of music. They have just passed, having two or three country lumpkins in company, to whom the soldiers have given their swords and exchanged their caps for their hats, with which the great boobies seemed as much pleased as a child with a rattle.

Sunday, [May] 21st. Attended divine service at the old church. This is a venerable building. It has a painted window; over the altar is a fine picture of our Saviour taking the cup at the Last Supper. The ceiling is also painted but the dampness arising from the floor (which is used as a burial place and covered with stone) has considerably injured it. Here are also several handsome monuments; one a beautiful piece of workmanship in marble representing an angelic figure weeping over the Flag of England. This was erected to the memory of two gallant officers, natives of Leeds, who fell at the battle of Talavera[206] in Spain. In one part of the church are hung the banner and armorial bearings of several knights. The preacher was tolerable; his subject was the piety of Cornelius the centurion.[207] There were fifty-one banns[208] of marriage published this morning; in addition to this several couples were joined in the holy bonds of matrimony previous to the beginning of the church service. The organ of this church is justly celebrated as being one of the finest toned ones in England. I dined at Mr. O.'s in company with the Mess Hoffman of Baltimore. The dinner was quite in the family style. Mr. O. remarked that his aunt was married by the celebrated Sterne,[209] and that a few days ago he had in his possession a whip which formerly belonged to that eccentric character. After we had dined the company walked out of town upon a visit to Kirkstall Abbey. I was no less delighted now than on my former visit. There were a number of common people rambling through the ruins of whom I asked a variety of questions respecting the antiquity of the place, and I received some very curious answers. We passed through the chapel at the end of which is a noble large window with some of its ornaments still remaining. In a small recess the font for holy water is still perfect, and the same is seen in a number of private chapels adjoining the great one. Ascending a flight of stone steps we came into a gallery from whence a circular staircase leads into one of the towers, but owing to the ruinous state of the steps we did not ascend. Several boys had however mounted to the top in quest of rooks' nests, those birds being the only inhabitants of this once splendid structure. Beneath the abbey is a dungeon, appropriated formerly as a place of punishment for refractory nuns and friars. The garden which is enclosed by the walls of the abbey is still kept in perfect order. The abbey, with the surrounding lands, belongs to the Earl of Cardigan, who endeavors to prevent the further decay of the edifice by employing a person to take care of it.[210]

In the evening I attended St. James' church a modern building, entirely destitute of ornament.[211] This being Trinity Sunday,[212] the sermon was appropriate to the occasion, and was delivered by the preacher without notes. The Psalms were read by a clerk with a broad Yorkshire dialect, and sung in a most discordant manner. At Mr. O's I was introduced to the Rev. Doctor Kewley of New York, whose church in Beekman Street having recently been burned he was enabled while it was rebuilding to leave upon a visit to his friends in England. He politely gave me his address with an invitation to call upon him should I visit New York.[213]

[Monday, May] 22nd. Departed this morning in the coach for Manchester. The passengers were three agreeable ladies and a clever loquacious Scotsman. The last person was a great admirer of Doctor Franklin,[214] whose works he had by heart and most liberally quoted from. The route was through Bradford and Halifax, large manufacturing places. The country was very hilly and afforded many fine views. The road in one part of our journey ran alongside a steep and dangerous precipice, where the least deviation of the horses would have hurled us to destruction. At such an immense height were we that the inhabitants of a village below in the valley looked not larger than crows. We dined at Halifax. Upon our entrance the landlord's ruby-colored nose was brightened up with renewed lustre and while rubbing his hands he congratulated us upon our arrival at his house "at (to use his own language) so fortunate a period, as he had a fine fresh turbot for dinner, an article that I do not have more than twice a year." But alas! this "fine, fresh turbot"[215] when it came upon the table, carried conviction to every nose that the landlord had been very much deceived with regard to its freshness, or had been like Roque[216] in the Mountaineers at "wonderful pains for a fortnight to keep it sweet."

At a small village before we entered Rochdale[217] it was their market day. The streets were crowded with women, men and children, the ugliest, dirtiest wretches I ever beheld. The women in particular were the most shocking. Old and young had on large caps with two flaps at each side which hung down to their shoulders. On our appearance in the coach a mob of children were immediately let loose to chase after us to beg a penny. When we entered the suburbs of Manchester the atmosphere underwent a total change; from its being very clear weather it became dull and foggy. The smoke which perpetually overhangs this city is the cause of it. The next day it rained incessantly. It seems as if this were forever the case. An anecdote is related of a foreigner asking a person from Manchester whether or not it had done raining yet! This city like almost all the large towns in Great Britain has an infirmary for the reception of the indigent sick. The building is placed in a fine situation and is a handsome structure. The people of this country are renowned for their charities. There is scarcely a place where there is not some institution supported by private munificence for the relief of the poor. They first are compelled to give largely by the "poor laws";[218] to this are added immense voluntary contributions. Were it not for these donations the streets would swarm with beggars, as it is, there are in the large towns a great many. I remarked an advertisement stuck upon the walls by the civil authority offering two guineas reward each for the apprehension of thirty-seven men who had absconded and left their families upon the parish! This is one of the blessings of manufactories.

[Wednesday, May] 24th Left Manchester for Liverpool. The country looked very fine. The fields of wheat in particular gave fair promise of a fine crop. When I passed through the country upon my first arrival there was written upon every fence "no corn bill"[219]— Government having passed a bill, for the encouragement of the farmers, prohibiting the introduction of flour or corn into the kingdom for sale, excepting the price was above 80 shillings per quartern. The manufacturing interest was violently opposed to the bill, upon the ground that if this restriction was off, foreign grain would be afforded much cheaper than the home-raised. The ministers replied that if corn could be imported, there would not be any inducement for the farmers to raise any, and that consequently they must be dependent upon foreign nations for their supply. In London the populace were so much exasperated at this bill that they attempted to tear down a member of Parliament's house for voting for it, and the government had to employ a military force to suppress the mob.[220]

Just at the entrance of Liverpool stands the mansion of Doctor Solomon, of Balm of Gilead memory.[221] He has gulled the world to some purpose, if one were to judge from the splendor of his establishment. The stage fare from Manchester to Liverpool, distance forty miles, is only six shillings. This is caused by the strong opposition, as there are eight or ten coaches continually running between those places. Besides the fare in the coach, you have to pay the coachman one shilling per stage of about thirty miles, and the same to the guard whose business it is to take care of the luggage, &c &c. Should the passenger refuse to pay the accustomed tribute he would inevitably be insulted. You must pay also, at the inns, the chambermaid sixpence a night, the "boots" (the person who cleans them) two pence a day, and the head waiter one shilling a day. The porter[222] who takes your portmanteau up stairs moves his hat with "pray remember the porter, Sir." In fact, it is necessary in travelling through England to have your pocket well lined with pounds, shillings and sixpences, otherwise you never can satisfy the innumerable demands made upon a traveller by landlord, waiters, chambermaids, and coachmen, &c. &c. My bill at Manchester for one supper, a dinner, a breakfast, and two nights lodging was five dollars. The beds at the inns are surprisingly neat and clean. In many of the inns in a large town, the chambermaids furnish the chambers and depend upon their fees for remuneration. The stagecoaches are very convenient and easy. No baggage is permitted to be taken inside, it being stowed away in the boot places before and behind the carriage for that purpose. Here it rides perfectly safe, not being liable to be rubbed, as they ride upon the same springs that the passengers do. A person can always calculate upon being at the place he takes the coach for (barring accidents) at a certain time, as the coachman is allowed a given time to go his stage. The guard always has a chronometer with him (locked up so that he cannot move the hands) as a guide with regard to time.[223]

In company with Mr. M. I went to the Liverpool Theatre. It is a neat building but the performers were miserable.[224] Many of the streets and squares in Liverpool are spacious and handsome.

St. James' Walk is a fine promenade. At the back of it is a public garden laid out in a tasteful manner. From the terrace is a commanding view of the town and Cheshire shore, with the shipping lying in the river. The stone quarry is very near here. The entrance is through a subterraneous passage 60 yards in length, hewn through solid stone. All the stones necessary for the formation of the docks are taken from this place. The stone resembles the Connecticut red stone: it is quite liable to crumble into sand, but I am informed that the water hardens it. The trade to Liverpool is immense. A multitude of ships are now in the liver waiting for a berth in the dock, which they can only gain by some other vessel's going to sea. The large warehouses near the docks, rising thirteen stories in height, and the bustle and noise in the streets show to the stranger that here "commerce is busy with her ten thousand wheels."[225]

[Thursday, May] 25th. Dined this day with Mr. B., a large company of ladies and gentlemen present. Among them was a venerable clergyman of the dissenting persuasion. He spoke in the highest terms of the American clergy, with many of whom he had been personally acquainted, but one lately had offended him by a breach of politeness; of him he observed to me that he was more conversant with religion than with good manners. Here again I was astonished at the amazing ignorance of a gentleman respecting the United States. He possessed such a knowledge of his own country that he led me to suppose that he was joking when speaking of ours. He first remarked that we could not live as cheaply in America as in England. I pointed out the mistake to him, when he again observed "True, you may live as cheaply but you are obliged to eat salted meat in winter." He was very much astonished when I informed him that even in that frozen and inclement season we had as good fresh provisions as were to be had in England. These errors respecting the United States have arisen from the misrepresentations of the English tourists and from its being the interest of the Government to keep up these impressions to prevent emigration.[226] I was asked the other day in the stagecoach if the Americans all spoke English,[227] and a genteel young lady at London was quite shocked to think I should prefer the "almost impenetrable woods of America" to England!

Mr. B. accompanied me to the Botanic Garden which is at the extremity of the town.[228] It is supported by private subscription and contains four thousand different trees, plants and shrubs. The garden is kept in perfect order. Each subscriber has the liberty of introducing strangers. The walks of it are much resorted to as a fashionable promenade, thus combining pleasure with instruction!

[Saturday, May] 27th. This morning went to the Herculaneum Pottery,[229] a short distance from town. Here both common and fine wares are manufactured. These works employ about two hundred persons, men, women and children. Having an introduction from a gentleman at Liverpool to the intendant of the place, I received every possible attention in viewing the processes of the work. Some of the china was quite elegant. There were a great many very genteel looking men and women at work drawing the landscapes upon the china; many women were also engaged in laborious work, much more suitable for men, such as beating heavy lumps of clay, &c &c. It is however quite the custom in Great Britain to make the fair sex bear at least one-half the burden of life, but I have frequently thought, when I have seen them ploughing, digging and reaping, that they have had the greatest part. On your entrance to the works you are presented with a card whereon is a request that you will not give the workmen any money, but if you are disposed, that you may contribute an offering to a fund appropriated to the instruction of the children of the workmen and to the relief of the sick. This is a praiseworthy regulation and should be adopted by every factory to which curiosity leads visitants, as the workmen always expect some little present which is almost invariably applied to furnish drinks.

In the afternoon went to Warrington. In the coach was a cotton dealer of Manchester with whom I had a spirited conversation respecting American affairs. The information he had concerning them he had obtained from British tourists and from letters of the officers of the army who had served in the United States. He was quite prejudiced; "the affair at New Orleans was a mere brush;[230] Sir Geo. Prevost was never beaten at Plattsburgh;[231] and with a force of fifty thousand men they (the English) could conquer the Northern States." This last information he had received from a publication entitled *The Military Chronicle*, wherein was a letter written by an officer who was at the capture of Castine[232] and expressed the above opinion and also stated his opinion of America generally, taking Castine as the place to govern his ideas of it. My travelling friend I could discover had taken pains to inform himself respecting America, but the sources from whence he had drawn his knowledge were miserably corrupt, and consequently had misled him. He had a general idea of the geographical situation of our country, but when he particularized he made me smile at the errors he committed. Speaking of Boston he observed that he thought that with ten thousand men they could take it with ease. I pointed out the impossibility of getting into our harbor; he replied that he knew the difficulty of passing by the Fort of Castle William,[233] and Noddles Island,[234] but that they could land at the back side of Bunker Hill (an odd place for an Englishman to land at), as their ships in 1775 had laid there with ease. He supposed from this that there was another passage to the sea. After we had conversed a long time together, he observed that he had just such another tête-à-tête with an American before and that his name was Silliman. Mr. S. mentions this gentleman in his work, but I cannot agree with him with regard to the gentleman's correct information.—My companion and I parted at Warrington where I for the first time heard ballad singers. They carry ballads for sale, at the same time singing them to allure purchasers. One of the women bore the appearance of having seen better days. She possessed a fine voice and sang but little inferior to many who sing at the London theatres.

[Sunday, May] 28th Went this morning to church. The place was neat. There were on the walls tablets with appropriate texts of Scripture inscribed on them. Part of the service was chanted in a very fine manner by a choir of women. The sermon, which was delivered in an oratorical manner, was upon the necessity of a renewal of the spirit to make us Christians. The congregation was extremely small, caused by the numbers which have seceded from the Church and joined the Dissenters.[235] After dinner my friend and myself set out for a farm house of his in a neighboring village, but being overtaken by a shower of rain we were compelled to seek shelter in a miserable hovel, which was occupied by a man who said he had been in the service of the Duke of Bedford for fourteen years. He was mixing some oatmeal cakes[236] for his supper, the materials for which were on his bed as he had neither stool nor table in the apartment, it being so small as to forbid the introduction of either. His fuel he kept under his bed, which of course was extremely dirty. On our jocosely asking him for his tap he told us that he had not tasted a drop of ale for six weeks. Amidst all this misery and wretchedness the poor fellow seemed to be cheerful and happy! The rain ceasing we were enabled to reach our destination. Here was a contrast to the last scene. Each apartment of the house was in the most perfect and neat order. Attached to it was a charming garden, filled with a variety of flowers in full bloom. Some strawberry vines were planted in a different manner from any I ever before noticed. Bricks were placed in the manner of steps upon the side of a terrace, between the interstices of which the roots were placed, and the tops lay upon the bricks. The rejection of the sun upon them serves to ripen the fruit, while they serve to prevent the berries from hanging into the dirt. I question however whether this manner of planting them would answer in America, as the bricks heated by our powerful sun would burn and destroy the vines. This way of cultivating them adds very much to the beauty of a garden.

[Tuesday, May] 30th Being a fine day we went to Northwick to view the salt mines.[237] The road lay through a charming country. We passed Belmont, an elegant mansion surrounded by an extensive park from which is an extensive view: the inhabitants upon this route are mostly employed in husbandry which may be plainly perceived by the neatness of their cottages and their comfortable appearance, contrasted with those in the manufacturing towns.

Budworth is a pretty little village with an ancient stone church. A little beyond here we called in at a farmhouse, the occupier of which told me he gave six hundred and fifty pounds rent and taxes, for his farm of two hundred acres. He shewed me fifty fine cows valued at 25 Guineas each. They were fine looking animals and appeared to be much superior to any I ever saw in America. He makes 7 tons of cheese Pr. Year. While he was here a wagon load of 3 tons weight was sent off to market to be sold. The dairy room was quite large, having vats of pewter to contain the milk which keeps better in this manner than in any other. The farmers do not put their hay into barns as our farmers do, but stack it out in the fields, first pressing it very hard. When they use it they are obliged to slice it off with a sharp instrument. A hay-mow half used looks similar to a loaf with slices cut from it. Here also was a garden laid out in the neatest manner imaginable. The gooseberry bushes hung down with the weight of their fruit, but the currants did not seem to flourish, nor did I ever see any bushes of that kind which seemed to bear well anywhere in England. After partaking of a glass of home-brewed ale, we proceeded to the salt pit, where four persons, including myself, were lowered in a tub down a shaft of three hundred and fifty-five feet in depth. I must confess that before I got one half of the way down I heartily repented of my journey, but upon my arrival at the bottom I was amply repaid for all my fears. The first thing that saluted my sight was a stable of five horses employed in removing the salt to the mouth of the shaft. The mine is excavated in length three-quarters of a mile, and width one-half. It is about fifteen feet in height. The sides and top are regularly and squarely hewn. There are regular streets cut at right angles. The roof is supported by pillars twelve yards square. One of the workmen blasted the rock which is so hard as to resist everything but gunpowder. The noise of the explosion reverberating through the chasms was awfully loud and rolled along the mine like thunder. The whole place made a most brilliant appearance when illuminated by our candles.' About a year since, Mr. Canning[238] visited this mine when it was lighted up with 1600 candles. I was not less alarmed in going up than in descending. The amazing depth of the shaft rendered apparently the light at the top like to a small star, but we arrived safely in the upper world after an absence of two hours. Here we saw the different processes of refining the rock. It is first soaked in a pit, the water of which becoming brine it is conveyed into a pan under which is a slow fire, where it remains until the water evaporates and the salt remains at the bottom. Then it is taken and put into baskets in the shape of a sugar loaf and carried into the drying room, when it soon becomes perfect and is fit for sale. The price of it for exportation is 4^d a bushel, but the people of England pay for home consumption (such is the enormous duty) 16 shillings for the same quantity. Excise men are always upon duty at the works to prevent any persons taking even the smallest quantity without the duty having been paid. So vigilant are they, and so heavy is the penalty for transgressing the law that should a piece of the rock be dropped by chance on the highway no one dares pick it up with an intent of using it!

[Wednesday, May 31] I returned the same night to Warrington and the next day went to the city of Chester.[239] At a short distance from the city we observed a gibbet[240] whereon hung the bodies of two men who were long ago executed for the robbery and murder of the postboy. The appearance of the city as you enter it is very pretty, the trees among the houses giving it a lively effect. The place is very ancient. That part of it designated "the old part" is surrounded by walls. The width of the walk on top of these is sufficient for three persons to go abreast. At small distances apart are remains of towers formerly used as watch-towers, and at a short distance from the wall on one of the corners (the West) of the city is a large tower in a state of dilapidation which was connected to the great wall by a smaller one.[241] The entrance to the town is through four spacious gates, situated north, south, east and west, the names the) bear. The modern part of the city is extended considerably beyond the wall. Directly under one part of the wall lies the race ground which is the most complete of any in England, with regard to its natural situation. The ground on which the horses run is a perfect plane, while the hills and wall which surround it form it into a circus.²⁴² There are several ancient churches here, and in some of them time has made sad havoc, as they are rapidly falling into decay. The foot passengers are in this city sheltered from the weather by the shops and houses projecting over in the form of a piazza having a walk under it. Chester Castle is a most noble building which stands upon an eminence and overlooks the city. The entrance to the yard is through a noble gateway. On the right stands the Armory and on the left the barracks for the soldiers stationed here. The principal building is appropriated as a house for the governor of the castle and as a court house and prison. The prison is conducted something similar to the State prison at Charlestown. The prisoners are confined in such a manner that the keeper can overlook them (while at work) from his apartment. The appearance of the governor's house with several young ladies dressed in high fashion was but illy calculated to inspire one with the gloomy thought of its being a place of pain and imprisonment. The whole edifice is formed of a light-colored stone and planned in such a manner as to conceal the purpose for which it was erected. The place where the courts are held is a pretty room, the ceiling being pannelled. In the bar is a trap door, beneath which is a sub-terranean communication with the cells of the prisoners, who are through it brought into court. In the bar is also an iron affixed for the purpose of confining the hands of those who are sentenced to be burnt in the hand, which punishment is put into execution in presence of the court.²⁴³ A short time ago a fellow thus sentenced bore the iron without flinching and then tore out with his teeth the disgraceful mark and spit it on the floor.

[Friday, June 2] Returned in the evening to Warrington and the next day set out for Manchester. On June 2nd in company with Mr. Bangs walked thirty-two miles to view the peak of Derbyshire. Our road was through Stockport, a large manufacturing town, with nothing worthy of notice excepting the narrowness of the street, and the steepness and length of its hills. The country generally was well cultivated. At a neat inn at Hazel Grove or Bullock Smithy²⁴⁴, we dined with an excellent appetite and afterwards continued on through the village of Dishley until we arrived at Whally-Bride,²⁴⁵—a most romantic situation. Directly under the window of the inn ran a small river over which was a bridge. Beyond this, upon the side of an eminence, stood a cluster of cottages whose white walls formed a charming contrast with the green vines which overspread them. At 5 in the evening we reached Chapel in the Forth, a tolerably neat village, and afterward ascended a very high mountain, from the top of which was a very extensive view. We took the wrong road and were progressing toward Chesterfield when we stopped at an alehouse, the master of which informed us of our mistake and directed us into a foot path whereby we might regain the right road; but we soon again missed the path and we were induced to think, as it grew dusky that we must be upon the "barren mountain starved," as there was no probability of our meeting any person to direct us. We continued on for some time in this uncertainty, until at last we espied at some distance a cottage, and after making up to it were directed on our way; following our directions we came to the ruins of an old castle, which we found situated upon an eminence directly over the village of Castleton. The immense height of the precipice made us shrink back with terror when we approached the brink and looked over it. After supper we retired to bed much fatigued from our long walk, and in the morning after having engaged a guide, we visited the Cavern, or Peak's Hole.[246] There is a small rivulet which takes its rise in or beyond the Cavern, over which we crossed by a little stone bridge to gain the entrance of the cave. This entrance is in the side of the mountain over whose brink we had looked the night before. In the mouth of the cavern are two small cottages inhabited by persons whose occupation is spinning of twine. One of them, an old woman, told us that she was born in this place and had always lived here. At a door beyond, candles are given you to light you into the interior, into which we proceeded until the roof became so very low that it almost seemed to touch a piece of water which reached athwart the cavern. We then entered a little boat and lay upon our backs while our guide waded into the water and shoved us along until we arrived at a cavern of great dimensions. Following our conductor we soon came to another cavern called Roger Rain's house, from its continual dropping water from the roof. Here we were surprised at the beautiful appearance of candles which some boys held in a gallery at a vast height above us. They appeared at an immense distance and resembled brilliant stars. We next descended into the Devil's Cellar the walls of which are inscribed with the initials of the visitors' names. The guide invited us to follow this example, but having no disposition to be in the Devil's books we did not accept the proposition.

 We proceeded until we came to the extremity of this wonderful cavern, which is 2250 feet from the entrance. The guide waded through the water under a low arch twenty five feet farther than visitors generally go. We were here saluted with a blast of gunpowder, the noise of which was tremendously loud and gave us a shock which electrified us. The water flows through a part of these caves in a beautiful streamlet, the bottom of it composed of white pebbles. It loses itself under ground, in one of them, and makes its appearance again at the mouth of the cavern. When we returned the daylight at the entrance of the cave was indescribably beautiful. After we had partaken of some refreshments we went to view the Speedwell mine.[247] This mine was worked for lead, but after the proprietors had expended fourteen thousand pounds sterling it was found not to answer the purpose. The guide to it lives in a little cot at its entrance. Here we descended one hundred and six steps at the bottom of them was a boat, into which we entered and were ferried through a passage cut out of solid rock just large enough to permit a person to sit upright in the vessel. This passage is 2300 feet in length, and terminates in a cavern called the Devil's Hall. Here we were 700 feet from the surface of the earth. The roof of the cavern has never been seen. Rockets have been sent up for that purpose, but without effect. Here is a grate which divides the cavern from the abyss down which the water tumbles, making a tremendous noise.

Our guide assured us that he had been lowered into this gulf for the distance of three hundred feet, until he arrived at the surface of the water which he tried with a line of one hundred and seventy feet in length, but could not find bottom. When the mine was worked, the rubbish that came out was for the period of five years thrown into this chasm, but to all appearance this has not in the least diminished its depth.

Castleton is romantically situated in a fertile valley, well watered by the stream proceeding out of the cavern.[248] The inhabitants are remarkably healthy. Their occupation consists of mining and husbandry. The church is a neat building and contains the following remarkable epitaph which is inscribed in Latin to conceal as much as possible the scepticism of the person who ordered it to be put upon his tombstone. The man's name was Micah Hall, who lived 79 years. It is as follows:

> "What I was you know not!
> What I am you know not;
> Whither I am gone you know not;
> Go about your business!"[249]

We were not a little surprised at our landlord's informing us that the way we came into Castleton was extremely dangerous, abounding in pits and precipices, where one false footstep would have hurled us to destruction! Having seen all the curiosities at Castleton, at five in the evening we took a post chaise for Buxton.[250] The road is through a valley which divides the mountains surrounding the Village. We passed the ebbing and flowing well. This is at the bottom of a steep hill. The water at irregular periods, according to the wetness, or dryness of the season, rises and falls in the manner of the tide. It was bubbling and discharging its waters when we passed it. Buxton is very charmingly situated, entirely surrounded with hills. The Crescent is a fine row of buildings built by the Duke of Devonshire for the accommodation of those persons who resort hither for the benefit of the waters. These waters are of great benefit in gouty and rheumatic complaints. There was a great deal of genteel company here. At a short distance from the Crescent is a fine walk through which flows a streamlet of water forming several cascades as it runs. The walks are planted with trees and at certain distances are seats for the promenaders. I think Buxton superior in beauty to any place I have seen in England, yet Bath is said to be much superior. In the afternoon of the next day, left in the coach for Manchester, where I arrived the same evening and found it the same dull, smoky, rainy hole as ever! I left Manchester without any regret at the possibility of my never seeing it again, and arrived at Liverpool. In the coffee-room of the Inn a traveller was giving a lively description of a pugilist's battle between two scientific fighters.[251] The bare recital of it I should suppose would make a person of humanity shudder. One of the combatants was carried off the field with his jaws broken, vomiting blood. This is called amusement for a refined people! An Englishman will say it serves to stimulate the courage of the common people! I am sure it brutalizes them and augments their ferocity, for no sooner does a little dispute chance to arise than an appeal to blows is resorted to, to settle it. So much are they in love with boxing that if two boys get to quarrelling, men, women and children will endeavour to add fuel to their resentment, just for the pleasure of seeing a little fun!

Being detained at Liverpool a few days by business, I passed my leisure hours in the Athenæum; this afforded much amusement and dissipated that time which otherwise would have hung heavy on my hands.

Sunday, 11th June. Attended this day (for the first time in England) a dissenting or Presbyterian church. Doctor Lewin,[252] the gentleman with whom I dined a short time since, was the preacher. He is 78 years of age, and was quite animated in his delivery. Generally speaking there is not that ignorance of the American nation among the people of Liverpool that there is in other places in England. It obviously arises from the great intercourse that is carried on between this port and the United States. I have scarcely passed a day without meeting some one whom I have seen in America. There is a degree of liberality shown here to our countrymen which is not shown in other places. This evening "God save the King" was called for at the theatre, when an American sailor loudly exclaimed from the gallery "God d——n the king and all the rest of 'em!" Yet the only notice taken of this was by a general laugh at Jack's republicanism. Had he been in London the mob would have torn him to atoms.

[Thursday] June 15th. In company with three of my fellow-countrymen, Thomas Dennie, Isaac Barnes and Abbot Lawrence,[253] I departed for London. There is something inexpressibly pleasant in meeting and associating in a foreign country with those with whom you have been acquainted at home. Our journey was very pleasant. On our road through Staffordshire we passed the potteries of Burslem and Hanley, as also several collieries[254] where at the mouth of the pits steam engines were erected to draw up the coals. Near Burslem, from the top of a very high hill, there is a commanding view of the county. Hanley is quite a pretty place and contains some fine houses. At Tutbury passed near the ruins of the castle of that name. It stands upon an eminence and entirely commands the town, which lies directly under its walls. This castle was once the prison of Mary, Queen of Scots.[255] The walls are now almost entirely demolished. At Uttoxeter we changed horses. The Inn was directly opposite an ancient church whose graveyard was filled by a rabble of boys, pedlars' stalls, etc. and seemed to be a common thoroughfare. It is shocking to behold the ashes of the dead outraged in this manner, but in this country I have remarked too often that the dead are trodden upon whenever it suits the convenience of the living. We dined at Burton, a, charmingly neat and clean town particularly famed for its good ale. Crossing the river, over which is a stone bridge, the next place we stopped at was Leicester, a place noted for its manufactory of stockings. This is also a very neat town. We passed a great many country seats, and at Northampton changed horses. The Inn where we stopped was in a large square which adds much beauty to the place. At a short distance from the town stands a stone cross, erected by Edward the First in memory of his beloved wife Eleanor,[256] whose body rested here on its way to London. Lace-making seems to be the principal employment of the people hereabout. "Pillow and bobbin appears to be all their little store"[257] in most of the cottages we saw. The day being fine enabled us to have a good view of London as we entered it. We arrived at five in the afternoon, being just thirty-six hours in travelling two hundred and ten miles. I found on my arrival a notice that all aliens should report themselves to the Mansion House.[258] Accordingly the next day I went thither and found the Lord Mayor examining a wretched looking woman with a child in her arms upon a charge of theft. The examination was conducted with much mildness on the part of the Mayor. He is a pastry cook by profession, and is still concerned with his nephew, who carries on the business not far from the Mansion House.[259] I received (after I had registered my name) directions to call in six days for a license to reside here. On going through the Royal Exchange I was peculiarly struck with the variety of dress in the crowd of merchants assembled there. Here were Christian, Turk and Jew. In walking the city a person meets such a variety of fashion in dress that it is impossible to tell the prevailing one. A man must possess considerable talent to make himself notorious for dress or equipage in this great city. Even Romeo Coates,[260] the amateur actor, when he first made his appearance in a dashing curricle ornamented with a cock as his crest, had to employ some boys to cry "Cock-a-doodle-doo" to bring it into notice.

Being near Eastcheap today I tried to discover the Boar's Head, but was unsuccessful. This is where Sir John Falstaff and Prince Henry had their "cup of sack."[261]

At a window in a print shop my eye was attracted by a print in glaring colors purporting to be the Capture of Washington. It represented a strongly fortified place, compared to which Quebec and Gibraltar were nothing. The British troops were marching over a breast-work of dead Americans in the face of a battery of cannon blazing at them. In the back-ground was the "President's Palace" (as the explanation informed me) and eight or ten seventy-fours[262] in flames. This is the mere idea, of the print seller, but the British Government tried all in their power to make this circumstance popular. They were unsuccessful. Many Englishmen have acknowledged to me that it was a stain on their national character which cannot be obliterated.

[Saturday, June] 17th In the evening went to the Opera.[263] This is a most splendid house, having five rows of boxes above which is a gallery to admit persons who are not in full dress, as they are excluded from all other parts of the house. The boxes are all private and are rented at from three hundred to one thousand pounds a season.[264] This immense building crowded with company in full dress is a charming sight. The scenery is elegant, but as the performances were in Italian I could not make out what the subject was that was represented.[265] The band is very large and the music excellent. There was some fine dancing, particularly Nestri's,[266] but the manner of the female dancing was very indelicate, to my ideas! In not understanding Italian I was in the same situation as the greater part of the audience, who attend here in preference to the English Theatre merely because it is fashionable! I was quite amused with the Bond Street loungers[267] who came into the gallery where I was, to look at the ladies. One of them, dressed in the extreme of fashion, with a chapeau under his arm, took his station opposite to two pretty girls who sat upon a seat in front of me, and taking out his quizzing glass[268] he most impudently stared them in the face as long as he could keep one eye open and the other shut. I have seen these fellows represented upon our stage and thought it a caricature, but I now think the original a great deal the worst.

Having a desire to see Royalty I attended the Chapel Royal, St James' Palace, to see the Princess Charlotte,[269] probably the future Queen of England. This chapel is in the courtyard of the palace. The entrance is through a small door into a dark and narrow passage which carries you into the chapel. This is quite a confined room and not at all elegant. The ceiling is panelled and ornamented with the coats of arms of the nobility. The Princess came in attended by several lords and ladies, and took her seat in the gallery opposite to where I stood. She has a pretty face and eyes, with the buxomness of a country lass. Her dress was a purple pelisse[270] edged with white, with a French fashioned bonnet and a wreath around it. She had not the least gentility of appearance and her manners were shockingly vulgar, particularly when she stood up. She had then a kind of rolling about, and kept her arms akimbo. She took very little notice of the service and seemed, from her uneasiness, to wish that it were ended. The singing and chanting of the service was very fine, as the first performers are here engaged. The preacher was a courtly looking man, who mounted the "rostrum with a skip," preached elegantly for half an hour about—nothing at all, made his bow and backed down the pulpit stairs (for he was too polite to turn his back upon royalty), and made his exit. I was much better pleased in the evening at the service of the Foundling Hospital, where the same preacher officiated whom I had heard some weeks ago. The anthem was sung by Mr. Pyne of Covent Garden Theatre. The subject of the discourse was "None of us liveth to himself."[271]

Some Bostonians of my acquaintance whom I visit, lodge in the coffee house so much frequented by Addison, Steele and Johnson, and from whence so many of their admirable essays are dated. It then went by the name of "Will's Coffee-house," but is now called "Richard's."

[Tuesday, June] 20th Last night went to Covent Garden Theatre to see Miss O'Neil as Euphrasia in "The Grecian Daughter."[272] Her representation of this character was exquisitely fine. Mr. Young[273] personified Evander. I never saw a tragedy which took such hold on my feelings as this did. Even the inferior parts were sustained by performers whose talents were above mediocrity.

The concluding scene where she stabs Dionysius drew forth repeated plaudits from a house filled in every corner: were it not for the attractions of the performances, the interesting sight of hundreds of well-dressed people in the pit and boxes would amply repay one for his attendance. The after piece was "The Forty Thieves,"[274] and I feel proud for the theatrical fame of America to be able to say that the representation, both as to acting and scenery, was quite inferior to that which we had on the Boston boards, when Mrs. Darley and Mr. Bernard took a part in the performance. Near Carlton House the residence of the Prince Regent, Mr. West's[275] two pictures of "Christ Rejected" and "Christ healing the Sick" are exhibited. The last is painted expressly for the hospital at Philadelphia, and, it is said, surpasses the original one which was painted for that institution and by the sale of which Mr. West incurred an imputation of ungenerous conduct. This he seems to be aware of, and has excited himself to produce this masterpiece of painting, for the loan of which for two years he has refused three thousand guineas. The meek and beautiful countenance of our Saviour, and the anxiety of the friends of the lame, halt and blind, together with a sick man borne along by two figures, to be healed, are admirably painted. The correctness with which the effects of the different diseases upon the human frame are delineated is the admiration of medical men, and shows with what attention and care the painting of this piece has been prosecuted. The picture of "Christ Rejected" I think far preferable to the one described. The meekness of Him who was borne "like a lamb to the slaughter"; the diabolical passions expressed by his persecutors; (the High Priest in particular); the grief of Peter who is "weeping bitterly," and the agony of the pious women from Galilee at beholding Him "whom they loved" bound as a malefactor, raises doubts in the mind of the spectator whether the scene is not real; and almost carries one to the hall of condemnation.

Carlton House is a gloomy pile of buildings faced by a colonnade; but the interior, it is said, surpasses most palaces in magnificence; behind it is Warwick House, an ill-shapen building, the residence of the Princess Charlotte.[276] All communication with her is through her father's palace, as all other entrances are closed up. This is caused by her running away from her keepers some time ago and jumping into a hackney coach, which carried her to her mother!

Mr. Tierney[277] made a motion in Parliament a few days ago that the amount of the Prince Regent's debts should be laid before the House. The result was that the debts amounted to six millions, five hundred and seventy-seven thousand, seven hundred and seventy-six dollars, and sixty-seven cents, of which one million, four hundred and sixty-six thousand six hundred and sixty-six dollars and sixty-seven cents remained unpaid the 1st of May, 1815. Here is one of the blessings attached to a regal government.

Going into a wholesale hosier's warehouse with a friend who was making purchases, we received an invitation to look at the hosier's race-horses: in the stable behind the warehouse were two which he kept for his amusement. One of them he offered to back against any horse in England for £500. He showed us a cup which this animal had won at Newmarket races. His parlor was ornamented with the portraits of these favorite animals. This I thought pretty well for a hosier![278]

Passing through St. James' Park after dinner I overheard two fashionable young men bidding each other "good morning!" The lateness of the hour impelled me to see what time it was; I found it just eight in the evening! These are imitators of the Prince, who never dines until nine at night.

[Thursday, June] 22nd. London is one continual scene of uproar and joy in consequence of the total defeat of Bonaparte at Waterloo by Lord Wellington.[279] This is announced by the Park and Tower guns and by placards upon the gates of the Mansion House[280]. It is also publicly declared that upon Friday and Saturday nights the public buildings are to be illuminated on the occasion.

Mr. D. of Boston having died suddenly, I was notified to attend his funeral, and accordingly went at 7 o'clock in the morning, being the time appointed. Those who were present were furnished by the undertaker with a pair of gloves, a mourning cloak and scarf.

The hearse was followed by mourning coaches, preceded by two mutes bearing black banners. At the graveyard the corpse was met by the priest who performed the service in the Episcopalian form. At the entrance of the yard on our return we were divested of our cloaks, weepers,[281] and gloves, the two latter of which we retained in remembrance of the deceased. Funerals here at this early hour are quite customary. Seldom is there any after one in the forenoon!

On Friday and Saturday night [June 23rd and 24th] all the public buildings and many private ones were illuminated. Many fanciful and beautiful devices were exhibited. Among those which were prominently beautiful were the excise office, the Bank, Post-office, Somerset House, Admiralty, Horse Guards, Carlton House, Foreign and Home Department (here the eagles taken from the French were displayed), Lord Liverpool and Lord Castlereagh's houses, etc. One house in St. James' was particularly fine. The whole front resembled a fortress, with cannon, flags, &c., formed by colored lamps. A publican who keeps a tavern with the sign of a cock, had a large transparency representing a game cock strutting over his fallen combatant, with the inscription "England the cock of the walk!" The crowd was very great, particularly in front of Somerset House. The mob would not suffer the coaches to pass excepting the coachmen and footmen took off their hats as an acknowledgment of the favor. Squibs and crackers[282] were plentifully distributed into the carriages, and the alarm which the ladies were consequently thrown into appeared to delight John Bull exceedingly. I did not return to my lodging either night till one o'clock. This was early, as it is not customary to get to bed here until twelve upon ordinary occasions. Of course the whole morning is lost in bed. At six in the morning there are but very few persons seen in the streets. The customary breakfast hour in the house where I boarded was from nine to ten. This too was called an early one!

Finding myself a little indisposed on Sunday morning, Mr. M. and I took a ramble into the country. On our way we observed a mean-looking brick building resembling a barn, on the walls of which was inscribed in very large letters "The House of God." It belongs to the followers of Joanna Southcott,[283] and is appropriated as their chapel. We returned to town to dine, and in the evening attended the Magdalen, the account of which I have given elsewhere.

[Monday, June] 26th. Went to day to the British Institution for the Encouragement of Fine Arts,[284] and Bullock's Museum. The institution contains a very large and splendid collection of paintings by Rubens, Rembrandt, Vandyk [*sic*] and other artists of the Dutch and Flemish schools. One picture (the subject an old woman by candle-light) was finely executed. After seeing the pictures in this gallery a person can readily believe what has been related of an ancient painter, that his works were so naturally executed that birds came and pecked at a bunch of grapes which he had! Bullock's[285] collection surpasses Peale's at Philadelphia[286] in some of the departments, particularly in some of the branches of natural history. There are several complete sets of armor used in this country in former times. The collection of fossils and minerals was respectable, but that of the birds and beasts was very fine indeed. The birds are in mahogany cases and are arranged in classes, being placed upon the boughs of trees. This gives them a very pretty effect, but the beautiful manner in which the beasts were disposed pleased me exceedingly. The spectator enters into a saloon the rustic appearance of which transports you at once into the wilderness. The thatched roof is supported by the trunks of trees, the branches from them mingling together form sashes which are glazed. Through the glass are seen the beasts, some roaming o'er the rocky cliffs, others crouching in their dens: in other parts are monkeys perched upon cocoa trees throwing the fruit to their companions. Interspersed among them were foreign trees and shrubs. Directly over the lions' den hung a large winter squash. Here it is esteemed a curiosity! In short I cannot do justice to this admirable collection. It was with pleasure I observed several mothers instructing their children (by the aid of books which are sold here for the purpose) in the history of these animals. Returning home I passed through Bond Street, and beheld a great display of fashionables. Some of the ladies were curiously dressed, their gowns were cut very low so as to leave their shoulders bare, while their clothes reached but very little below their knees. In the Strand are a great many jeweler's shops. At the window of one was exhibited a large assortment of snuff-boxes,[287] the prices varied from 150 to 700 Guineas each. That he finds purchasers I have but little doubt, for the other day an advertisement appeared in the public papers announcing the sale of Sir Gregory Turner's "splendid collection of ninety-one superb snuff boxes."[288] In the Strand is also to be seen a full grown ox with five legs; the fifth one grows out of his back and has a perfect shoulder resembling much a lobster's claw. The English are forever upon the alert to make money out of everything. No sooner was the dreadful slaughter of the battle of Waterloo known than half a dozen advertisements appeared in the newspapers offering mourning to the

Figure 10 Dancers and celebrants in front of the highly illuminated orchestra pavilion at Vauxhall. The illustration by Pugin and Rowlandson appears in Volume III of Acerkman's *Microcosm of London* (1808-1811), 204. Courtesy of the James Noel Smith Collection, Louisiana State University in Shreveport.

relatives of the deceased, and one person offered to contract with them to remove the dead bodies to England, he having (as he states) formed a connection in Brussels for that purpose.

[Tuesday, June] 27th. Went to Vauxhall Garden,[289] which to attempt an adequate description of would be impossible! The entrance is through a gloomy passage at the end of which you pass through a small door and are immediately transported into one of the fairy scenes of the Arabian Tales, as it all appears enchantment. It is lighted up with variegated lamps, fancifully arranged so as to give a brilliant effect. The walks are very long and have at their side seats and tables set out with refreshments sufficient for accommodating several thousands. The rotunda is illuminated by a chandelier and is ornamented with paintings. Adjoining is the saloon, at the corners of which are emblems of the four quarters of the globe. Here is an orchestra, with a band habited in the Scottish costume and it plays only Scotch tunes. In the centre of the garden is the grand orchestra wherein a fine band amused the company. Mr. Bland[290] sang one song with great effect. Each verse ended with these words:—"a sweet little bird warbles No! no!" This "no, no" was echoed by another performer from a recess of the garden.

At 10 o'clock upon the ringing of a bell the company scampered down a long walk where was exhibited a curious piece of mechanism[291] in a scene where there was a bridge and miller's house, beyond a real waterfall, the water tumbling down the rock and running under the bridge, a little boat is seen having in it a sportsman who shoots and kills a little bird flying over his head. Horses and carriages are passing over the bridge;—that of a stage-coach, the guard blowing his horn, was quite natural. The scene is then changed to an encampment with a triumphal procession of horse and foot-soldiers to conclude. At the extremity of another walk was the representation of a sea-light; to help the illusion, the noise of real water dashing against the sides of ships was produced. In another part of the garden a man performed several tunes upon seven instruments at once. This he did by the aid of his feet, which he seemed to have a perfect command of. At eleven o'clock the nobility and fashionables began to enter, when there was a grand display of dress, for most all who are here appear in full dress. I should imagine there were from four to five thousand persons promenading the walks this night. At twelve the fireworks commenced. These were exhibited at the end of dark walks. They surpassed anything of the kind I ever beheld! At two o'clock the party to which I belonged left the garden, as the dances had begun, this being the signal for the departure of respectable ladies. Fifteen thousand lamps are lighted in these gardens each night they are opened. As I was coming through Finsbury Square one evening, I saw a man with a large telescope in the street, intent upon looking at the stars, and upon my expressing my surprise at its singularity, my companion informed me that this person stood there to accommodate any one to look through the instrument, for which he charges two-pence. This is one of the wonderful variety of ways they have of making money in London![292]

[Saturday, July 1] On Saturday night attended Drury Lane Theatre to see the comedy of "Wild Oats"[293] represented. It was excellently well performed, the parts being sustained by Elliston,[294] Dowton,[295] Munden,[296] and Knight.[297] The last performer, in the character of Sim, excelled beyond everything. I went into the pit which was crowded with ladies and gentlemen so full that I was obliged to stand

Figure 11 A cartoon accompanying Thomas Hood's poem "Love and Lunacy" (*Hood's Own*, 1855) depicting an enterprising man selling views through his telescope and simultaneously making more than two pence charge per view. Author's collection.

up for some time until a gentleman by hard squeezing contrived to let me have a part of a seat, just affording me room sufficient to half sit down. I was soon relieved from this awkward situation by a lady (who was it appears an old attender on the playhouse) having brought in a small stool upon which she sat down directly behind me, and as there was not room sufficient otherwise, thrust her lap directly under me and furnished a comfortable seat during the rest of the evening.

[Sunday, July 2] Sunday I passed at Camberwell-grove, a sweet village about three miles from London. I think this place a delightful spot. The grove resembles the Boston Mall, and is one mile in length. On each side are genteel houses with gardens laid out in a tasteful manner; at the upper end of the grove are two pretty cottages with thatched roofs, one of them having a fountain before it, in the centre of which is a sea-god upon a throne of shells, &c. The residents of these houses are principally merchants who here retire from the bustle and noise of the city. After tea we took a ramble into an adjoining village from which is a fine view of London and Greenwich, and at night returned to the city. Lord Cochrane of whose confinement I have spoken in my visit to the King's Bench prison, yesterday revenged himself upon the ministry (whether intentionally or not I do not know) in a manner which has caused much public conversation. His term of imprisonment was ended the 18th of last June, but as he refused to pay the £1000 fine he was detained in prison. The ministry have lately brought forward a bill in Parliament granting the Duke of Cumberland £6000 per annum additional income upon his marriage with the Princess of Salm Salms.[298] This bill not being popular, Lord Castlereagh had to drum up all the absent ministerial members to vote it through, when as they were taking the question, Lord Cochrane, having paid his fine and obtained his discharge, came into the House of Commons and by his single vote negatived the bill. On the back of the bank-note which he paid to government he wrote a protest, stating that he was forced to comply as the ill state of his health demanded that he should be liberated.

[Wednesday] Fourth of July. Dined with a friend at Dolly's chop-house.[299] This house was formerly kept by a woman whose name was Dolly, and to perpetuate her name, a female servant attends upon customers (which is not the case in other chop-houses) who, let her name be what it will, is still called Dolly. This place is much frequented by the booksellers, as it is adjoining Paternoster Row, where the principal book-sellers prosecute their business. I was not a little amused at meeting near London with a party of sailors having the American flag displayed in honor of Independence Day. They were headed by a Jew playing upon a hand-organ. Each one had his girl with him, and the procession was closed by two large negroes each with a white girl under his arm.

[Friday, July] 7th. Went to Covent Garden Theatre. The play was the Exile of Siberia,[300] with the entertainment of The Critic, or Tragedy Rehearsed. In this piece, Matthew, in Sir Fretful Plagiarist [*sic*],[301] exhibited his uncommon comic powers. During the evening a row was raised in consequence of Miss Stephens'[302] not coming on to sing, as was announced in the bills. Babel was quiet and still in comparison with the house, nor was order restored until one person was taken by main force from the boxes.

The Fishmongers' stalls and Butcher Shops are worthy of notice for the neatness and high perfection in which the articles for sale are kept. Although the fish was brought a great distance yet they are perfectly fresh and look as bright as when first taken. Many of them have white marble benches to display them upon. The meat also in the Butcher shops is displayed in as nice a manner; indeed the way in which everything for sale is shown in London exceeds description. Last night during my walks I discovered a fire and after following the direction of the light for some time found that it was near the Tower, the turrets of which were beautifully illuminated by the flames. The crowd around the fire was immense; the bustle of the firemen and people moving their effects made the scene "confusion worse confounded." The place consumed was a gunmaker's shop, from whence some powder exploded and wounded several people.

[Saturday, July] 8th. Went into a room in the Strand where a man exhibits the process of glassmaking in miniature.[303] This he does by means of a lamp through the blaze of which a current of air passes and blows the flame upon the metal until it melts. You pay a shilling for entrance, to be returned in ware, but he takes care to sell nothing less than eighteen pence. The alternative then is, to save a shilling you have to throw away sixpence. The room was crowded with spectators, among whom were several ladies with children to whom they were explaining the process of glass-making. It being the Jewish Sabbath I was induced to visit the Synagogue near Duke Street,[304] the residence exclusively of these Shylocks.[305] The church is a neat edifice. It is lighted with seven chandeliers, the pulpit, or desk, where the priests stand being in the centre: at the end is the altar or holy of holies, toward which they turn their faces and bow while repeating their prayers. The men sit with their hats on. The women are in a screened gallery, apart from the men. The service was chanted in Hebrew, the congregation joining in at times in "din most horrible."[306] I came away disgusted with the little reverence they seemed to pay to that Being who pronounced them His chosen people!

I spent the Sabbath at Camberwell Grove. In the afternoon attended church and heard a good discourse from the nephew of the unfortunate Dr. Dodd.[307] On Monday I chanced to pass through Smithfield Market. Being market day I had a fair view of the great mart of flesh; the quantity of sheep and cattle sold here upon these days is immense, and amounts to an incredible number in the course of a year.[308]

Opposite Somerset House is erecting the Strand Bridge. This magnificent structure is entirely of stone, having nine arches of great width. The pillars are twelve feet in thickness, ornamented with Tuscan columns. When it is completed it will be one of the most elegant structures of the kind in the Kingdom. It was begun in 1811 and will probably be finished in another year. This is designed as a toll bridge.[309] The other bridges are all free. To give an idea of the passing in London I will make an extract from an account of the numbers which are computed to pass over the respective bridges daily, viz.,[310]

Several other bridges are projected, but none are begun excepting the Vauxhall one, which progresses but slowly.

[Wednesday, July] 12th Today the Prince Regent prorogued both Houses of Parliament.[311] I went to see the splendid procession usual upon these occasions, and was fortunate enough to procure a situation opposite the door of the House of Lords and close by the state-coach which was in waiting for the Prince. I was enabled thereby to have a fair view of his person: his form is perfectly elegant, but his countenance exhibits the marks of intemperate habits. He was dressed in uniform. When he made his appearance there was but

	Blackfriars	London
Foot passengers	61,069	89,640
Wagons	533	769
Carts & drays	1,502	2,924
Coaches	990	1,240
Gigs	500	740
Horses	822	764

London Bridge is the great thoroughfare to the Continent.

little acclamation among the people. "Now and then a voice cryd [*sic*] God save King Richard" and that was all! The state coach is a great lumbering vehicle, carved and gilded all over. The inside was lined with crimson velvet hung around with silk damask curtains. It was drawn by six cream-colored horses, each horse led by a groom in gold and scarlet livery. Their harnesses were crimson morocco with massive gold trimmings, and their manes and tails braided with blue ribbons. There were also many noblemen's carriages in the procession, whose livery and equipages were so splendid that they appeared to try which should most outvie each other. The whole of the way from Carlton House to the House of Lords was lined with horse guards and the State carriage was surrounded by the Prince's own regiment.

[Thursday, July] 13th. This morning went to see Barker's panoramas[312] of the Isle of Elba and of the battle of the Heights of Montmartre before Paris in 1814. He is esteemed as the first artist in this line in the world, and after viewing his works no one, I am sure, would be disposed to dispute his claim to the title. The battle appears to be raging around you, and you are at once carried by imagination amid scenes of horror and carnage. Through the smoke of the cannon is a view of Paris and its environs. The view of Elba is, I think, superior to the battle, it being so beautifully illusive as to make one almost forget he is in London and carries one at once to the far-famed residence of Bonaparte. The whole is incomparably well done. The water in particular appeals of the same hue and the same glassy surface as reality. So deceiving is it that I am informed a Newfoundland dog belonging to a gentleman jumped over the railing which divides the painting from the spectator and made a plunge at that part representing water, so much was he deceived by it. Crowds of spectators attend daily to repay the artist for his admirable work.

The whole town has for some time past been agitated by the suicidal death of Mr. Whitbread.[313] Many reports have, as usual upon such occasions, been circulated as to the cause, and many high eulogiums have been made upon his character even by his political opponents. The opposition party have by his death received a blow from which they will not for a long time recover.

Lackington's Bookstore,[314] near Finsbury Square, is a capacious building, containing an immense number of volumes of books for sale. In this place they were extremely polite to strangers. I was desired to walk through the building. There were five large rooms, entirely filled with books and as many circular galleries filled likewise,—the whole lighted from the top by a skylight. This place is well worth visiting. Lackington himself has retired to the country and takes no active part in the business.

[July 16] Sunday there was a collection at St. Andrew's Church for the sufferers by the battle at Waterloo. A Mr. Price delivered the sermon from Zechariah 14th, 6th and 7th. The substance of the discourse was similar to that in those beautiful lines of Dr. Beattie, viz.

—One part ' one little part we scan,
Through the dark medium of life's feverish dream,
Yet dare arrange the whole stupendous plan
If but that little part incongruous seem
Nor is that part perhaps what mortals deem
Oft from apparent ills our blessings rise
Oh ' then renounce that impious self-esteem
Which Aims to know the secrets of the skies,
For thou art but of dust, be humble and be wise[315]

[July 17] On Monday, in company with a small party, took an excursion to Richmond. The road, lying upon the Thames bank was ornamented with many pretty houses and gardens. Kew Gardens, the favorite residence of George III, lay upon our right. The road was pretty, yet I think that many places in the United States can boast of as handsome seats, particularly around Boston, Hellgate near New York, and those which adjoin the banks of the Delaware near Philadelphia. But when we ascended Richmond Hill—in the language of the poet:

"Heavens! what a goodly prospect spread around,
Of hills, and dales, and woods and lawns and spires,
And glittering towns, and gilded streams, till all
The stretching landscape into smoke decays
Enchanting vale! beyond what ere the muse
Has of Achaia or Hesperia sung!
O vale of bliss! O softly swelling hills!
On which the Power of cultivation lies,
And joys to see the wonder of his toil."[316]

I was quite enchanted with the scene before me! The winding of the "silvery Thames," the beautiful lawns gradually sloping from the houses upon its banks, and its charming walks overshadowed with trees, conspired altogether to render it a charming place. Numerous parties were enjoying themselves, either upon the grass plat or in sailing in pleasure boats on the river. One company was footing it to the music of the pipe and tabor.[317] All appeared to be exhilarated! Here it was that Thomson[318] wrote his *Seasons*, and doubtless received inspiration from the enchanting views around him. Our time did not permit us to visit that spot which he so much loved. I much wished it but was compelled to be content with drinking a glass of wine to his memory, having in view from the windows of our apartment those scenes which his pen has immortalized. We rambled through a part of Richmond Park, from which is a fine view of St. Paul's and Westminster Abbey. Upon the hill are many houses in the occupation of the nobility and gentry. One of them is built in imitation of a castle having its turrets fallen to decay and overgrown with ivy. The town of Richmond has nothing worthy of notice excepting the Bridge across the river. This has a very pretty effect at a small distance below it. When our carriage was ready I sincerely regretted to leave this sweet spot, and I think that one must be utterly insensible to the beauties of nature not to admire such a scene as Richmond Hill. The view from Milton Hill[319] near Boston bears a, faint resemblance to that of Richmond, and has I think the preference in one particular,—the view of the sea! while that of Richmond is "one boundless landscape"[320] only terminated by the horizon.

[July 18] On Tuesday I received a note from Mr. C. informing me of the sudden death of his child. I immediately waited upon him and found him and Mrs. J. in the greatest affliction. Mrs. C.'s case was peculiarly distressing, sustaining the loss of an only child in a foreign land and not being acquainted with any female who could sympathize with her and offer consolation. Two English gentlemen who were entire strangers to them, having heard of their misfortune kindly offered their advice and services, and tendered the assistance of the female part of their family to Mr. C. One of them had the family grave opened to receive the body. The funeral took place upon Thursday morning. A priest of the dissenting persuasion attended on the occasion and offered prayers at the apartments of Mr. C. and also an address and prayer at the grave, which was in the same churchyard in which John Bunyan, author of *Pilgrim's Progress* lies buried.[321] His tombstone was pointed out to me.

Lounging in the park today I turned into the street which leads to Westminster Abbey, and went in once more to view that venerable building. I was not less interested than on my former visit there. I could not walk through this receptacle of the ashes of kings, warriors, statesmen, poets and their great men without instructive lessons on the vanity and shortness of life. Many of the monuments are so crumbled by the hand of Time that their inscriptions are scarcely legible; many are entirely effaced! Yet with this knowledge of the folly of outstanding the lapse of ages, vanity still raises yearly new monuments, which three or four hundred years hence will puzzle the antiquarian in discovering for whom they were erected. I purchased a book here which gives a particular description of the Abbey. In it is an extract not inappropriate to be inserted here, Speaking of this building the author says "I have wandered with pleasure into the most gloomy recesses of this last resort of grandeur, to contemplate human life, and trace mankind through all the wilderness of their frailties and misfortunes, from their cradles to their graves I have reflected on the shortness of our duration here, and that I was but one of the millions who had been employed in the same manner, in ruminating on the trophies of mortality before me: that this huge fabric, this sacred repository of fame and grandeur would only be the stage for the same performances: would receive new accessions of noble dust would be adorn'd with other sepulchres of cost and magnificence, would be crowded with successive admirers: and at last by the unavoidable decay of time bury the whole collection of antiquities in general obscurity, and be the monument of its own ruin."—[322]

[July 22] Saturday evening I attended the little theatre at the Haymarket.[323] This house is only open in the summer for the exhibition of petit comedies and farces. One of the pieces represented this evening satirized the English character for the prevalence of suicide; the other was an admirable production from the French, called the Beehive, wherein Matthews[324] represented an old inn-keeper (the master of the Beehive). His comic Powers [sic] kept the whole house in a roar. One of the dramatis personae was an officer who described everything by technical language. The one who sustained that part bore a strong resemblance to the late Col. Tuttle[325] and often reminded me of him.

[July 23] Sunday I walked to Highgate,[326] a small village placed upon an eminence four miles from London. Thompson in his description of Richmond Hill denominates it one of the "sister hills." The prospect from this place is extensive, embracing a fine view of the city. Here is a causeway[327] built across a valley through which one of the great roads of London runs. It is of sufficient width for carriages to pass, and is formed of stone with a composition railing. I returned to the city by another road for the purpose of varying the excursion.

It is almost incredible as to the number of persons who leave town on the Sabbath here for a ramble into the country. Vehicles of every description, from the elegant barouche and chariot[328] to the humble horse-cart, are put in requisition, and thousands of pedestrians, men, women and children, crowd all the avenues of the city upon this day, being by their occupations so much engaged on week-days as to prevent their enjoying this comfort.

Being in want of a passport to enable me to leave the country, I was obliged to wait upon Mr. Adams,[329] the United States Minister to the British Court, to obtain a paper to enable me to obtain one. I went accompanied by Dr W. After walking about four miles, we found him at the west part of the town, in lodgings at a house in Harley Street. Over the front door was a signboard in large characters denoting that warm and vapor baths were to be had here. We were not at all pleased that the representative of the American nation should be so meanly lodged. This we thought was carrying his Republican simplicity a little too far! Mr. Adams treated us politely and furnished me with the necessary passport, being most particularly expressed in the following manner, viz.,—"Age 26 years, Stature 5 feet, 10 inches, Forehead high, Eyes blue, Nose aquiline, Mouth common, Chin round, Hair dark brown, Complexion clear, & Face oval." After we had called upon Mr. A. we went to visit Messrs. Alston [sic], Leslie and Morse, American painters.[330] Mr. Morse was on the eve of setting out for Liverpool to embark from there to the United States. He shewed us a painting of his which he had just finished to be exhibited at the Academy, they having proposed the subject, for a prize. Mr. A., being very much engaged, was with us but a few minutes. Mr. Leslie I was extremely pleased with. He is possessed of very prepossessing manners. His celebrity and that of Mr. Alston [sic] as professional men is daily gaining ground and they bid fair to fill part of the chasm which will be formed by the death of West, who is now much advanced in life.

There is never a dearth of novelty to a stranger in the streets of London. Numerous ways are resorted to by the beggars to attract attention and gain a halfpenny. One poor fellow who had lost both his legs, has a board before him upon which he chalks in so elegant a manner that it would not disgrace a copperplate engraver, any word that the spectator desires, beginning at the end and writing them bottom upward, thus ʎɐʍ sıɥʇ uı. Having often heard of "rag fair" and accidentally mentioning it at dinner, one of my fellow lodgers offered to be my guide thither. We accordingly went to that celebrated mart of cast-off garments. Just before we got there we were pestered with Jews in front of their shops who gave us pressing invitations of "pleshe to valk in, Shur, and puy a shecond-hand coat shust as coot as new." When we arrived in the midst of the fair, a scene presented itself which almost baffles description. Millions of cast-off habits, of every fashion and quality, and in all stages of decay were here exhibited for sale. In one part was seen a fellow striving to thrust himself into a coat, and in another an old hag cheapening[331] a pair of worn-out shoes. I came away highly entertained with my visit to this place.

Sunday, 30th. This day I passed at Camberwell grove and attended a church near that place. The preacher was extremely eloquent and delivered extempore a very pathetic and elegant discourse upon the necessity of our "living unto God" but most unfortunately his paying a greater attention to the displaying of a brilliant ring gave me an impression that he was one of those who "shewed us the steep and thorny road to heaven while he the path of dalliance kept."[332] My serious impressions were by this deportment in the preacher dissipated.

[Monday, July 31] The following day I went to the East India House[333] for the purpose of viewing its museum of curiosities. The opulence of the company and the power they have acquired by their conquests in India have thrown into their possession the greatest and richest collection of eastern curiosities in the world. We were first conducted into the Library, containing a splendid collection of Eastern literature, among which is a book of dreams in Tippoo Sahib's[334] own handwriting, the Poems of Hafiz,[335] and innumerable other Indian, Chinese and Persian manuscripts. Here is also a collection of minerals, shells, &c. In the next room are some Hindu idols, bricks from Babylon, a marble covered with characters from the same place and which is supposed to contain some matter relative to the history of that magnificent city.

Many learned men have studied it to decipher it, but have not succeeded as the characters are totally unknown at the present day. In the same room is a curious piece of mechanism representing a tiger having in his fangs a figure dressed in the English costume. By turning a handle in the manner of an organ the screeching of distress and the roaring of the beast are produced; at the same time the hand of the man is moved to ward off the paws of the beast. Playing upon this instrument was Tippoo Sahib's chief amusement![336] Enclosed in a glass case is a head of a tiger which stood at the foot of the sultan's throne, it is of solid gold, the eyes and teeth being of crystal. It now lies on a carpet of crimson velvet studded with gold, which was used as a cover to the throne. The Chinese gardens in this apartment are very beautiful. The trees are of silver, the birds and beasts of gold, and the water of mother-of-pearl. We were also shown a medal struck for the Company by the celebrated Bolton of Birmingham,[337] The workmanship of it is so exquisitely fine as to require a magnifying glass to discover the representation of a battle upon it which this was designed to commemorate. Several port-folios of views in India executed by the first artists and amounting to several hundred pictures were also shown to the visitor. The collection of curiosities in this place is very grand, and the bare amount of the precious metals must be immense.

In company with Dr. W. took a ride to Kensington Gardens, situated at the extremity of Hyde Park.[338] It is by far the most beautiful promenade that London or its immediate vicinity affords. The grandeur and wildness of the woods more strongly reminded me of the American forest scenery than any other place I have seen, in England. There is a palace here which has nothing remarkable in its external appearance, from the terrace in front is a fine view of lawn and a piece of water. Beyond, the woods are of such impenetrable thickness that a person would suppose he was a long distance from a city. The gardens contain three hundred and fifty acres laid out in charming walks, groves, etc. The trees are principally oak and chestnut. These gardens are open to the public except to liveried servants and persons carrying bundles. Park keepers are stationed at the gates to preserve order and decorum, and at proper distances are seats for the company. At the gates, several footmen in splendid liveries were waiting for their masters or mistresses who were here promenading.

Being obliged to take Mr Adams's[339] passport to the Alien Office[340] for the purpose of obtaining Lord Sidmouth's[341] license to leave the country, I chanced to meet a friend on the way thither who informed me that a small douce[342] would be a great facility in enabling me to get it, although the Alien Act expressly provides that they shall be given gratis. When I came to the office I received the pass from a man of gentlemanly appearance, who with many profound bows excused himself for making me wait, &c. &c. at the same time looking me in the face as if he were saying "you must be a stupid fellow if you don't understand me?" I put four shillings into his hand and received many polite assurances as to the pleasure it would afford him to be of service to me in renewing the passports, and that if I wrote from Liverpool I might depend upon a speedy answer to my letter. It is true the law did not compel me to give the man anything, but if I had not, and it should have happened that I wished for a renewal of the paper, it might have been delayed and I had cause to regret not having paid the accustomed tribute.

Since my residence in England some of the most important events in modern history have occurred, the most prominent of which is the downfall and captivity of Buonaparte. London has been agitated many times in consequence of reports that apartments had been fitted up in the Tower for his reception, and so much were these believed that some thousands of the populace waited a long time upon London Bridge in order to see him pass. It is now, however, understood that he is to be sent to St. Helena, there to remain a prisoner for life. Thousands have gone from all parts of England to Plymouth to catch a glimpse of the disturber of the world. He is now confined on board of the Bellerophon Frigate,[343] on board of which no one is allowed to go. The boats which daily sail around this vessel for the purpose of carrying persons to see him are estimated at two thousand.

[Sunday] 6th August. Parted with Mr. M.'s family at Camberwell Grove.[344] During my stay in England they had paid every attention to me, endeavoring to make my absence from home as pleasant as possible. It was with real regret that I took a last farewell of this family. One of the most serious counterbalances to the pleasure of travelling is that after having formed an acquaintance with those whom you would esteem through life you are obliged to part, and this without a hope of ever again meeting them!

Having been introduced a few weeks ago to a Mr. C., a fellow of Trinity College, Oxford, it luckily chanced that he was going there on a few days' visit, and hearing of my intention of taking that place into my route to Birmingham, very politely invited me to join him and stop a day or two in that city. As such an opportunity was too fortunate to be declined, I accepted the invitation and accordingly having taken our seats upon the top of the coach, we on Monday morning took our departure from London. Fortunately the day was fine, and as some rain had fallen the night previous we were not incommoded with the dust. We passed through Kew. The palace lay upon our right and appeared to be as devoid of elegance as all the royal residences in this country are.[345] We continued on through the neat village of Hammersley,[346] and Slough. A little before we came to the latter place we had a charming view of Windsor Castle which lay at about a mile distant on our left. It is situated upon an eminence from which is an extensive view. Its exterior appearance is much more elegant than any other palace I have seen. It is at present the residence of King George, who has always given the place a preference. Our route lay over Hounslow Heath (a barren and desolate spot, so much celebrated for the robberies committed here), through Maidenhead to Henley on the Thames. Here we crossed this river over a stone bridge leading to the town, which is truly a charming place, possessing an air of neatness, with a fine situation which renders it superior to any other village I have seen in England. I regretted that the rapidity of our travellng did not permit me to pass a few hours in this pretty place. Ten miles this side of Oxford we crossed the Isis and entered Dorchester,—a dirty, mean-looking village. The entrance to Oxford inspires a favorable impression of that beautiful city, the towers of many churches and colleges are seen through the foliage of the fine trees with which this city abounds After passing a handsome bridge we entered High Street, esteemed the most beautiful street in Europe. On the right is the front of Magdalen College,[347] and it is adorned with the fronts of several other colleges and halls. My companion and myself alighted at the inn, and after we had deposited our baggage he hurried me away to a livery stable to look at some favorite horses which belonged to him. I soon found that Latin and Greek had but few charms for him when compared to his favorite amusements of hunting and racing. He kept three horses and about a dozen dogs for those purposes, nor was he alone in this, as there were many other animals here belonging to the fellows of the respective colleges. It being the long vacation, and but few collegians in the city, Oxford appeared quite dull. Mr. C. took me to his chambers in Trinity College, which were pleasantly situated. Attached to his college is a church of uncommon elegance.[348] The ceiling is most exquisitely painted and the altar adorned with some fine carved work in marble. In the garden belonging to the college is a secluded walk in the manner of an arbor, the top of it being formed by the intermingling of the branches of the lime tree. The hawthorn hedge which surrounds the ground is curiously cut so as to bear a resemblance to a board fence. In the New College[349] church the painted windows are estimated as the first work of the kind in the kingdom. That from a design by Sir Joshua Reynolds is very fine. Many ancient painted windows adorn this chapel. The colors of them are in the highest perfection although many hundred years have elapsed since they were painted. In a small cabinet adjoining the altar is kept the crosier which formerly belonged to William of Wykeham,[350] one of the founders of the church. It is of silver gilt surmounted with small gothic images. The altar piece of this church is also carved out of marble. The Theatre where all the prize poems are recited is a fine building. The ceiling of it is estimated a great curiosity, as it is entirely unsupported by pillars although its dimensions contain 5600 square feet. It is painted by Sir James Thornhill.[351] The chairs used by the Allied sovereigns during their visit last year are in an ante-room.[352] They are made of gold burnished with silk crimson velvet! Near to the theatre is the Clarendon printing office, where Bibles and Prayerbooks are printed. The expense of its erection was defrayed from the sale of Lord Clarendon's manuscript history, which was given for that purpose. The Bodleian Library[353] contains 35,000 volumes and 60,000 manuscripts, as also a gallery with a large collection of pictures and busts. The ceiling is adorned with the arms of the respective colleges. Among the pictures are some copies of the cartoons of Raphael. An incident occurred here which made me smile. Mr. C., whose love of Greek and Latin was not excessively ardent, indignantly shaking his fist in the face of a bust of Homer exclaimed, "If it had not been for your writing that cursed hard book my brains would have escaped many a puzzling!" Two windows in this gallery are entirely formed from the relics of painted windows from different parts of the kingdom which are most curiously cemented together. Opposite here is Hertford College,[354] now in a state of decay. Charles James Fox[355] was a fellow of it. It now has but two or three belonging to it, and they are esteemed as eccentrics, and almost as great curiosities as the old edifice. The Radcliffe Camera[356] is another fine building. It stands in the centre of a beautiful area. The architecture of it is admirable, particularly the staircase composed of stone and so formed as to appear unsupported. The books are arranged in cabinets. From the dome, which you ascend by a stone cylindrical staircase, is an extensive view of the city and adjacent country. There is no place in the world where there are so many public buildings in so small a space as the city of Oxford, nor are there many which can vie with it in elegance! On the floor of the library stand two marble candelabra of superb workmanship. They were found in the ruins of the Emperor Hadrian's palace at Tivoli. One of the principal embellishments to this city is the college gardens, as most of them have very large ones, laid out in charming walks: that of the Magdalen in particular is one mile and a half in length.

The following day, in company with Mr. C. and mounted on his horses, we took our way to Woodstock to visit Blenheim, the seat of the Duke of Marlborough. Woodstock is a small neat village, famed for its manufacture of leather and fine steel work. Hard by is the princely mansion of Blenheim,[357] which stands in the midst of a park which contains 2700 acres of land and 800 of water. The walls are twelve miles round. You enter this park through a gate of the Corinthian order and are at once presented with a view of the mansion. Opposite is a lake having an elegant bridge thrown over it. Directly in front of this upon an eminence stands a lofty pedestal having upon it a statue of the great Duke. Upon it are recorded in marble his various achievements and the Acts of Parliament granting this place as a reward for his services. The interior of the house is superbly elegant. We were shown through the following apartments: the Hall, "Bow-window room," Duke's Dressing-room, East Drawing-room, Grand cabinet, Blue Drawing-room, State Drawing-room, Dining-room, Saloon, Green drawing-room, State bedchamber, Winter drawing-room, Library, Chapel, Theatre, and La Titian gallery; the whole containing an immense collection of statues, and paintings by the first artists, and otherwise furnished in a style of great splendour. The library is quite elegant. The number of volumes of books is 24,000. In the chapel is a monument to the memory of the great duke and his duchess, and a very fine picture over the altar by some Dutch artist. The theatre is a pretty little place, capable of containing 200 persons. The scenery is in perfect order although there have been no performances here for twenty years. Far different, this reward for services, to our country, which even denies a monument to the memory of him who is acknowledged as her saviour!

We spent three hours in viewing this palace. On our return to Oxford the duke passed us in his carriage. He is an old man of 77 years of age, and is great grandson to the famous Duke.

In the afternoon I mentioned to my companion the necessity of my going the next morning to Birmingham, &c. In reply he pressed me to stay a day or two longer, observing that Oxford was far pleasanter than those damned cotton-spinning places. In the morning I took my leave and having mounted upon the box seat alongside the coachman, bid farewell to Oxford. I was much entertained by the coachman who was, as he informed me, a freeholder,[358] and who took considerable interest in an election of a member of Parliament by distributing to those of his side the house handbills, a bundle of which he carried with him for the purpose. We changed horses at Stratford-upon-Avon, immortalized as the birthplace of Shakespere [*sic*]. While this was doing, curiosity impelled me to visit the house, which is one of the most wretched hovels I ever beheld, and is now used as a butcher's shop. An old woman (who, as she informed me, was a descendant of the poet) was my conductor. Many things which belonged to the bard were shewn me, such as his chair, which is cut almost up for relics, a bench, sword, iron box, picture, linstock,[359] table, candle-sticks, some coins, &c. &c. I continued my ride to Birmingham. The entrance to the town is quite pretty and quite agreeably disappointed me who had anticipated beholding a den fit only for the Cyclops! From seeing the interior of the place I am decidedly of opinion that it is preferable to Manchester and most other manufacturing towns (as a place of residence!). Here I went through a pin manufactory, and was surprised at the number of persons who are necessary to the formation of a single pin. As usual, here was a number of wretched little boys and girls confined at work from morn to night.

Thomason's show rooms are considered as one of the "lions" of Birmingham.[360] Here is exposed for sale almost every article which is made in the place. The rooms are fitted up in great taste, and the style in which the articles are displayed tempt almost every one who visits here to become a purchaser. The attendants are uncommonly polite in showing the articles to strangers. They were manufacturing in an outer room a copper vase modeled after a marble one dug from the ruins of Herculaneum[361] which is now deposited at Warwick Castle. This vase when done will cost £1500. The original is exquisitely carved and this is to be an exact copy. I did not visit any of the manufactories, as the proprietors of most of them are particularly averse to the introduction of strangers, especially Americans.[362] This is the same throughout England. The next morning set out for Liverpool upon the outside of the coach. The early part of the day was remarkably fine, but at noon it began to rain, and I arrived early in the evening at Liverpool completely drenched by the torrents which poured down, the latter part of my journey.

Finding that the ship in which I have taken my passage did not sail for a fortnight, I took lodgings instead of being at an inn. I have two rooms, a parlor and bedroom, for which I pay a very moderate sum compared to the inn charges. When I take my meals at my room, my landlady charges me the first cost for the articles, the expense for preparing them being included in the rent of the apartments. I found this to be a much more comfortable way of living than I had anticipated. Wishing to bathe I went as directed a small distance from town where a number of bathing machines is kept.[363] These are drawn into the sea by a horse. These machines are quite comfortable and the charge for using them moderate, being only sixpence. At a short distance from where I was there were some women bathing. They seemed not at all disturbed at a number of us being so near them. Although this is quite customary here, I think the indelicacy of it is not commendable.

 Mr. W. of Warrington having heard of my arrival at Liverpool sent his son in a gig[364] after me to go on a visit to his house. I returned with him and on Sunday dined at a country seat of Mr. A. G. at Walton, a short distance from Warrington. After dinner we took a short ride. The road was uncommonly pretty, running most of the way between the Duke of Bridgewater's canal and the River Mersey.[365] At about five miles from Walton stands Halton Castle, now a ruin. One of its walls forms part of the wall to an inn, much resorted to as a place of recreation. The site of the hall is now a bowling green. Some of the window arches are in tolerable preservation and some few specimens of ornamented stone work still remain. The eminence upon which this ruin stands rises up almost perpendicularly. The village of Halton directly underneath adds much to the beauty of the landscape. On the other side is a view of Norton Priory, standing in a fine park, the seat of Sir Richard Brook.[366] The view altogether is very extensive. When upon the walls it appeared like being in the centre of a vast panorama; having nothing to obstruct the view on every side the eye was presented with cultivated fields, woods, rivers, canals, and villages. At the entrance of the village the traveller is notified by an inscription upon the castle walls that an inn is kept there. The road winds round the hill and leads to the top. There were several groups of lads and lasses seated upon the ruins of the walls, partaking of refreshments. I could not help drawing in my imagination the contrast between the scene and the scenes here exhibited a few centuries ago, when

> "From yon high tower the archer drew
> With steady hand the stubborn yew,
> While fierce in martial state,
> The mailed host in long array,
> With crested helms, and banners gay,
> Burst from the thundering gate"[367]

 This castle was destroyed by Oliver Cromwell in the civil wars. There could not be a situation better calculated for defence than this: there is no way by which a foe could approach undiscovered as the battlement commanded a view of the country to along distance in every direction, and the steepness of the eminence rendered it almost an impossibility to storm the walls. Most of the strongholds of ancient days are remarkable for being erected in such situations as rendered them inaccessible. One mile from here is the village of Runcorn. This place is much resorted to by the people of Manchester and Liverpool as a place of amusement.[368] Here I saw for the first time an English steamboat.[369] Compared with our boats of the same description they are as far behind in point of improvement as our stagecoaches are to those of this country; nor are those boats which are upon the River Clyde in Scotland and which are much praised here to be (as I am informed) compared to those in America. The deficiency of improvement in both cases may be accounted for in their superiority of roads and number of population and the natural advantages of our rivers over theirs.

Monday, went to a fair or wake[370] in the village of Winwick; among the sports of this place was a bear bait.[371] Bruin after being muzzled was tied to a stake and the dogs were set upon him. I was at first shocked at the inhumanity of depriving the poor animal of resistance and then thus tormenting him, but I soon discovered that the bear was fully equal to his adversaries. The first dog set upon him was a large bull-dog, to whom he gave the "hug à la françois"[372] and sent him off howling. So well was he satisfied of his reception that all the coaxings and threatenings of his master could not induce him to repeat it. Many others were served in a similar manner without the bear's being in the least injured, as his hair was grown to such an immoderate length as to entirely prevent the least laceration of the flesh from the dogs' teeth.

The baiting continued for some time until the bear grew angry, when he broke his rope and after laying his keeper sprawling set off in full chase after the mob of men, women and children who fled over hedges and ditches in all directions. The ludicrous scene that then was presented would require (to give an adequate idea of it) the pencil of Morland.[373] The rest of the amusements were similar to those of our fairs. The church in this village is quite ancient. It is adorned with a handsome spire. Upon the base of the tower is sculptured the figure of a hog with a bell around his neck. The design of this curious figure I could not learn.[374] While we were viewing the church, a person (whom we afterwards found to be the head gardener to the rector) very politely invited us to view the grounds of the Rectory, which was opposite the church. He conducted us round the park through the shrubbery into the gardens where he treated us with some fine peaches and nectarines, and showed us the way back to the village through another part of the grounds. At parting we wished to make him a present for his civility, which he refused. This I mention as being a singular case, as it was the first money I offered in England to a guide or servant which was refused. The rectory belongs to the Earl of Derby and is estimated as the richest living in this part of England.

At Warrington is a manufactory of files. The proprietor of it very politely showed me the different processes of the making of them. The teeth of the files are cut by a chisel, and it is astonishing with what precision and regularity the workmen move their hands even while looking off their work. Some of these files were of such exquisite fineness that it required a glass to discover the teeth. These are for jewellers' and watchmakers' use. The steel is first softened to receive the impression of the chisel, and afterwards hardened by being plunged while red-hot into a prepared liquid.[375] The proprietor complained sadly of the drunkenness of his workmen. It was now Tuesday, and many of them had not yet made their appearance. He presumed they had not spent all their last week's wages, as they seldom came from the alehouse until it was entirely expended. Being some time with the proprietor and conductor of an extensive manufactory, I had a fair opportunity of observing the habits of the workmen, and can without any hesitation declare that with very few exceptions they are of the worst kind; their only care and ambition seems to be to earn a daily pittance which they invariably spend the most part of at the alehouse. This arises from their ignorance; not knowing the common rudiments of learning, their only enjoyment is beastly indulgence and insensibility.

[August 16] On Wednesday, with Mr. A. took a short tour into Wales. We stopped with our gig at Chester and proceeded on foot along the banks of the River Dee to Eaton House,[376] the seat of Earl Grosvenor. I cannot do justice to the description of this fairy structure. It is but just finished. The house is of the gothic order and finished both interior and exterior, in a superb manner. The furniture corresponds to the building, and the offices around it are of the same older of architecture. It is in the centre of an extensive park. If the ancient buildings the ruins of which still remain visible, were at their erection as truly beautiful as Eaton House (and judging from those I have seen, I have no reason to question that they were) one of the least pretensions to taste must sincerely deplore that barbarism which tempted the destruction of these ornaments to Great Britain. We walked back to Chester, and after having dined resumed our ride. Shortly after leaving that place we came into Wales and our first stop was at the village of Hawarden. In the park and near the mansion of Sir Stephen Glynn[377] stand the ruins of a castle which is so embosomed in the midst of a wood as to render the top only visible. The owner has erected a wall around to preserve the ruin from further decay. The park is an intermixture of hill and dale.

One of the valleys is very picturesque, having a small white cot overspread with vines at the bottom of it. As we continued our way the road became more mountainous, and afforded many fine views of the sea-coast. At the foot of the hills we overtook an interesting little Welsh girl who with her brother had been upon an errand to a neighboring village. We asked some information respecting the road. This she gave us and in return requested permission to run behind the gig. During the run, which lasted a mile or more, we had much conversation with her, highly amused at the quickness and propriety of her replies to our numerous inquiries. She as well as her brother spoke Welsh as well as English. I asked her if she would go home with me. She said she would if I would stop and "let her see her father and mother a bit first." Her name was Martha Owings. She was quite handsome and had a peculiar sharp, although innocent and artless manner which interested us very much. A short distance from the road side was a cluster of cottages, into one of which she entered after dropping us a curtsey and bidding us goodbye! We soon arrived at Holywell, and as soon as we alighted, as our time was limited, found our way to St. Winifred's Well.[378] This is called one of the wonders of the world. It throws out one hundred tons of water every minute. The stream proceeding from it is sufficient to supply a number of mills and manufactories erected close by. The water is used for bathing in rheumatic complaints. It is so remarkably clear that the minutest object is distinctly seen at the bottom of a very deep basin. There is a gothic building over the well upon the roof of which are hung the crutches of those who have been so relieved of their complaint by the application of the water as to enable them to offer them as a testimony of its virtues. We descended into the body of the bath by a flight of stone steps and found one of the baths occupied by a young lady who was not in the least disturbed at our entrance, but continued her employment. One of the nymphs of the fountain who was as ugly as sin and almost as old, presented us with a glass of water direct from the spring. I could observe nothing extraordinary in the taste of it. There is a legendary tale respecting this well which requires no small share of faith to believe. It is said that St. Winifred, having made a vow of chastity, was afterwards addressed by a heathen prince who, finding his passion unrewarded, in a rage cut off her head which rolled down the hill and stopped at the very place where the spring now is and which then sprang up! One of the saints of the church took the head up and placed it on her body. It immediately re-united and she lived many years afterwards.

Holywell is pleasantly situated upon the side of a mountain from which is a view of the sea and of the English shore:[379]—near it the River Dee[380] flows into the Channel. In its vicinity are numerous lead mines, which are very productive and afford the proprietors great incomes.

The income of Earl Grosvenor from this source alone is £80,000 per annum. If I were to form an opinion from the small specimen this jaunt afforded me of the Welsh inns, I should without the slightest hesitation say they were quite inferior to the inns of England. The waiter at the best inn in Holywell was one of the most polite, palavering dogs I ever saw. Upon our requesting to be called in the morning he assured us (to use his own expressions) "that we might rely upon it that everything should be done according to our wishes," at the same time bountifully pledging his honor that the hostler should have our horse in readiness at 4 o'clock, the hour appointed. When I awoke in the morning it was past 4, and no waiter had made his appearance. I descended into the stable yard and could not find the hostler, but the noise I made disturbed his understrapper[381] who slept in the hayloft. Feeling a little angry at thus being neglected I addressed myself to him as being the cause of it, and after scolding away for some time discovered from the vacancy of the fellow's countenance that he did not understand a word of English. Finding we could do no better we tackled the horse in ourselves and proceeded back by the same road we came, to Warrington. The next day, left that place and arrived at my quarters at Liverpool.

Being obliged to go to the custom house to obtain a clearance as a passenger in the Liverpool Packet, I experienced a great delay from the inattention of the officers. These officers are universally complained of by every one who has any business to transact at the Custom house. Those who attend on board the vessels are a vile set, whose appearance denotes poverty and who for the pitiful bribe of a shilling will assist in smuggling anything on shore.

At the close of my journal it may not be improper to make a few remarks respecting the people of Great Britain. I found them hospitable in the extreme, zealous in paying every attention to a stranger, and this so delicately expressed as not to leave an impression that they had conferred an obligation At breakfast you generally find tea and toast. The manner of preparing the tea is different from ours. They either have an urn on the table or a small kettle upon the grate, thus keeping the water hot. They consider "steeping" it by the fire as unnecessary. Upon the whole I think this way preferable to ours, as the tea is always hot. Meat is scarcely ever introduced upon their breakfast tables. I have often made the ladies stare at my description of an American breakfast, particularly when I named over some of the etceteras, such as pickles, apple-sauce, potatoes, &c. The dining hour is somewhere about 4 o'clock. Their table is not spread at this meal unlike ours, but you are never asked to drink before you sit down to dinner. Soon after the dessert and wine, tea is served in another apartment, when you meet the ladies who always retire when the wine begins to move round. In the evening at ten or eleven o'clock a supper is brought in, and afterwards liquors with hot and cold water to mix them with. There is so trifling a difference between their customs and ours that a stranger feels but little inconvenience in the society of Englishmen.

Business was my only object in visiting England. At my leisure moments I noted down the foregoing observations which I wish considered as the casual ones of a stranger. I have endeavoured as much as possible by associating with Englishmen to obtain correct ideas of their country, still I am sensible that many things appeared to me different from what they otherwise would have done had I had sufficient leisure to have made further researches. I however trust that these observations are divested of prejudice other than that honest and rational one which inevitably arises in the breast of one sincerely attached to his native land. I am not conscious of having like the traveller in New Jersey (as related in *Salmagundi*[382]) noted down all the people of a town as fat and cross-eyed merely because the landlord and waiter were so. Respecting England there is much to admire and much to dislike, yet the former predominates so far that I have no hesitancy in saying that if I were not an American I should wish to be an Englishman. The Americans are not in the habit of viewing England in the light in which she should be seen. We either represent her as too faulty or too faultless; one party represents her as striving to destroy our country by every means in her power, and pains are taken to persuade the people that the inhabitants are almost to a man inimical to the prosperity of America. I am satisfied by my intercourse with Englishmen and from many conversations I have had with them respecting the late unhappy contest, that they were opposed to it, and that had their government been purely elective like ours they would have thrown the same obstacles in the way of their ministry in prosecuting it as the opposition of the United States did towards Mr. Madison and his party. I have never seen one who did not deprecate a quarrel with us. I wish that the same sentiments respecting England more generally prevailed in the United States than they do, and that we were not so accustomed to hear such intemperate language towards the people of England. On the other hand, the Federalists are apt to imagine that England is perfect.[383]

These feelings arise from the commercial intercourse which the Northern States have more immediately had with her; and from the habit of considering her as their mother country, they look upon her faults with the same feelings as a child would those of a parent.[384] As to the oft told magnanimity which some warm advocates of her say she displays towards America, I believe it is ideal, and that her Government shows none but what is perfectly consonant to her own interest. Self-interest governs nations as well as individuals! The government is undoubtedly jealous of our manufactures and more especially so of our navy, yet that jealousy carries not with it that deadly animosity so often expressed by our Jacobins.[385] Her existence depends upon the welfare of trade and commerce. Whenever the period arrives that the manufacturing interest decays, from that moment I date her declension!

Having closed my concerns, on the 8th of September [Friday] went on board the Liverpool Packet, which dropped down the river, but owing to the lightness of the wind was obliged to anchor opposite the rock. My fellow passengers' names are White, Barnett, Prince, Todd, Hall, Hayward, and Aiken.

[Saturday, September] 9th Continued at anchor.

[Sunday, September] 10th In the same situation. In the afternoon a party of us went on shore and bathed.

[Monday, September] 11th. No prospect of a fair wind, nor any encouragement from the pilot that we shall have one very soon. I cannot conceive a more irksome situation than to be thus detained.

[Tuesday, September] 12th Tried this morning to pass the rock, but were unsuccessful. I was awakened by the pilot's exclaiming "Let go the anchor!" It sounded harsher in my ears than thunder. After breakfast we all went on shore and amused ourselves with rambling about until dinner time, soon after which we weighed anchor and bade farewell to the little Island.

At 6 o'clock Mr. Ford, the custom house officer, with two or three gallows-looking fellows having lanterns with them came on board to search our baggage and examine our crew. One of them came into my stateroom and told me it was a pity that I should trouble myself to open my trunk and hoped that I would give him a shilling to enable him to drink my health and a pleasant passage. This I did, when he at once told Ford that all was correct in my baggage. After getting their fees they all departed in good humour, having, as they expressed it "done their duty." The "Milo"[386] passed us just at sundown. She kept at a small distance ahead most of the evening, which was enlivened by a brilliant moon.

[Wednesday, September] 13th Today the wind has been ahead but the weather continues delightfully pleasant. This relieves in a way the tediousness of confinement. Our employments to pass away the time are various; some are reading and writing in the cabin, while others are pacing the deck in conversation.

[Thursday–Friday, September] 14th and 15th. Beating about near the Tuscar Light [sic],[387] myself and some of my companions very sick.

[Sunday, September] 17th. A gale of wind with the uncomfortable assurance that we were on a lee shore and the tide driving us upon it. The captain was extremely anxious all day, scarcely stirring from the deck. Just at 5 in the afternoon the wind instantaneously changed, and threw the ship aback. All hands were called to extricate her from the perilous situation, which was quickly effected, when we had the pleasing satisfaction that we were running from a dangerous shore.

[Monday, September] 18th. Light winds and fair, but made very little progress in our voyage.

[Tuesday, September] 19th. About seven in the morning spoke the ship Indian Trader from Jamaica, seven weeks out. Gave the crew some newspapers and potatoes.

[Wednesday, September] 20th. The wind fair, and going at the rate of 8 knots. This evening the appearance of the setting sun was uncommonly beautiful and grand.

[Thursday, September] 21st. Wind blowing fresh but fair. The ship rolled very much and shipped some seas, which afforded much amusement to us in beholding the agility of the old cook who tried to escape them by dodging into his caboose.[388]

[Friday–Tuesday, September] 22nd, 23rd, 24th, 25th & 26th. A gale of wind from the Northwest.

[Wednesday, September] 27th. The wind tolerably fair, but the small progress we have made in our voyage is truly discouraging. Were it not for the pleasant society aboard the time would indeed hang heavy on my hands. It is singular that all of us passengers, eight in number, are Bostonians. Six were born in that town and four were school fellows together. From this time until the 18th of October the wind continued dead ahead. On that day it came partly fair and enabled us to lay almost on our course.

[Thursday, October] On the 19th in the morning in lat. 40 long. 40,[389] passed by a small earthen barrel, but being under full sail could not get it. It gave rise to many speculations among us, such as the possibility of its containing letters from persons in a shipwrecked vessel.

[Friday, October] 20th. The wind fair but increased to a tremendous gale. The ship was laid to, but having moderated toward night we proceeded on our course.

[Saturday, October] 21st. At 12. o'clock we were all electrified by the man at the masthead crying out "a boat ahead!" Sail was instantly taken in and preparations to lower the boat made when we discovered it to be the wreck of a vessel of about 80 or 90 tons burden, which had apparently been stripped of everything that was valuable. The hatch was off and the only article upon deck was an old water cask. Her cabin windows were washed out and an old sail hung over them, apparently for the purpose of keeping the water out. She appeared to be quite light, and her bottom was much covered with barnacles.

[Sunday, October] 22nd. Wind still fair. About twelve discovered a sail under our lee bow. She fired a gun and made us bear down upon them. She proved to be the English Gun Brig Cora, five weeks out from New Providence. Supplied them with Steel's Army & Navy list and some newspapers, also some vegetables for their sick. They sent us in return a fine green turtle and six bottles of spirit.

[Monday, October] 23rd. Calm in the morning, but at ten o'clock a fine breeze sprang up which wafted us along at 8 knots. We observed several flocks of birds and some shoals of fish, which gave us notice of the approach to land. Among the fish were some of the flying species, which resembled a swallow in skimming the surface of the water.[390] Toward night the wind increased into a violent gale, and blew tremendously. At the same time it was so dark that it was impossible to see from one side the ship to the other. The appearance of the sea was truly beautiful. Our vessel seemed to be making her way through a mass of liquid fire.

[Wednesday, October] 25th. This day it blew a violent gale of wind, at times increased by heavy squalls. One took the foreyard short off, another took the staysail over board. It abated at twelve o'clock, when all hands were employed in repairing damages. By night a new yard was got up and everything looked a little more ship-shape. The captain had suffered exceedingly with his fatigue and our ill luck.

From this time until our arrival at Cape Ann[391] on the 9th November [Thursday], nothing remarkable happened. I got into Boston at 8 at night, and found all friends in good health, although almost despairing of ever seeing me again.

Appendix A

The Treaty of Ghent

In 1814, British and American delegations met to negotiate peace in the Belgian city of Ghent, prompted, in part, by Czar Alexander of Russia who was interested in solidifying Britain's attention to the fight against Napoleon. Among the American diplomats or "peace commissioners" who participated in the negotiations were John Quincy Adams, James A. Bayard Sr., Henry Clay (who was Speaker of the House), and the Swiss-born Albert Gallatin, who had only recently served as Secretary of the Treasury. The English negotiators included Admiral James Gambier and Henry Goulburn, who was undersecretary for war and the colonies, and William Adams, a specialist in maritime law. The following excerpts highlight a few of the major issues that emerged from the negations, including the restoration of lands and negotiation of boundaries (Article Five). The return of goods, including slaves, was highly problematic for England given that the Slave Trade Act of 1807 made the trading of slaves illegal throughout the British Empire. In the final analysis, perhaps following the sentiments of Article Ten, England purchased the slaves in question rather than return them to the United States.

Treaty of Peace and Amity between His Britannic Majesty and the United States of America

His Britannic Majesty and the United States of America desirous of terminating the war which has unhappily subsisted between the two Countries, and of restoring upon principles of perfect reciprocity, Peace, Friendship, and good Understanding between them, have for that purpose appointed their respective Plenipotentiaries, that is to say, His Britannic Majesty on His part has appointed the Right Honourable James Lord Gambier, late Admiral of the White now Admiral of the Red Squadron of His Majesty's Fleet; Henry Goulburn Esquire, a Member of the Imperial Parliament and Under Secretary of State; and William Adams Esquire, Doctor of Civil Laws: And the President of the United States, by and with the advice and consent of the Senate thereof, has appointed John Quincy Adams, James A. Bayard, Henry Clay, Jonathan Russell, and Albert Gallatin, Citizens of the United States; who, after a reciprocal communication of their respective Full Powers, have agreed upon the following Articles.

ARTICLE THE FIRST. There shall be a firm and universal Peace between His Britannic Majesty and the United States, and between their respective Countries, Territories, Cities, Towns, and People of every degree without exception of places or persons. All hostilities both by sea and land shall cease as soon as this Treaty shall have been ratified by both parties as hereinafter mentioned. All territory, places, and possessions whatsoever taken by either party from the other during the war, or which may be taken alter the signing of this Treaty excepting only the Islands hereinafter mentioned, shall be restored without delay and without causing any destruction or carrying away any of the Artillery or other public property originally captured in the said forts or places, and which shall remain therein upon the Exchange of the Ratifications of this Treaty; or any Slaves or other private property; And all Archives, Records, Deeds, and Papers, either of a public nature or belonging to private persons, which in the course of the war may have fallen into the hands of the Officers of either party; shall be, as far as may be practicable, forthwith restored and delivered to the proper authorities and persons to whom they respectively belong. Such of the Islands in the Bay of Passamaquoddy as are claimed by both parties shall remain in the possession of the patty in whose occupation they may be at the time of the Exchange of the Ratifications of this Treaty until the decision respecting the title to the said Islands shall have been made in conformity with the fourth Article of this Treaty. No disposition made by this Treaty as to such possession of the Islands and territories claimed by both parties shall in any manner whatever be construed to affect the right of either.

* * *

ARTICLE THE FIFTH. Whereas neither that point of the Highlands lying due North from the source of the River St Croix, and designated in the former Treaty of Peace between the two Powers as the North West Angle of Nova Scotia, nor the North Westernmost head of Connecticut River has yet been ascertained; and whereas that part of the boundary line between the Dominions of the two Powers which extends from the source of the River St Croix directly North to the above mentioned North West Angle of Nova Scotia, thence along the said Highlands which divide those Rivers that empty themselves into the River St Lawrence from those which fall into the Atlantic Ocean to the North Westernmost head of Connecticut River, thence down along the middle of that River to the forty fifth degree of North Latitude, thence by a line due West on said latitude until it strikes the River Iroquois or Cataraquy, has not yet been surveyed: it is agreed that for these several purposes two Commissioners shall be appointed, sworn, and authorized to act exactly in the manner directed with respect to those mentioned in the next preceding Article unless otherwise specified in the present Article. The said Commissioners shall meet at St Andrews in the Province of New Brunswick, and shall have power to adjourn to such other place or places as they shall think fit. The said Commissioners shall have power to ascertain and determine the points above mentioned in conformity with the provisions of the said Treaty of Peace of one thousand seven hundred and eighty three, and shall cause the boundary aforesaid from the source of the River St Croix to the River Iroquois or Cataraquy to be surveyed and marked according to the said provisions. The said Commissioners shall make a map of the said boundary, and annex to it a declaration under their hands and seals certifying it to be the true Map of the said boundary; and particularizing the latitude and longitude of the North West Angle of Nova Scotia, of the North Westernmost head of Connecticut River, and of such other points of the said boundary as they may deem proper. And both parties agree to consider such map and declaration as finally and conclusively fixing the said boundary. And in the event of the said two Commissioners differing, or both, or either of them differing, declining, or wilfully omitting to act, such reports, declarations, or statements shall be made by them or either of them, and such reference to a friendly Sovereign or State shall be made in all respects as in the latter part of the fourth Article is contained, and in as full a manner as if the same was herein repeated.

* * *

ARTICLE THE TENTH. Whereas the Traffic in Slaves is irreconcilable with the principles of humanity and Justice, and whereas both His Majesty and the United States are desirous of continuing their efforts to promote its entire abolition, it is hereby agreed that both the contracting parties shall use their best endeavours to accomplish so desirable an object.

* * *

ARTICLE THE ELEVENTH. This Treaty when the same shall have been ratified on both sides without alteration by either of the contracting parties, and the Ratifications mutually exchanged, shall be binding on both parties, and the Ratifications shall be exchanged at Washington in the space of four months from this day or sooner if practicable.

In faith whereof We the respective Plenipotentiaries have signed this Treaty, and have hereunto affixed our Seals. Done in triplicate at Ghent the twenty fourth day of December one thousand eight hundred and fourteen.

GAMBIER
HENRY GOULBURN
WILLIAM ADAMS
JOHN QUINCY ADAMS
J. A. BAYARD
H. CLAY
JON. RUSSELL
ALBERT GALLATIN

Appendix B

Vauxhall

Vauxhall Gardens, on the south bank of the Thames, was a retreat for entertainment ever since the late seventeenth century. Built on the proper of Jane Fauxe (or Vaux), the site grew to encompass several buildings and stages that allowed for orchestral and vocal performances. Other entertainment included fireworks and displays of

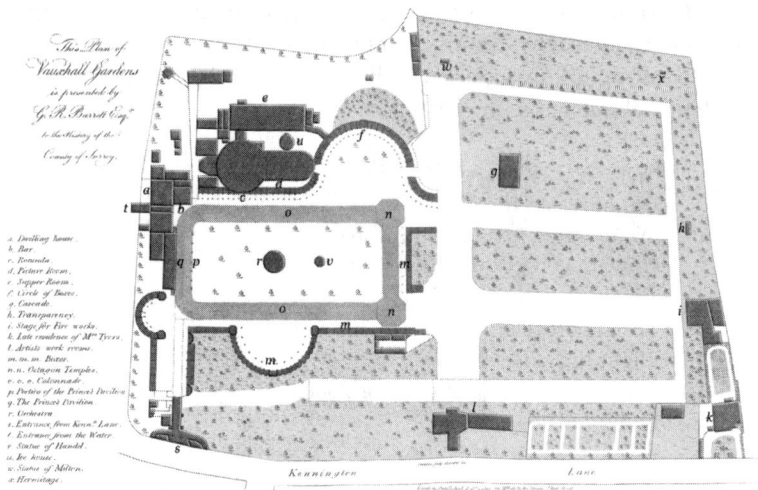

Figure A1 George Rogers Barrett was manager and joint owner of Vauxhall Gardens from 1809 to 1825. This plan of the garden is roughly contemporary with Ballard's visit. (I have enhanced the letters on the map itself to assist readers in locating the sites of the garden.) Courtesy Prints George Image Bank.

ballooning and parachuting. Certain areas of the ground were illuminated and meant to be social venues, while the remainder of the grounds was planted with vegetation and so served as a retreat for lovers. A similar venue, Ranelagh Gardens, could be found in Chelsea, closer to London. It was known for its great rotunda in which members of society could promenade, mingle, and be seen. Unlike Vauxhall, which retained some distinction until the mid-nineteenth century, Ranelagh began its decline in the late eighteenth century, which culminated in the demolition of the Rotunda in 1805.

William Wordsworth recalls the splendors of Vauxhall Gardens and Ranelagh in Book 7 of *The Prelude*:

> Vauxhall and Ranelagh! I then had heard
> Of your green groves, and wilderness of lamps
> Dimming the stars, and fireworks magical,
> And gorgeous ladies, under splendid domes,
> Floating in dance, or warbling high in air
> The songs of spirits!

ll. 119-126

Among Vauxhall's entertainments was a resident hermit who was "hired" to occupy a picturesque grotto and thus add some Romantic charm to the gardens.[1] In his brief history of Vauxhall Gardens, W. S. Scott cites the following poem, which expressed bemused interest in the Vauxhall hermit's profession:

> "Father, your salary of course
> You must receive," I said:
> "Your sitting here is not by force:
> How do you get your bread?"
>
> The sage replied, "Alas! my son,
> I light the lamps by day:
> The hermit's work, at evening done,
> Brings me no extra pay."

From a poem (Anon) about the Hermit at Vauxhall Gardens[2]

The hermit also appears in Chapter 6 of William Thackcray's *Vanity Fair*[3] (1847-1848) when Captain Dobbin wanders around on his own:

APPENDIX B   117

Captain Dobbin had some thoughts of joining the party at supper: as, in truth, he found the Vauxhall amusements not particularly lively—but he paraded twice before the box where the now united couples were met, and nobody took any notice of him. Covers were laid for four. The mated pairs were prattling away quite happily, and Dobbin knew he was as clean forgotten as if he had never existed in this world.

"I should only be *de trop*," said the Captain, looking at them rather wistfully. "I'd best go and talk to the hermit,"—and so he strolled off out of the hum of men, and noise, and clatter of the banquet, into the dark walk, at the end of which lived that well-known pasteboard Solitary. It wasn't very good fun for Dobbin—and, indeed, to be alone at Vauxhall, I have found, from my own experience, to be one of the most dismal sports ever entered into by a bachelor.

Benjamin Silliman's detailed account of Vauxhall in *A Journal of Travels in England, Holland, and Scotland . . . 1805 & 1806* may well have motivated Ballard to visit the attraction, which clearly exercised its charms even on the stately Professor Silliman:

In the evening, I went with a party of Americans to Vauxhall gardens. They are situated about a mile and a half from London, on the south side of Lambeth, on the Surry [*sic*] side of the river. The gardens cover a number of acres, the whole surface is perfectly smooth, free from grass, and rolled hard. Avenues of lofty trees are planted every where, and the confines are filled with shrubs. I came to the gardens with the impression that I was about to see something excelling all other splendid objects which I had hitherto beheld. Nor was I disappointed. For, as we entered, a scene presented itself splendid beyond description, exceeding all that poets have told of fairy lands and Elysian fields.

From the trees, even to their very tops and extremities, from the long arched passages, open at the sides and crossing each other in geometrical figures, from the alcoves and recesses which surround the whole, and from the orchestra and pavillions, such a flood of brightness was poured out from ten thousand lamps, whose flames were tinged with every hue of light, and which were disposed in figures, exhibiting at once all that is beautiful in regularity, and all that is fascinating in the arrangements of taste and fancy—that one might almost have doubted whether it were not a splendid illusion which imagination was playing off upon his senses. Do not suspect me of exaggeration, for, what I have now written can give you but a faint idea of this abode of pleasure.

The arched passages to which I just now alluded, cross the gardens at right angles with each other, and yet, not in such a manner as to obscure the trees. In the recesses which bound the gardens on several sides, and also beneath the trees, tables are placed, furnished with cold collations, confectionaries and other refreshments. Transparent paintings rendered conspicuous by lights behind them, terminate several of the avenues, and all the arbours and walks are painted in a splendid manner.

The rotunda is a magnificent room; it is finely painted, its walls are covered with mirrors and gilding, and two of the principal arched passages cross each other here. The flags of several nations are suspended within, accompanied by paintings characteristic of the several countries.

The orchestra is erected nearly in the centre of the gardens. It is in the form of a Grecian temple; the second story is open in front, and there the musicians are placed.

About 10 o'clock, thousands of well dressed people thronged the gardens. The first entertainment consisted of vocal and instrumental music from the orchestra, and then a noble company of musicians, in number about thirty, most splendidly dressed, and known by the name of the Duke of York's band, performed in a very superior style. The orchestra itself is one of the most beautiful objects that can be imagined. It is a Grecian temple of no mean size, and it is illuminated with such a profusion of lamps arranged in the lines of the building that its appearance is extremely splendid. These lamps are simple in their form but very beautiful in their effect. They are somewhat spherical, open at the top and suspended by a wire. The wick floats in the oil, and the whole forms a little illuminated ball.

The entrance to the gardens presents you with double rows of these lamps arranged in perpendicular lines on the pillars, and then with other rows, corresponding with the form of the roof of the arched passage under which you enter. Along the concave of this roof, extending a great way into the gardens, other lamps are suspended so as to represent the starry heavens. Conceive farther that these lamps are thus disposed in every part of the gardens, in very various and beautiful forms, among the trees and green leaves, in the alcoves, recesses, and orchestra, and that some are green, others red, others blue, &c. thus transmitting rays of these colours only, and you may then form some idea of the gardens of Vauxhall.

Our little party in the gardens was under the direction of an American captain, who was familiar with the place. As soon as the band had finished performing, he told us to run after him, which we did with all possible speed, and we saw every body running that way, although we knew not why. Having reached the end of one of the arched passages, the captain, in language perfectly professional told us to *haul our wind* and *lay our course* for the fence. This we did, and the mystery was soon explained. For, down in a dark wood, we perceived a curtain rise, which discovered London bridge, and the water-works under it nearly as large as the original. The scene was produced by a combination of painting and mechanism. An old woman was sitting and spinning at the foot of the bridge; the mail and heavy coach passed over into town, and a fierce bull followed driving before him an ass. The thing was very well done, and it was at once so odd, unexpected and puerile, that it afforded us more diversion then a fine strain of wit could have done.

After this exhibition there was music again from the orchestra.

It was not past eleven o'clock, and the bell rung for the fire-works. These were exhibited from the bottom of a long dark avenue, terminated by a grove. They were very splendid, and as the night was uncommonly dark, they produced their full effect. It is impossible to give any adequate idea of them by description.

After the fire-works there was an intermission, while every body that was disposed sat down to the cold collation. Our party had engaged a table in one of the boxes, as they are called. They are, in fact, little apartments without doors, closed on three sides, and opening into the gardens. I was now no longer at a loss for the meaning or propriety of the proverbial expression, *a Vauxhall slice*; for the ham was shaved so thin, that it served rather to excite than to allay the appetite. We sat, until the music, beginning again, animated the company to new feats.

Beside the musicians in the orchestra, several other bands now appeared in different parts of the gardens, seated on elevated platforms, railed in, and covered with splendid canopies. Music now broke out from various quarters, and a new entertainment was opened to the company. The assemblies in these gardens always include a crowd of genteel people, among whom are, frequently, some of the nobility, and occasionally, even the king and queen and royal family appear at Vauxhall.

But, in addition to these, no small part of the crowd is composed of courtesans. They are of that class who dress genteely, and whose manners are less indecorous than is usual with persons of their character. The renewal of the music was, it seems, a signal for them to commence dancing. This they did in several groups in various parts of the gardens, and the young men readily joined them. There was among these dancing females a large share of beauty and elegance, and some of them could not have been more than fifteen or sixteen years of age. Their manners and modes of dancing, while they were not so gross as necessarily to excite disgust, were such as I ought not to describe. I can hardly believe what I heard asserted, that some respectable ladies, of more than common vivacity, and less than common reflection, occasionally, in a frolic, mix in these dances. However this may be, it is certain that both ladies and gentlemen, and little misses and masters, are always spectators of these scenes, and I saw numerous instances where young men would leave ladies who were under their care, and join the dances, and then return to their friends again.

This scene continued till half after one o'clock in the morning, when our party came away, and I was told that it would probably continue till three o'clock.

Appendix C

Labor Conditions

Ballard's eagerness to visit England as soon as the Treaty of Ghent was signed had much to do with the need to restore the transatlantic flow of both raw and manufactured goods. England, having clearly emerged as a country at the vanguard of industrial innovation, was advancing factory-based manufacturing at a breathtaking rate. The increasing number of factories and the reliance on steam power to increase productivity was problematic, however, for laborers who saw their jobs disappearing and wages diminishing. Some radicals, loosely called Luddites or frame breakers, broke into factories in order to destroy the machinery, which they saw replacing their individual labor. What's more, working hours and conditions were abominable, particularly amongst children who were shamelessly exploited. The conditions moved Friedrich Engels, who had been living in Manchester, to write *The Condition of the Working Class in England* in 1844.

Although there was no single solution to the increasingly tense relationship between factory owners (masters) and laborers, one renowned manufacturer, Robert Owen (1771–1858), sought to create a factory setting in New Lanark that was sympathetic and supportive of its employees. Owen's objective, though not fully socialist, was to provide decent housing, reasonable hours, education, and some benefits to support the mental and physical health of his workers. As progressive as many of Owen's views were (expressed in *A New View of Society* (1813) [Address prefixed to Third Essay]), his approach to industry is fully in line with emerging capitalism. His references in the excerpt below to workers as "living machinery" who, if properly maintained, "would return you, not five, ten, or fifteen per cent for your capital so expended, but often fifty, and in many cases a hundred per cent," leave little doubt about the objectives of industry.

Address prefixed to Third Essay

To the superintendents of manufactories, and to those individuals generally, who, by giving employment to an aggregated population, may easily adopt the means to form the sentiments and manners of such a population.

Like you, I am a manufacturer for pecuniary profit, but having for many years acted on principles the reverse in many respects of those in which you have been instructed, and having found my procedure beneficial to others and to myself, even in a pecuniary point of view, I am anxious to explain such valuable principles, that you and those under your influence may equally partake of their advantages.

In two Essays, already published, I have developed some of these principles, and in the following pages you will find still more of them explained, with some detail of their application to practice under the peculiar local circumstances in which I took the direction of the New Lanark Mills and Establishment.

By those details you will find that from the commencement of my management I viewed the population, with the mechanism and every other part of the establishment, as a system composed of many parts, and which it was my duty and interest so to combine, as that every hand, as well as every spring, lever, and wheel, should effectually co-operate to produce the greatest pecuniary gain to the proprietors.

Many of you have long experienced in your manufacturing operations the advantages of substantial, well-contrived, and well-executed machinery.

Experience has also shown you the difference of the results between mechanism which is neat, clean, well-arranged, and always in a high state of repair; and that which is allowed to be dirty, in disorder, without the means of preventing unnecessary friction, and which therefore becomes, and works, much out of repair.

In the first case the whole economy and management are good; every operation proceeds with ease, order, and success. In the last, the reverse must follow, and a scene be presented of counteraction, confusion, and dissatisfaction among all the agents and instruments interested or occupied in the general process, which cannot fail to create great loss.

If, then, due care as to the state of your inanimate machines can produce such beneficial results, what may not be expected if you devote equal attention to your vital machines, which are far more wonderfully constructed?

When you shall acquire a right knowledge of these, of their curious mechanism, of their self-adjusting powers; when the proper mainspring shall be applied to their varied movements you will become conscious of their real value, and you will readily be induced to turn your thoughts more frequently from your inanimate to your living machines; you will discover that the latter may be easily trained and directed to procure a large increase of pecuniary gain, while you may also derive from them high and substantial gratification.

Will you then continue to expend large sums of money to procure the best devised mechanism of wood, brass, or iron; to retain it in perfect repair; to provide the best substance for the prevention of unnecessary friction, and to save it from falling into premature decay?—Will you also devote years of intense application to understand the connection of the various parts of these lifeless machines, to improve their effective powers, and to calculate with mathematical precision all their minute and combined movements?—And when in these transactions you estimate time by minutes, and the money expended for the chance of increased gain by fractions, will you not afford some of your attention to consider whether a portion of your time and capital would not be more advantageously applied to improve your living machines? From experience which cannot deceive me, I venture to assure you, that your time and money so applied, if directed by a true knowledge of the subject, would return you, not five, ten, or fifteen per cent for your capital so expended, but often fifty, and in many cases a hundred per cent.

I have expended much time and capital upon improvements of the living machinery; and it will soon appear that time and the money so expended in the manufactory at New Lanark, even while such improvements are in progress only, and but half their beneficial effects attained, are now producing a return exceeding fifty per cent, and will shortly create profits equal to cent per cent on the original capital expended in them.

Indeed, after experience of the beneficial effects from due care and attention to the mechanical implements, it became easy to a reflecting mind to conclude at once, that at least equal advantages would arise from the application of similar care and attention to the living instruments. And when it was perceived that inanimate mechanism was greatly improved by being made firm and substantial; that it was the essence of economy to keep it neat, clean, regularly supplied with the best substance to prevent unnecessary friction, and by proper provision for the purpose to preserve it in good repair, it was natural to conclude that the more delicate, complex, living mechanism would be equally improved by being trained to strength and activity and that it would also prove true economy to keep it neat and clean; to treat it with kindness, that its mental movements might not experience too much irritating friction; to endeavour by every means to make it more perfect; to supply it regularly with a sufficient quantity of wholesome food and other necessaries of life, that the body might be preserved in good working condition, and prevented from being out of repair, or falling prematurely to decay.

These anticipations are proved by experience to be just.

Since the general introduction of inanimate mechanism into British manufactories, man, with few exceptions, has been treated as a secondary and inferior machine; and far more attention has been given to perfect the raw materials of wood and metals than those of body and mind. Give but due reflection to the subject, and you will find that man, even as an instrument for the creation of wealth, may be still greatly improved.

But, my friends, a far more interesting and gratifying consideration remains. Adopt the means which ere long shall be rendered obvious to every understanding, and you may not only partially improve those living instruments, but learn how to impart to them such excellence as shall make them infinitely surpass those of the present and all former times.

Here, then, is an object which truly deserves your attention; and, instead of devoting all your faculties to invent improved inanimate mechanism, let your thoughts be, at least in part, directed to discover how to combine the more excellent materials of body and mind which, by a well-devised experiment, will be found capable of progressive improvement.

Thus seeing with the clearness of noonday light, thus convinced with the certainty of conviction itself, let us not perpetuate the really unnecessary evils which our present practices inflict on this large proportion of our fellow subjects. Should your pecuniary interests somewhat suffer by adopting the line of conduct now urged, many of you are so wealthy that the expense of founding and continuing at your respective establishments the institutions necessary to improve your animate machines would not be felt, but when you may have ocular demonstration, that, instead of any pecuniary loss, a well-directed attention to form the character and increase the comforts of those who are so entirely at your mercy, will essentially add to your gains, prosperity, and happiness, no reasons, except those founded on ignorance of your self-interest, can in future prevent you from bestowing your chief care on the living machines which you employ. And by so doing you will prevent an accumulation of human misery, of which it is now difficult to form an adequate conception.

That you may be convinced of this most valuable truth, which due reflection will show you is founded on the evidence of unerring facts, is the sincere wish of

THE AUTHOR

Appendix D

Monarchy, Regency, and Politics

The focus of Regency politics, complicated though they were, was, of course, the Prince Regent, later George IV. Perhaps the most scandalous moment in the Regency occurred in 1820, a few years after Ballard's return to the United States when George attempted to divorce Caroline. Still, the issues that eventually led to the Pains

Figure A2 George Cruikshank's 1820 caricature of George and Caroline reduced to green bags of evidence to be used as part of the divorce proceedings in Parliament. Courtesy of the Library of Congress.

and Penalties Bill of 1820, a scheme to have authorized a divorce on the basis of Caroline's adultery, were very much on people's minds in 1815. The bill was eventually withdrawn, but Caroline was not admitted to George's coronation in 1821. She died later that year. Satirical cartoons of George and Caroline abounded, but Cruikshank's depiction of them trapped in the evidence of their own indiscretions (Figure A2) captures the prevalent attitude toward both monarchs.

Trial evidence, in Parliament, was typically contained in a green bag. The satire is clear in Cruikshank's caricature but slightly more subtle as Becky Sharp in Chapter Four of William Thackeray, *Vanity Fair*, assembles a green purse which eventually traps Jos. Sedley.

"Let us have some music, Miss Sedley—Amelia," said George, who felt at that moment an extraordinary, almost irresistible impulse to seize the above-mentioned young woman in his arms, and to kiss her in the face of the company; and she looked at him for a moment, and if I should say that they fell in love with each other at that single instant of time, I should perhaps be telling an untruth, for the fact is, that these two young people had been bred up by their parents for this very purpose, and their banns had, as it were, been read in their respective families any time these ten years. They went off to the piano, which was situated, as pianos usually are, in the back drawing-room; and as it was rather dark, Miss Amelia, in the most unaffected way in the world, put her hand into Mr. Osborne's, who, of course, could see the way among the chairs and ottomans a great deal better than she could. But this arrangement left Mr. Joseph Sedley *tête-à-tête* with Rebecca. at the drawing-room table, where the latter was occupied in knitting a green silk purse.

"There is no need to ask family secrets," said Miss Sharp. "Those two have told theirs."

"As soon as he gets his company," said Joseph, "I believe the affair is settled. George Osborne is a capital fellow."

"And your sister the dearest creature in the world," said Rebecca. "Happy the man who wins her!" With this Miss Sharp gave a great sigh.

So the conversation went on. I don't know on what pretext Osborne left the room, or why, presently, Amelia went away, perhaps to superintend the slicing of the pine-apple; but Jos was left alone with Rebecca, who had resumed her work, and the green silk and the shining needles were quivering rapidly under her white slender fingers.

"What a beautiful, *byoo-ootiful* song that was you sang last night, dear Miss Sharp," said the Collector. "It made me cry almost; 'pon my honour it did."

THE DANDY OF SIXTY

Figure A3 A caricature of George IV (as Regent) replacing the traditional ostrich feathers of the Prince of Wales with the peacock feathers of a dandy. Drawn by George Cruikshank, the illustration was used in antigovernment pamphlets prepared by William Hone. Author's collection.

"Because you have a kind heart, Mr. Joseph; all the Sedleys have, I think."

"It kept me awake last night, and I was trying to hum it this morning, in bed; I was, upon my honour. Gollop, my doctor, came in at eleven (for I'm a sad invalid, you know, and see Gollop every day), and, 'gad! there I was singing away like—a robbin."

"O you droll creature! Do let me hear you sing it."

"Me? No, you, Miss Sharp; my dear Miss Sharp, do sing it."

"Not now, Mr. Sedley," said Rebecca, with a sigh. "My spirits are not equal to it; besides, I must finish the purse. Will you help me, Mr. Sedley?" And before he had time to ask how, Mr. Joseph Sedley, of the East India Company's service, was actually seated *tête-à-tête* with a young lady looking at her with a most killing expression; his arms stretched out before her in an imploring attitude, and his hands bound in a web of green silk, which she was unwinding.

In this romantic position Osborne and Amelia found the interesting pair, when they entered to announce that tiffin was ready. The skein of silk was just wound round the card; but Mr. Jos had never spoken.

"I am sure he will to-night, dear," Amelia said, as she pressed Rebecca's hand; and Sedley, too, had communed with his soul, and said to himself, "'Gad, I'll pop the question at Vauxhall."

Another caricature of George IV by Cruikshank (Figure A3) can be found in *The Political House that Jack Built* by William Hone (London: W. Hone, 1819), 8, accompanied the following satirical poem:

> This is THE MAN—all shaven and shorn,
> All cover'd with Orders—and all forlorn;
> THE DANDY OF SIXTY, who bows with a grace,
> And has *taste* in wigs, collars, cuirasses and lace;
> Who, to tricksters, and fools, leaves the State and its treasure,
> And, when Britain's in tears, sails about at his pleasure:
> Who spurn'd from his presence the Friends of his youth,
> And now has not one who will tell him the truth;
> Who took to his counsels, in evil hour,
> The Friends of the Reasons of lawless Power;
> That back the Public Informer,
> Who would put down the *Thing*,
> That, in spite of new Acts,
> And attempts to restrain it, by Soldiers or Tax,

Will *poison* the Vermin, that plunder the Wealth
That lay in the House,
That Jack Built.

The "wealth" is the Magna Carta, Bill of Rights, and right of *habeas corpus*; the "thing" is a printing press.

Appendix E

Cab Fares and Street Life

Few people in London either owned their own coaches or could afford to hire a coach for special occasions. Much of the cost, beyond the vehicle itself, was to keep horses in the livery. Some individuals who were genuinely wealthy and fashionable and could afford this kind of lifestyle, such as Henry Tilney in *Northanger Abbey*, maintained a curricle that was drawn by two horses. The pompous and buffoonish John Thorpe, by contrast, owns a gig that is drawn by a single horse. Nevertheless, Thorpe tries to impress Catherine Morland by describing his recently purchased gig with the same inflated rhetoric and bravado of someone trying to impress someone with their new (but used) sports car:

> Curricle-hung, you see; seat, trunk, sword-case, splashing-board, lamps, silver moulding, all you see complete; the iron-work as good as new, or better. He asked fifty guineas; I closed with him directly, threw down the money, and the carriage was mine. (Chapter 7)

Getting around in London was difficult at best, and given that the weather was always unpredictable and the streets were dirty and often unsafe at night, a regulated (licensed) system of cabs and hackney coaches emerged. Derived from a type of two-wheeled carriage called a cabriolet, the term cab came to apply to any public carriages for hire (which were often painted yellow and later, red). Cab stands could be found throughout London, and while regulated by the city, the condition of the vehicles themselves, to say nothing of the horses, was often dubious. Dickens offers a view of cab life in London in "The Last Cab-driver" in *Sketches by Boz* (1839).

Stagecoaches could be taken at specific inns, such as the Golden Cross Inn near Charing Cross, for travel outside of London. The post office ran "mail" coaches (black and red with the insignia of the monarch), which were exempt from paying tolls on turnpikes and thus were considered the most rapid form of travel.

THE COST OF TRAVEL:

The Hackney Coach and Cabriolet Pocket Companion; Containing Upward of 7,000 Fares From the Principal Coach Stands in the Metropolis, Alphabetically Arranged. London: H. C. Hodson, 1824. Advertisement.

In the following List of Fares, they are reckoned *from* the Coach, as stated at the head of each stand, to the nearest point of the various streets mentioned; except where otherwise expressed. This should be particularly observed as it will frequently make a difference of 6 *d.* or 1 *s.* whether the Coach be taken at one end of the stand or the other.

The Fares to Places of Amusement are reckoned in a similar way.

CABRIOLETS

The Cabriolet Fares are very easily calculated from the following [l]ist; as they are exactly *one-third less*. Thus is the Coach Fare is 1 *s.* 6 *d.*—[T]he Cabriolet Fare will be 1 *s.*,&c.&c.

Fares to the Theatres, Opera House. Vauxhall, &c. Drury Lane, Covent Garden, Opera House, Vauxhall Gardens, Surry Theatre, Astley's Theatre. Sadler's Wells.

	Drury Lane	Covent Garden	Opera House	Vauxhall Gardens	Surry Theatre	Astley's Theatre	Sadler's Wells
Gray's Inn Lane, New road end	2s 0d	2 0	3 0	4 6	3 6	3 6	1 0
Piccadilly, near the Haymarket	1 0	1 0	1 0	3 6	2 0	1 6	3 0

Figure A4 The Quicksilver Royal Mail, as depicted by coaching artist James Pollard (1792–1867), was supposed to be the speediest coach on English roads. Author's collection.

Figure A5 An illustration by the German immigrant George Scharf (1788–1860) of street vendors, hawkers, and signpost carriers. Author's collection.

Appendix F

Celebrating the Defeat of Napoleon ["Boney"][4]

The following evocative and celebratory ballad collected by John Ashton in his collection, *Modern Street Ballads* (1888),[5] suggests some of the excitement that was felt at Napoleon's capture. Ballads and broadsides were, in general, an important mode of communication in early nineteenth century London (and to some extent in England overall).

THE WONDERFUL WONDERS OF TOWN.*

Good neighbours, pray listen—nay do but come round,
I've a tale that shall puzzle your heads I'll be bound;
From London I've 'scap'd pretty glad to get down,
And tell you the wonderful wonders of town.

The streets 'luminated I walked every night,
And the devil a bit I could see for the light;
Such pictures, lamps, feathers, stars, anchors, and jokes,
With Boney, the devil, and all sorts of volks.[6]

Lords, pickpockets, ladies, lamplighters, girls, boys,
I didn't think Peace could have made such a noise.
Push'd, bump'd, lump'd, and thump'd, when I tried to retire,
I was out of the frying pan into the fire.

---

* A song relating to the celebration (in London) of the Peace of 1815.

Then the Emperor's fist was at every one's call,
Till princes and kings went for nothing at all;
And, English good manners to show so polite,
We pulled 'em and hauled 'em, from morning till night.

Then the Cossack Horse Soldiers as fought with our foes,
We kill'd 'em with kindness, as all the world knows,
And gave 'em such welcome and hearty good cheer,
They'd no time to get shav'd all the time they were here.

Two jolly old lions we must not forget,
To Platoff[7] and Blucher, how much we're in debt;
The Mob cried, Come out, like wild beasts, 'twas so droll,
I expected to see 'em stirred up with a pole.

The Sarpentine river,[8] it looked if so be,
All the cock boats[9] i' Lunnun had put out to sea;
Grown up to great ships their gay canvas now swells,
As big, pretty near, as at Saddler's Wells.

You never see'd yet a procession so fine,
As when into the City the Kings went to dine;
I gap'd with mouth open, like many an elf,
Till no dinner I got to put in it my self.

Next Peace were proclaimed, when King Charles on his horse,
Counts the coaches as start from the old Golden Cross;[10]
And the Herald, so call'd who cried down wars alarms,
Looked like the Kings Head stuck a top of his arms.

Now safely return'd, for lost time I'll make up,
So down with the bacon, and round wi' the cup;
And I'll drink may *Peace* also the Yankees subdue,
And turn their *Merry ca*, into our merry cue.

One word more—of all sights that in town I did see,
There was one sight worth all the whole bundle to me,
Great Wellington's self who has made the world ring,
With glory, God bless him, and God save the king.

Appendix G

British Currency

The main unit of currency in the United Kingdom was the pound (designated by £ or l), which was composed of twenty shillings (designated by s. or /-). The value of a shilling was twelve pennies (designated by d.), and so the value of a pound was 240 pennies.

When documenting currency, for example three pounds six shillings and tuppence, the notation would be as follows: £3/6/2d. *or* £3-6-2d.

A shilling could also be referred to as a "bob" and pennies were subdivided into farthings (¼ of a penny), and a halfpenny (½ of a penny), pronounced as "haypnee."

A Guinea was a gold coin valued at one pound and one shilling and was used primarily as currency among the upper classes. After the recoinage of 1816, it was replaced by the "Sovereign."

Notes*

Preface

1. Brief excerpts of Ballard's book are cited in Henry Steele Commager's *Britain Through American Eyes* (New York: McGraw Hill, 1974) and Allison Lockwood's *Passionate Pilgrims: The American Traveler in Great Britain, 1800–1914* (Madison: Fairleigh Dickinson University Press, 1981).
2. The fierce pride of early Americans is not in doubt. John Adams, responding to a question about whether he had remaining family in England, answered indignantly, "I have not one drop of blood in my veins but what is American" (cited in David McCullough, *John Adams* [New York: Free Press, 2002], 329). Still, as McCullough and other historians demonstrate, the relationship between the United States and Great Britain as two formerly linked countries was nothing if not complicated.

Introduction

1. "Anon." *Times of London*, Tuesday, March 14, 1815, Issue 9468, E3.
2. Excerpts from the treaty can be found in Appendix A.
3. Packets, according to the 1918 edition of the *Encyclopedia Americana* (Chicago: Encyclopedia American Corporation, 1918–20), were "swift but capacious vessels, large carriers for their tonnage, with accommodations in the cabin for first-class and between decks for steerage passengers" (659). A voyage from the United States to Liverpool would last anywhere from fourteen to twenty days.
4. See Boyd Hilton's *A Mad, Bad, and Dangerous People?: England 1783–1846* (Oxford: Oxford University Press, 2006), 237.
5. See Joseph Ballard Crocker's "Introduction" to the text.
6. Ballard is familiar enough with the work of Washington Irving (1783–1859) to cite from his *Salmagundi* (1809), which suggests that he had a disposition to humorists and to travel narratives. Elsewhere, Ballard

---

* Notes within brackets are notes from the original text.

demonstrates that he is very well read by quoting from Shakespeare, Cowper, Young, Barbauld, and Beattie.
7. Francis Henry Allen (1866–1953) joined Houghton Mifflin shortly after attending the Roxbury Latin School and was part of the editorial staff by 1894. Because of financial constraints, he did not attend Harvard. An amateur ornithologist, Allen was an expert on Thoreau and served as Roger Tory Peterson's first editor.
8. Houghton Library, Harvard. Archives of the Houghton Mifflin Papers—No. A7733: MS Storage 245, carton 8.
9. The 1913 edition, which was contained in a black slipcase, was bound in gray boards.
10. See, for example, "Notes and News," *The American Historical Review* 18, no. 4 (July 1913): 848–86.
11. For readers unfamiliar with terminology regarding England as a country, it is worth knowing that while "England" is often used (unadvisedly) to refer to England, Scotland, and Ireland collectively, it literally refers to the Kingdom of England and the principality of Wales. The Act of Union of 1707 joined the Kingdom of Scotland with England, forming the Kingdom of Great Britain. A subsequent Act of Union (discussed later) was passed in 1801, incorporating Ireland into the union and forming the United Kingdom of Great Britain and Ireland, which remained viable until 1920 when the Republic of Ireland was formed.
12. The poet Walter Savage Landor (1775–1864) summed up the Georgian era in his scathing but comical verse, *The Georges*, which first appeared in 1855:

> George the First was always reckoned
> Vile, but viler George the Second;
> And what mortal ever heard
> Any good of George the Third?
> When from earth the Fourth descended
> (God be praised!) the Georges ended.

Later, in 1861, the novelist William Makepeace Thackeray (1811–1863), whose *Vanity Fair* (1847) takes place during the Regency, published a series of comical essays called *The Four Georges* in the *Cornhill Magazine*.
13. The designation of George I occurred after the Act of Settlement in 1701.
14. The Industrial Revolution has become a cliché and should not be construed as a simple historical moment that instigated change. Rather, as Colin Jones and Dror Wahrman begin to suggest in their collection, *The Age of Cultural Revolutions* (Berkeley: University of California

Press, 2002), it should be broadly conceived as part of a "cultural revolution" that redefined the self (and the idea of society) in the late eighteenth and early nineteenth centuries.
15. Jenny Uglow's *The Lunar Men* (New York: Farrar, Straus, and Giroux, 2002), provides a fascinating overview of the circle of scientists and engineers that included Erasmus Darwin, James Watt, Joseph Priestley, Josiah Wedgwood, and Matthew Boulton.).
16. In 1788 Prime Minister William Pitt, perhaps recognizing that he would have to turn to the young and impetuous Prince of Wales, who was then twenty-six and already had to be bailed out of a marriage to the Catholic Mrs. Fitzherbert, to say nothing of his the enormous debts, managed to forestall a regency when George III recovered. In 1789, when George III's health declined again, a regency bill was drafted for Parliament, but once again, to Pitt's relief, the king recovered.
17. Brummell was eventually alienated from the Prince Regent and died in France where he had gone to escape his creditors. See Ian Kelly's *Beau Brummell: The Ultimate Man of Style* (New York: Free Press, 2006) for a thorough treatment of Brummell's life.
18. *Northanger Abbey*, though probably completed in 1799, was not published until 1818, shortly after Austen's death.
19. Cant referred to vocabulary adopted by Regency wags that was meant to be clever, if not witty, and restricted to their particular set.
20. Muslin was a finely woven cotton.
21. See Steven Parissien's *Regency Style* (London: Phaidon, 1992) for a comprehensive overview of fabrics, furniture, architecture, and decorative objects in the Regency.
22. Silliman, *Journal of Travels in England, Holland, and Scotland* (New Haven: Converse, 1820).
23. Simond and Hibbert, *An American in Regency England: The Journal of a Tour in 1810–1811* (London: Maxwell, 1968).
24. Cooper, *Gleanings in Europe, England* (Albany: State University of New York Press, 1982).
25. Colton, *A Voice from America to England* (London: H. Colburn, 1839).
26. Bartlett, *What I Saw in London Or, Men and Things in the Great Metropolis* (Auburn, NY: Derby and Miller, 1852).
27. Born in Groton, Massachusetts, Bigelow studied at Harvard College and then entered the Divinity School from which he graduated in 1817.
28. Ballard met Adams briefly (probably on Monday, July 24, 1815) when, toward the end of his stay in England, he needed to secure a passport to travel back to the United States.
29. Rush, *A Residence at the Court of London* (1833; London: Century, 1987), 45.

30. Southey, *Letters from England* (1807; London: Cresset, 1951).
31. Ibid., 362–63.
32. Hoare and Thompson, *The Journeys of Sir Richard Colt Hoare Through Wales and England, 1793–1810* (Gloucester [Gloucestershire]: A. Sutton, 1983).
33. Ibid., 101.
34. For the sake of comparison, it is worth looking as far back as Daniel Defoe's (1660–1731) *A Tour Through the Whole Island of Great Britain (1724–1726)* (Harmondsworth: Penguin, 1975), to mark some of the changes in the landscape, the process of travel, and social customs.
35. The East India and the West India companies, among others, were already well established, and it was apparent, particularly after the Napoleonic Wars, that English colonial power and wealth would only increase. For a very brief summary of London in the early nineteenth century, see Roy Porter's *London: A Social History* (Cambridge: Harvard University Press, 1995).
36. Feltham, *The Picture of London, for 1809 Being a Correct Guide to All the Curiosities, Amusements, Exhibitions, Public Establishments, and Remarkable Objects, in and Near London* (London: Printed by W. Lewis for Richard Phillips, 1809).
37. Competing for the London tourist audience was Samuel Leigh, whose *Leigh's New Picture of London; or, A view of the Political, Religious, Medical, Literary, Municipal, Commercial, and Moral State of the British Metropolis: Presenting a Luminous Guide to the Stranger, on all Subjects Connected with General Information, Business, or Amusement. To which is subjoined, a description of the Environs. Embellished with Numerous Views, a Correct Plan of London, and a Map of the Environs* (London: Samuel Leigh, 1818) remained in print from 1818 until 1833.
38. Feltham also published *A Tour of the Isle of Mann in 1797–1798* (Bath: C. Dilly, 1798).
39. The lasting association between the notion of troublemakers and the pairing of "Tom and Jerry" is no small tribute to Egan.
40. Ackermann was born in Stolberg, Saxony, and emigrated to England where he operated a gallery in the Strand called The Repository of Arts. He also printed works such as *The Microcosm of London* and a periodical called *The Repository of Arts, Literature, Commerce, Manufactures, Fashions, and Politics.*
41. Shepherd, *Metropolitan Improvements Or, London in the Nineteenth Century* (1827–31; New York: Benjamin Blom, 1968).
42. Knight, *Pictorial Half-Hours of London Topography* (London: Knight, 1851) is a useful source that contextualizes the structures of the city and how they changed through the Victorian era.

43. Charles Lemercier de Longpré, Baron d'Haussez (1778–1854) was implicated in the July Revolution of 1830, which sent a number of Charles X's ministers into exile, when he was replaced by Louis-Phillipe. Baron d'Haussez was tried in exile and traveled in Europe until the amnesty of 1839, when he returned to France.
44. See Prince Hermann Pückler-Muskau's *A Regency Visitor. The English Tour of Prince Pückler-Muskau Described in his Letters 1826–1828*, ed. Peter Quennell (New York: Dutton, 1957) and Frederick Raumer's *England in 1835, Being A Series Of Letters Written To Friends In Germany, During a Residence in London and Excursions into the Provinces* (Shannon: Irish University Press, 1971).
45. Dickens, *Pickwick Papers* (New York: Penguin, 2000), chap. 15.
46. Tyler and Kierner, *The Contrast* (New York: New York University Press, 2007). 100.
47. Dickens, *Memoirs of Joseph Grimaldi* (1838; New York: Stein and Day, 1968).
48. A map of Vauxhall and some additional materials about the gardens can be found in Appendix B.
49. See Malcolm Thomis's *The Luddites: Machine- Breaking in Regency England* (New York: Schocken, 1972).
50. For the system of coinage and its terminology in 1815, see Appendix G.
51. Rowlandson's more illicit (not to say pornographic) images reflect a side of British culture that, while not always documented, was omnipresent.
52. Figurines could also be purchased from "image-boys," who were typically Italian and who sold their wares, balanced on a board (frame) on their heads, in the streets of London. It is not clear how early these vendors appeared in London, but Wordsworth recalls them from his youth, in Book VII of *The Prelude* (New York: W. W. Norton, 1979):

> The Italian, as he thrids his way with care,
> Steadying, far-seen, a frame of images
> Upon his head;
> (ll. 214–126)

53. For the single most comprehensive and engaging overviews of the practices of reading in this period, see William St. Clair's *The Reading Nation in the Romantic Period* (Cambridge: Cambridge University Press, 2004).
54. Barbauld, Kraft, and McCarthy, *Selected Poetry and Prose*, ed. William M. McCarthy and Elizabeth Craft (Orchard Park, NY: Broadview, 2002), ll. 39–49, 162–63.

55. Shelley, "England in 1819," ll. 1–5.
56. See Galperin's *The Historical Austen* (Philadelphia: University of Pennsylvania Press, 2006), 3–5.
57. See Thompsons's *Gentrification and the Rise of Enterprise Culture* (Oxford: Oxford University Press, 2001), 22. Thompson notes the existence of a large group of "pseudo-gentrifiers" in the early nineteenth century who "sought to emulate some of the values and lifestyles which percolated down from the aristocracy and gentry."
58. Alliances such as this were prevented by the Royal Marriages Act of 1772.
59. The Delicate Investigation was an unsuccessful attempt from 1806–1807 to inquire into the affairs of Princess Caroline and to determine whether a four-year-old boy, William Austin, who traveled with the Princess, was her illegitimate child.
60. His name is variously cited as Pergami or Bergami.
61. For a comprehensive view of the relationship between Dorothy Jordan and the duke of Clarence, see Claire Tomalin's *Mrs. Jordan's Profession: The Actress and the Prince* (New York: Knopf, 1995),
62. See John Nash's *Views of the Royal Pavilion* (London: Pavilion, 1991).
63. Plowright (London: Routledge, 1996) characterizes the Corn Laws as "selfish class legislation which ran counter to the national interest and the new ideas of free trade." Implementation of the laws," he continues, "merely encouraged inefficiency and greed" (13).
64. Plowright notes that the national debt "rose from £238 million in 1793 to £902 million in 1816" (ibid., 10).
65. Many of the names later implemented for geological time periods, including the Devonian, Cambrian, Silurian, and the Ordovician periods, were derived from place-names or tribal names in England and Wales. The Carboniferous Period owes its name to the abundance of coal in the United Kingdom and Europe.
66. See William Albert's *The Turnpike Road System in England 1663–1840* (Cambridge: Cambridge University Press, 1972).
67. See *The Penny Magazine for the Diffusion of Useful Knowledge*, June 30–July 31, 1833, 133.

1. Bromfield Street, in the heart of Boston, intersects with Tremont Street and is only a few hundred yards from the Boston Common.
2. "Livery and hack" simply refers to a stable where horses and small carriages (hacks) were available for hire.
3. This appears to have been an award for top scholars in Boston schools. There was also a Franklin Medal awarded by the American Philosophical Society in Philadelphia.
4. Franklin medals were awarded to the most deserving boys in the upper class in the Latin, writing, and grammar schools. In 1801 Ballard was one of twenty-one recipients of the medal presented by John Adams, who had just been defeated in the presidential election. See the *Annual Report of the School Committee of the City of Boston, 1877* (Boston: Rockwell and Churchill, 1878), 40–41.
5. Standfast Smith, who was born in Edgeworth, Gloucester, England in 1762, married an American woman and established an import business, eventually taken over by John and Joseph Ballard, in Boston.
6. The Treaty of Ghent, a "Treaty of Peace and Amity between His Britannic Majesty and the United States of America," which ended the War of 1812, was signed on December 24, 1814. The treaty, however, was not ratified by President Madison until mid-February, less than a month before Ballard's departure.
7. [Professor J. W. Webster, convicted of murdering Dr. George Parkman on November 23, 1849, and later hanged.] A chapter describing the murder, including the attempt to incinerate Parkman's body is provided by H. B. Irving in *A Book of Remarkable Criminals* (London: Cassell, 1918). Webster, a professor of chemistry at Harvard, was in financial debt to Parkman.
8. [The *Boston Daily Advertiser* of March 13, 1815, gives list (sic) of passengers as follows—Samuel S. Barnett, Joseph Ballard, Isaac Bangs, Charles Blanchard Jr., John W. Webster, George Wheelock, George Wright, and William B. White, all of Boston, Nathan Plummer of Newport, and J. C. Neilson of Baltimore.]
9. [The following extract from Southey is appropriate to my sensations upon this day and better descriptive of them than any observations of my own:

> "Tis pleasant, by the cheerful hearth, to hear
> Of tempests and the dangers of the deep,
> And pause at times, and feel that we are safe,
> Then—listen to the perilous tale again,
> And, with an eager and suspended soul,
> Woo terror to delight us. But to hear
> The roaring of the raging elements;

To know all human skill, all human strength,
Avail not, to look round, and only see
The mountain-wave incumbent with its weight
Of bursting waters: on [*sic*] the reeling bark:
O God! this is indeed a dreadful thing:
And he who hath endured the horror once
Of such an hour, doth never hear the storm
Howl round his home, but he remembers it,
And thinks upon the suffering mariner."]

This passage is from Robert Southey's (1774–1843) epic poem *Madoc* (1805). Southey's poem is about the Welsh hero Madoc (Madog) who, according to legend, crossed the Atlantic and landed on the southern coast of North America in the twelfth century. Southey, who was poet laureate from 1813 until his death, was an early friend of both Coleridge and Wordsworth, but his poetry was parodied and ridiculed by Byron.

10. The "black fish" Ballard refers to are probably pilot whales of the genus *Globicephala*; these mammals are related to dolphins and travel in pods of twenty or more.
11. "Musquito," is simply a variant of the more modern spelling. The *Mosquito*, a British naval vessel, seems to have been acting as escort to the convoy for sixty or so merchant vessels. It was active in the Battle of Navarino, which occurred in 1827, just west of the Peloponnese, as part of the Greek War of Independence.
12. A brig of war is a two-masted, square-rigged vessel carrying a relatively light armament.
13. Ballard lends out his newspapers because the boarding officer is doubtful that the "Old man," the commanding officer of the *Mosquito*, will lend his copies.
14. Frigates lacked the heavy armament of line-of-battleships. However, frigates were fast and versatile warships, somewhat analogous to twentieth-century cruisers. By 1815, frigates were three-masted ships that displaced over a thousand tons and carried at least thirty-eight guns.
15. Because news traveled so slowly, especially for ships at sea, it is not surprising that the ship on which Ballard was sailing is commanded to "heave to" more than once. Firing warning shots to "bring to" another vessel for examination was common maritime practice in this period.
16. In this period, British naval vessels often mounted a more numerous armament than indicated by their official ratings. In part, this reflected the introduction of "carronades," short-range weapons much lighter than the traditional "long guns." *La Pique* was a thirty-eight-gun frigate built by the French but captured by the British in 1795.

17. The British may have heard rumors about "The Hartford Convention," which brought together representatives of some of the "northern" states and territories, such as Massachusetts, Connecticut, and Maine, which contemplated seceding rather than pressing forward with the war.
18. Napoleon's remarkable escape from Elba, to which he was exiled on May 14, 1804, occurred on February 26, 1815. The event tested everyone's credulity but was probably even more astonishing to Americans who learned of Napoleon's first exile much later than their European counterparts.
19. Ballard was evidently confused here in identifying the ship as a "brig." Perhaps the vessel described had one mast temporarily dismantled, giving a landsman the impression of a brig (two-masted) rather than a three-masted line-of-battleship rated as mounting seventy-four guns.
20. The captain's concern, however unlikely, is that some of the crew of the *Liverpool Packet* might have been taken by force (impressed) by the Americans and are, thus effectively, prisoners of war. Given that the impressment of American seamen by the Royal Navy had long been a source of international tension, Ballard clearly sees this as a positive gesture for the improvement of Anglo-American relations.
21. According to Lloyd's list, which recorded arrivals and departures of ships from major ports, the *Liverpool Packet* arrived in Liverpool, Friday, April 7, 1815.
22. The Liverpool Arms in Castle Street, according to *The Stranger in Liverpool: or, An Historical and Descriptive View of the Town of Liverpool and its Environs* (Liverpool: Thomas Kaye, 1807), was relatively new in 1815 and run by an innkeeper named Lillyman.
23. [Benjamin Silliman (1779–1864), noted American scientist; wrote a journal of travels in England, 1810; was first lecturer at the Lowell Institute, 1838.] Silliman's travel narrative, *A Journal of Travels in England, Holland, and Scotland, and of Two Passages over the Atlantic in the Years 1805 and 1806* (Boston: Howe and Deforest, and Increase Cook and Co., 1812), enjoyed broad readership in the United States.
24. The uncertainty of trade during wartime had a significant impact on currency values, thus gold was considered extremely desirable.
25. The symbol "&c." represents the term *et cetera*, for which we now use the abbreviation "etc."
26. The Liverpool Athenaeum, one of several private subscription libraries established at this time, was founded in 1797.
27. The Frenchman Louis Braille (1809–1852) developed his system of writing for the blind in 1821. Prior to that, however, raised-type print systems did exist, both for the blind and for transmitting military secrets.

28. The "Asylum for the Indigent Blind" was established in 1790 by the Rev. Henry Dannet. See John Aikin's *The Country from Thirty to Forty Miles Round Manchester* (1795; Newton Abbot: David & Charles, 1968.), 348.
29. Thomas Kaye's guidebook, *The Stranger in Liverpool, Or, An Historical and Descriptive View of the Town of Liverpool* (Liverpool: Thomas Kaye, 1812) describes this site as "an institution of this kind, under the appellation of a School for the Indigent Blind has been established, and carried on in Liverpool since the year 1791, with remarkable success. The stranger, in his transient visit to this valuable institution will find his feelings and curiosity equally gratified; and the inhabitant justly regards as one of the proudest honours of the town the place where the greatest of human misfortunes is alleviated, and where a class of beings, otherwise wretched, are, by proper culture, rendered happy themselves, and useful members of society" (111).
30. Vice Admiral Horatio Nelson was celebrated for his many victories during the Napoleonic wars, particularly the Battle of Trafalgar in which he was killed. In earlier battles, Nelson lost sight in his right eye, and in the Battle of Santa Cruz de Tenerife, he lost his right arm. (He is depicted with his right sleeve pinned to his uniform in the sculpture atop Nelson's Column in London's Trafalgar Square.) Aside from his naval victories, he is remembered for his affair with Emma, Lady Hamilton, a striking woman who rose from life in a brothel to marrying William Hamilton, a peer of the realm. The striking sculpture by Richard Westmacott Jr., RA (1775–1856), depicts a shrouded image of death reaching out to touch the figure of Nelson near his heart. Inscribed with Nelson's famous motto, "England expects every man to do his duty," the monument is still situated behind the elegant Town Hall (completed in 1754 and refurbished after a fire in 1795) designed by John Wood (1704–1754).
31. One could ride on the outside of a coach, often on top, for a reduced fare. Outside seating was not only dangerous in the case of accidents but also could be very unpleasant during inclement weather and potentially lethal when temperatures dropped below freezing.
32. While, strictly speaking, Ballard may be accurate here, given the fact that coach interiors were very cramped and often foul smelling, the pricing structure reflected a difference between riding on the inside or the outside of a coach. Around 1830, according to William T. Jackman's *Development of Transportation in Modern England* (Cambridge: Cambridge University Press, 1916), "the general average fares by mail coaches were 5 *d.* [pence] per mile inside and 3 *d.* per mile outside; and by the stage coaches 3 *d.* inside and 2 *d.* outside" (344). Mail coaches, which did not have to stop and pay tolls on private turnpikes, were much faster than standard stagecoaches and hence more expensive.

33. Edward Smith Stanley, twelfth Earl of Derby (1752–1834), served briefly in the House of Commons and subsequently, when he succeeded to become the twelfth earl after the death of his grandfather, in the House of Lords. A friend of the radical Charles James Fox and of the Prince Regent, the earl was also an enthusiast of cricket and cockfighting. Horseracing, however, was his passion and he was responsible for creating the Epsom Derby (pronounced "Dar-bee" and named after himself), which remains a prestigious thoroughbred race for three-year-olds. Also know as the Derby stakes, it is run on the first weekend of June. Elizabeth Farren (1759?–1829) performed at Drury Lane for over twenty-four years and was described by Horace Walpole as the "Queen of Comedy."
34. Warrington, aside from its manufacturing role with respect to wire, the production of leather, etc., was also home to the Warrington Academy (1757–1786), which was an independent educational institution (college) established by Dissenters, particularly Unitarians. The poet Anna Lætitia Aikin Barbauld (1743–1825) and her brother and sometime collaborator, the writer John Aikin (1747–1822), joined the Warrington community when their father was appointed the instructor of theology at Warrington. Joseph Priestley (1733–1804), the chemist, political reformer, and founder of Unitarianism, also taught at Warrington. As an outspoken dissenter, Priestley became a central focus of religious intolerance in England. This intolerance culminated in the Birmingham riot (1791) in which his home and laboratory as well as several meeting churches were burned to the ground. Priestley, a friend of Benjamin Franklin and correspondent of Thomas Jefferson, in 1794, emigrated to the United States in 1794 and lived, until his death, in a home he built in rural Pennsylvania.
35. St. Monday was ostensibly a "holiday" for journeyman workers who could not or would not attend work after a weekend. The term still has some cultural resonance, at least in England, having been used by Billy Bragg (1957–) on the 2002 CD *England, Half English* (London: Cooking Vinyl CD 222, 2002).
36. Child labor laws were very lax and often entirely ignored around this time. Even after the Cotton Factories Regulation Act of 1819, children could be employed at nine years old and were made to adhere to a twelve-hour workday. At the New Lanark mills, Robert Owen (1771–1858), author of *A New View of Society* (London: Privately Printed, 1813), was driven to develop a system of education for children at New Lanark as well as a socialist model of manufacturing. In 1825, Owen attempted, unsuccessfully, to create a utopian community in New Harmony, Indiana.
37. John (Joao) VI, King of Portugal (1767–1826), only five years younger than George IV, became Prince Regent in 1792 when his mother,

perhaps ill from the porphyria (which was the apparent cause of George III's madness), took ill. In 1816, after her death, he succeeded as king. By that time, however, he had been living in Brazil after having escaped Napoleon's invasion of Portugal in 1807. He returned to rule Portugal in 1821 until his death in 1826. The remarkable expense of this glassware suggests something of the luxury that the Regent brought to Rio de Janeiro, where he ruled in exile.

38. Among the people who joined the clergy were second sons of well-to-do families who, unlike their elder brothers, had no inheritance. Yet, having been raised in the lap of luxury, their objective was for a comfortable "living" that would not require too much adherence to the letter of religious law. In *Northanger Abbey* (published in 1817), Jane Austen offers the example of Henry Tilney, a second son who eventually marries the heroine Catherine Morland and becomes small town parson, offering a positive picture of the clergy. However, in *Pride and Prejudice*'s (1813) Mr. Collins, we see a picture of a simple-minded, grasping cleric whose primary allegiance is to the wealthy aristocracy. Decades later, Charlotte Brontë begins her novel *Shirley* (1849) with a scathing depiction of lazy and self-indulgent curates (a level in the church below rectors and vicars).

39. A "living" refers to the income associated with a position, particularly a clerical position in the Anglican Church. While individuals who were given livings were ordained by the Church of England, they often paid "curates" (assistant clerics) to run services, give sermons, and serve the parish. Desirable livings, such as the one described here, were often given to second sons who, not having the first son's right of inheritance, turned to the church as a source of employment.

40. [This living was probably at Winwick, and was held by Rev. John James Hornby, the nephew of this Earl. The living is still one of the richest in England,—£2,400 per annum.] According to Aikin's *Description*, the living in 1795 was valued at "a little short of £3000 per annum" (309) and was occupied by the Rev. Geoffrey Hornby, who died in 1812.

41. [This date should either be 1715 or 1745, on both of which dates the Scottish rebels were in the vicinity of Warrington.]

42. The acronym for a "Hundredweight" (exactly 100 pounds) was established by American merchants in the early nineteenth century.

43. "Boots" is a term used for a boy (servant) who polishes and takes care of one's boots.

44. Windows were considered something of a domestic luxury, and households were taxed on the basis of the number of windows in the structure. The tax was considered a hardship on the middle classes, who occasionally bricked up a window to reduce tax rates, but it was not repealed until 1851.

45. The Portico Library, a private subscription library in Manchester, included the scientist John Dalton (1766–1844) and the physician Peter Mark Roget (1779–1869), who also compiled *Roget's Thesaurus*, among its first members. It is a beautiful example of a library of its time and can be found at 57 Mosley Street in its original structure, built in 1806.
46. The cathedral is dedicated to St Mary, St Dennis, and St George. It was built in 1421 and was known as the Collegiate Church until it became the cathedral in 1847. It was also known as Christ Church in the early nineteenth century. See http://www.genuki.org.uk/big/eng/LAN/Manchester/Cathedral.shtml.
47. The performances attended by Ballard were probably at the Theatre Royal in Manchester, built in 1806. The theater, located at the intersection of Fountain Street and Charlotte Street, was close to the Portico Library. In 1844, the theater was destroyed by a fire and was rebuilt on Peter Street.
48. *The Battle of Hexham, or Days of Old*, first produced in 1789, was a very popular musical historical drama written by George Colman (the younger; 1762–1836).
49. *The Miller and His Men* (1813) was one of many popular plays written by Isaac Pocock (1782–1835), who was also a well-known painter.
50. John Bull, the nickname given to the "typical" British citizen, is often featured as a stocky individual dressed in the clothes of a country squire. John Bull functions in illustrations and cartoons in the same way as Uncle Sam in an American context. The American author Washington Irving (1783–1859) described John Bull as follows:

> John Bull, and has no relish for frippery and nicknacks. His very proneness to be gulled by strangers, and to pay extravagantly for absurdities, is excused under the plea of munificence—for John is always more generous than wise.
>
> [He is] a plain, downright, matter-of-fact fellow, with much less of poetry about him than rich prose. There is little of romance in his nature, but a vast deal of a strong natural feeling. He excels in humour more than in wit; is jolly rather than gay; melancholy rather than morose; can easily be moved to a sudden tear or surprised into a broad laugh; but he loathes sentiment and has no turn for light pleasantry. He is a boon companion, if you allow him to have his humour and to talk about himself; and he will stand by a friend in a quarrel with life and purse, however soundly he may be cudgelled. . . . [He is] a plain, downright, matter-of-fact fellow, with much less of poetry about him than rich prose. There is little of romance in his nature, but a vast deal of a strong natural feeling. He excels in humour more than in wit; is

jolly rather than gay; melancholy rather than morose; can easily be moved to a sudden tear or surprised into a broad laugh; but he loathes sentiment and has no turn for light pleasantry. He is a boon companion, if you allow him to have his humour and to talk about himself; and he will stand by a friend in a quarrel with life and purse, however soundly he may be cudgelled. *The Sketch-book of Geoffrey Crayon, Gent* (New York: Maynard, Merrill, 1906), 432–33.

51. Although the Scots have always had a strong sense of national pride and independence, these traits were particularly strong at this time, particularly because of the "Scottish Enlightenment," which included notable figures such as the philosopher David Hume (1711–1776), the poet Robert Burns (1759–1796), the economist Adam Smith (1723–1790), the geologist James Hutton (1726–1796), the chemist Joseph Black (1728–1799), and the inventor, James Watt (1736–1819) to name only a few individuals. By 1815, Sir Walter Scott (1771–1832), who had been well established as one of the United Kingdom's greatest poets, turned to writing fiction—fearing that his poetry was being eclipsed by the work of Byron (1788–1824). In 1814, Scott published (anonymously) *Waverley*, a historical novel in which the English hero, Edward Waverley, joins the unsuccessful Scottish in 1745 to restore "Bonnie Prince Charlie" to power (thereby restoring the Stuart dynasty). The novel was a remarkable success and led to a series of Waverley novels and other works of fiction, all attributed to "the Author of Waverley."

52. This is almost certainly a reference to another private subscription library, the Leeds Library, which was established in 1768 and moved to its present location, in the heart of Leeds, at 18 Commercial Street in 1808. Joseph Priestley, the scientist and radical, was one of the early members and, in later years, Charlotte Brontë visited the library with her friend Ellen Nussey.

53. Heckmondwike is a town in West Yorkshire.

54. The satiric dramatist and novelist Henry Fielding (1707–1754) was one of the early pioneers of the novel. His work includes *Tom Jones* (1749), which remains his best known work, and *Joseph Andrews* (1742), which is a satirical twist on Samuel Richardson's (1689–1761) melodramatic novel, *Pamela, or Virtue Rewarded* (1740). Fielding later became a magistrate in London and helped establish the "Bow Street Runners," the precursor to what became the London police force.

55. Parson Adams, a central character in Samuel Richardson's *Joseph Andrews* who is traveling to London to try to publish his sermons, finds himself in a number of small inns and alehouses and on one occasion, has to borrow money from a peddler to pay his bill.

56. These were probably "oat-cakes" (also called Haver Cakes) that were allowed to dry on wooden racks called "brade-fleigh." See J. H. Nodal and George Milner, *A Glossary of the Lancashire Dialect* (Manchester: Alexander Ireland, 1875), 51.
57. "Paniers," typically spelled "panniers," are large baskets. Children would collect the scraps of coal that had fallen off larger wagons and then sell them for pennies.
58. Given the enormous weight of twenty-eight fully loaded wagons (perhaps an exaggeration on Ballard's part), it is likely that the engine in question was not a locomotive engine but rather a stationary device that pulled wagons along a track. Nevertheless, Matthew Murray (1765–1826) of Leeds collaborated with John Blenkinsop (1783–1831) to develop a locomotive in 1812 that was capable of hauling ninety tons at about four miles per hour. The two engines that were built, the Prince Regent and the Salamanca (the latter named after Wellington's victory in Salamanca in 1812), transported coal from the Middleton Colliery to Leeds. The engines relied on dual piston engines and, for added traction, on geared wheels that meshed with a cogged rail system. The Salamanca is depicted in the background of George Walker's 1814 illustration of a coal worker in *The Costume of Yorkshire* (Leeds: Robinson & Son, 1814).
59. [Probably the Marquis of Rockingham.] The Needle's Eye is a pyramidical stone structure about thirty-eight feet tall that still stands on what was the coach road, known as the "Great North Road," heading to the village of Brampton near Wentworth. The arched passageway is probably wide enough to admit some of the cramped, narrow coaches used at the time, if driven carefully, but the more grand coaches and carts may have had to divert around it. Ballard might have read about Charles Watson-Wentworth, second marquess of Rockingham (1730–1782), given that he was a strong supporter of the American Revolution. In fact, in one of his brief periods as prime minister, Rockingham repealed the Stamp Act, which the colonies saw as a serious burden and imposition. It is uncertain whether the Needle's Eye was built to reflect Rockingham's Masonic connections (which might well be tied to American symbolism) or, as legend has it, to win a bet proving that the marquis could drive a coach through the "eye of a needle."
60. Because of the availability of coal and iron ore in and around Sheffield, the city was already the center of cutlery production in England by the seventeenth century. The Company of Cutlers in Hallamshire (now the southern district of Yorkshire) was established as a guild by an act of parliament in 1624. Sheffield's cutlery production retained its preeminence well into the early twentieth century.
61. Workhouses that emerged as the parish system of relief for the impoverished, as set up under the Poor Laws, proved inadequate for the

number of individuals seeking work in newly industrialized cities, like London. Residents in a workhouse were given lodging and food in return for their labor, but conditions, as is clear from *Oliver Twist*, were often harsh and unsympathetic. The following description of the workhouse of St. James Parish, which was just north of Picadilly and bordered by Marshall and Poland Streets, offers some insight into workhouse life:

> The average number of people in this asylum amounts to seven hundred and fifty. In the school of industry there are three hundred children, and two hundred are at nurse at Wimbledon; who, when they have attained the age of seven years, are transferred to the establishment in London. Those who are able to work, are employed in needle-work, slop-work, pulling and winding cotton for tallow chandlers, spinning mop and carpet yarn, picking horse-hair for upholsterers, making hat-boxes, &c. They are supplied with clothes made of very good second cloths; but are not distinguished by any particular livery, [242] or compelled to wear a parochial badge. For their food, they are allowed the best ox beef, legs, shoulders, and necks of mutton, four days in the week; on the other days, soup and puddings.
>
> The officers of the house consist of a master, to superintend the men, and a matron to overlook the women; a schoolmaster and schoolmistress, with the necessary attendants. There are also a surgeon, an apothecary, and a chaplain.
>
> The men and the women are separated from each other; and the common room, used by the latter, form the subject of the *plate*.
>
> Each parish in London has a similar institution.

See *Microcosm of London*, vol. 3 (London: R. Ackermann, 1808–11), 241–42.

62. Ballard appears to be conflating the lives of Joseph Gales Sr. (1761–1841) and his son, Joseph Gales Jr. (1786–1860), who was editor and part owner of the *National Intelligencer* in Washington DC. The elder Gales, a radical newspaperman and printer, left England after being accused of distributing weapons to reformers. After briefly living in Philadelphia, he eventually settled in Raleigh, North Carolina, where he continued his work in print and journalism, starting the *Raleigh Register* in 1799. He also served as mayor of Raleigh for almost two decades. Gales Jr. moved to Washington after graduating from the University of North Carolina at Chapel Hill and took over the *Intelligencer* with his brother-in-law, William W. Seaton. They served as the official printers of Congress from 1819 to 1829, and their publications, taken as a whole, constitute an important predecessor to the Congressional Record. Gales Jr. was mayor of Washington from 1827 to 1830.

NOTES TO PP. 25-56   157

63. [James Montgomery, 1776–1854. Best known as the author of many hymns.] Journalist, poet, and hymn writer James Montgomery (1771–1854), according to the Dictionary of National Biography, was born in Scotland but eventually settled in Sheffield. He was known as something of a radical. When Ballard arrived in Sheffield, Montgomery had recently published the epic poem *The World Before the Flood* (1812), which, though popular, received mixed reviews particularly from Francis Jeffrey (1773–1850), editor of the *Edinburgh Review*. Both Sir Walter Scott (1771–1832) and Robert Southey (1774–1883), however, were enthusiastic supporters of Montgomery. Ballard might have been aware of Montgomery's 1809 poem, *The West Indies*, which supported the abolition of the slave trade in England. The poem, composed of four parts, opens as follows: "Thy chains are broken, Africa, be free/Thus saith the island-empress of the sea."
64. An impressive structure, the abbey (now St. Alban's Cathedral) is the second longest cathedral in England and dates back to 1077 AD. The first draft of the Magna Carta was written in the abbey in 1213.
65. The New England Coffee House was at 59–61 Threadneedle Street near the Royal Exchange.
66. Drury Lane Theatre was London's premier venue for theater, as is clear in this passage from Feltham, *Picture of London for 1809* (200-1):

> This immense and superb theatre exhibits externally a magnificence of plan, and internally a refinement of taste, which are at once an honor to Mr. Holland, the architect, and to the nation. It was raised on the site [*sic*] of the old house, and opened in the year 1794. It contains four elegant tiers of boxes, an ample pit, and two galleries; beside which, there are a number of private boxes, ranging along the sides of the pit, and so contrived as to afford the occupiers a perfect view of the stage without exposing their persons to the observation of the rest of the audience. Drury-lane seems to be the favorite [*sic*] theatre with people of fashion, at which indeed, we cannot be surprised when we consider the splendid talents by which it is recommended. The various powers of Mr. Kemble; the nervous, dignified, and impressive manner of Mrs. Siddons; the forcible declamation of Mrs. Powell . . . etc.
>
> The price of admission to the boxes is six shillings, to the pit three shillings and sixpence, and to the second gallery one shilling. The doors are opened at half past five and the performance begins at half past six.

See Feltham, *Picture of London for 1809* (London: R. Phillips, 1809), 200–201.
67. *The Unknown Guest* was ostensibly reveiwed by Samuel James Arnold (1774–1852), who was the joint manager of Drury Lane (he would resign later in 1815). Although Ballard seems to have enjoyed the

production, the review by William Hazlitt was scathing: "The Unknown Guest (said to be from the pen of Mr. Arnold, the manager) is, we suppose, to be considered as a dramatic trifle: it is one of the longest and dullest trifles we almost ever remember to have sat out. We think in general, that the practice of making the manager bring out his own pieces on the stage, is a custom which would be 'more honoured in the breach than the observance.'" W. Hazlitt, A. R. Waller, and Arnold Glover, *The Collected Works of William Hazlitt*, vol. 8 (London: J. M. Dent, 1903). 224–25.

68. "The Woodman's Hut" was a melodrama by Samuel James Arnold (1774–1852); it was published in 1814.
69. Mrs. Darley (1780–1849) was born Eleanor (Ellen) Westray in London. Along with her two sisters, she sang and acted, primarily in Boston and Philadelphia. She married John Darley (1765–1863) in 1800. Images of Ellen Darley have been archived at the Robert Cushman Butler Collection of Theatrical Illustrations at Washington State University and can be found online at http://content.wsulibs.wsu.edu/.
70. Joseph Shepherd Munden (1758–1832), was a comic actor known for his ability to contort his facial features in remarkably effective ways. He was much admired by William Hazlitt, Charles Lamb, and Leigh Hunt.
71. John Bernard (1756–1828), born in Portsmouth, England, was a comic actor who was popular both in regional theater and at Covent Garden. He lived in America from 1797 through 1820, working as an actor and theater manager in a variety of locations, most notably in Boston, where Ballard probably saw him in one of his many performances at the Federal Street Theatre.
72. Describing the Bank of England, Feltham wrote, "The business of this room will greatly amuse the curious stranger, although he comprehends nothing of the detail, for the throng, the hurry, the seeming confusion, and the busy eager countenances, he will perceive there" (*Picture of London for 1809* [London: R. Phillips, 1809], 96). Feltham's observations are confirmed in the description provided in Ackermann's *Microcosm*: "Here, from the hours of eleven to three, a crowd of eager money-dealers assemble, and the avidity of gain displays itself in a variety of shapes, truly ludicrous to the disinterested observer." *Microcosm of London*, vol. 1 (London: R. Ackermann, 1808–1811), 41.
73. A beadle was a parish constable who, despite his elaborate uniform, was primarily responsible for minor tasks such as bringing defendants to court, circulating announcements as a kind of town crier, and executing the low-level beadle in *Oliver Twist*.
74. Guildhall is "the public hall of the city of London; in which are held the various courts of the city; the meeting of the citizens to chuse [*sic*]

their parliament, lord-mayor, sheriffs, &c. and in which most of the grand city entertainments are given." Feltham, *Picture of London for 1809*, 102.

75. Chatham refers to William Pitt (the elder), the first Earl of Chatham (1708–1788) who entered the House of Commons in 1735 and quickly rose in popularity and power. An advocate of military strength in the service of mercantile gain, he supported the acquisition of colonies and the advancement of trade, leading to the growth of what would be known as the "British Empire." He briefly served as prime minister for which he was given a peerage, allowing him to serve in the House of Lords but alienating him from the public who had come to call him "the great commoner." The city of Pittsburgh is named in his honor. His son, William Pitt (the younger; 1759–1806), was the youngest prime minister on record (achieving the post at the age of twenty-four) and served in that capacity from 1783 to 1801 and then from 1804 to 1806. The monument to the elder Pitt was designed by John Bacon (the elder; 1740–1799).

76. The memorial to William Pitt (the younger; 1759–1806), was sculpted by J. G. Bubb (1782–1853) and erected in 1812 at a cost of £4,078 17s. 3d. John Thomas Smith, *The Streets of London: Anecdotes of Their More Celebrated Residents* (London: Bentley, 1861), 392.

77. The memorial to Lord Nelson by James Smith was installed in 1811 and cost £4,442 7s. 4d.

78. [William Beckford, 1709–1770, Lord Mayor of London, 1762 and 1769. Speech mentioned was made May 28, 1770, and he died June 21, 1770.] The monument was sculpted by John Francis Moore (d. 1809) in 1772 at a cost of approximately £1300.

79. Gog and Magog, derived from a biblical source, were two giants variously represented as defenders of London or as the victim (as Gogmagog) of the hero Corineus, after whom the area of Cornwall is named.

80. The Royal Exchange, established in 1563, was London's center of commerce and a gathering place for merchants.

81. The Theatre Royal, Covent Garden burned down in September 1808 but was quickly rebuilt, following a design by the architect Robert Smirke, and reopened the following September in 1809.

> The price of admission to the boxes is six shillings; to the pit three shillings and sixpence; to the first gallery two shillings; and to the second gallery one shilling. The doors are opened at half past five, and the performance commences at half past six.
>
> N.B. *The Half Price* at both these theatres [Drury Lane as well] commences at the end of the third act of the play, generally a little after eight o'clock. Places for the Boxes may be previously engaged, on paying a small fee of one shilling or sending a servant

to keep them. Either theatre may be seen behind the scenes for a small compliment, on proper application at the stage door, and to persons, who never saw the machinery of a theatre, they afford a most interesting spectacle. Constables always attend at the doors to take improper persons into custody. Feltham, *Picture of London for 1809*, 203.

82. [Eliza O'Neil, afterwards Lady Becher, born in Ireland 1791, died 1872. Made her debut as Juliet at Covent Garden Theatre in 1814. Was for five years until her marriage England's most popular actress.]
83. [George Frederick Cooke died in New York in 1811 [*sic*], and was regarded by Edmund Kean as the greatest of actors.] George Frederick Cooke (1756?–1812) was primarily known in England for his work in provincial theaters, although his portrayal of Richard III in London was greatly admired. Troubled by alcoholism, he left England for the United States in 1810 and toured in New York, Boston, Baltimore, Philadelphia, and Providence where he performed as Richard III or as Sir Giles Overreach in Philip Massinger's *A New Way to Pay Old Debts*. Ballard may well have seen Cooke in Boston, where he performed in the early month of 1812.
84. Five-act dramas were typically followed by a short (one or two acts) farce or pantomime. Less well-to-do theatergoers could pay a reduced fee to enter the theater after the third act of the main production and thereby see the conclusion of the main production and the subsequent two-act entertainment.
85. This may be an original transcriber's error. According to an advertisement in the *Times of London* (Wednesday, April 19, 1815, Issue 9499, E3), the afterpiece on this evening was "Zembuca, or, The Net Maker and his Wife, a dramatic romance in two acts" by Isaac Innes Pocock (1782–1835).
86. *Tekeli, or, The Siege of Montgatz* (which was three acts in 1806 and was then condensed to two acts in 1809) by Theodore Hook (1788–1841) was an English play derived from a French drama by Pixerecourt's French drama of 1803, which was itself based on the life of Emeric, Count Tekeli (1656–1703), a Hungarian revolutionary who opposed Austrian rule.
87. John Liston (1776–1846) was an actor renowned for low comic roles. As a young man, his physique was admired, but atop his five-feet-eleven-inch frame was what Leigh Hunt called an "exquisitely ridiculous face." See Leigh Hunt's *The Autobiography* (London: Constable, 1903), 147. Hazlitt commented that Liston had "more comic humour, more power of face" than any other actor, and observed that "his drollery oozes out of his features, and trickles down his face." Cited in Jim Davis, "'They Shew Me Off in Every Form and Way':

The Iconography of English Comic Acting in the Late Eighteenth and Early Nineteenth Centuries," *Theatre Research International* 26, no. 3: 248.

88. Gas was first used in 1807 to illuminate Pall Mall, a major thoroughfare in London, which, at the time, was the site of many gentlemen's clubs as well as Christie's auction house (Numbers 83–84) for a brief period of time. With the establishment, by Royal Charter, of the Westminster Gas Light and Coke Company in 1812, gas illumination was becoming more common in central London.
89. The Old Bailey is the central criminal court of England.
90. Captain John Wesley Wright (1769–1805), a British naval officer, was captured by the French and accused of being a spy. While in a French prison he apparently committed suicide by cutting his own throat, although the popular attitude in England was that he was murdered, or, at the very least, would have been murdered.
91. The Tower of London is one of the oldest structures in London. It was built in about 1090 on the site of Roman ruins adjacent to the Thames and has served as a palace, a prison, an armory, the home of the Crown Jewels, and of course, a tourist attraction. In Ballard's time, the "Tower Menagerie," a collection of wild animals, was open to the public. Most of the animals were transferred to the London Zoo after it opened in Regent's Park in 1828.
92. The "Yeomen" are the guards who are popularly called "beefeaters" but are officially the "Yeoman Warders."
93. On March 31, 1815, a woman named Margaret Moore attempted to steal the king's crown while taking a tour of the Tower of London. Moore accumulated some debt and was reputed by friends and acquaintances to be deranged or "insane." Still, when asked why she attempted to steal the crown, she testified, "I thought it a pity that so valuable a thing should remain there, while half the nation was starving, for want of bread! I wished, also, at the time, to take the whole of what was there, and give it to the public!" Cited in John Ashton *Social England Under the Regency* (London: Ward and Downey, 1890), 11.
94. [Sir Francis Burdett, who published in *Cobbett's Register* in 1810 a letter denying the right of the Commons to imprison for libel. His arrest being ordered he created quite a sensation by barricading his house and resisting arrest for four days.] Sir Francis Burdett, a former member of parliament, advocated radical and reform-driven positions often in opposition to the House of Commons. Perhaps to make a public example of him, he was held for a short time in the Tower of London in 1810 for questioning the authority of the House of Commons to imprison individuals for free speech. In the United States, the First Amendment, guaranteeing the right to free speech, had been ratified since 1791.

95. In 1483, Richard, Duke of Gloucester (1542–1485; later, Richard III), had the two children of his brother King Edward IV (1442–1483) declared illegitimate and then imprisoned in the Tower of London, where they disappeared and were no doubt murdered.
96. Guy's Hospital was widely known in London and was included in Feltham's *Picture of London for 1809* (147–48):

> There are twelve large wards, containing 432 beds for so many in-patients; besides whom charity relieves 2000 out-patients every year.
>
> Wednesday is the day for receiving patients. Behind the hospital a small neat building has been lately erected for the reception of lunatic patients. At the theatre on Saturday evenings, a debating society is held during the winter, on subjects connected with medical science and is respectably attended; and to which members are at liberty to introduce a stranger or a friend. A library is attached to this institution; and a collection of anatomical preparations.

97. Ballard is mistaken here; the statue is of Edward VI (1537–1553), who reopened the hospital in 1551. In his guidebook, *Some Account of London* (London: Faulder, 1813), the author and artist, Thomas Pennant, described the statues as follows: "In the middle of the second court is a statue in brass of Edward VI and beneath him the representation of the halt and maimed. In that of the third court is a stone statue of Sir Robert Clayton' knight, lord mayor of London, dressed in character, in his gown and chain" (69).
98. Sir Robert Clayton (1629–1707) was a banker and former Lord Mayor of London who served as president of St.Thomas' Hospital. The hospital was greatly improved through his own donations and fundraising.
99. A roasting jack was a spit for roasting meat over a fire. Many jacks had spring mechanisms that could be wound so that the spit would automatically rotate the meat.
100. In nineteenth-century British currency, twelve pence (abbreviated with letter *d.*) comprised a shilling (abbreviated with the letter *s.*) and twenty shillings comprised pound (abbreviated with the letter *l.* or the symbols £ or /). Prices were listed in three categories: pounds, shillings, and pence, or *l.*, *s.*, and *d.* A guinea, which was used in special circumstances, was one pound and one shilling, but the last minting of the coin itself was in 1813. Sovereigns, coins that were the value of a pound, were minted in 1817.
101. Astley's Amphitheatre, on the south bank of the Thames, was well known for staging enormous spectacles often involving horse races. "The prices of admission are four shillings, two shillings, and one shilling," Feltham notes, and "the doors open at half past five, and the performances begin at half past six" (Feltham, *Picture of London*

for 1809, 207). The advertisement for the performance that Ballard attended reads as follows: "Horsemanship by 12 celebrated Equestrians. A new splendid Serio-Comic Equestrian Pantomime called THE LIFE, DEATH, and RESTORATION of the HIGH METTLED RACER; or Harlequin on Horseback. In the course of 21 interesting scenes will be introduced a REAL HORSE RACE and REAL FOX CHACE. 'Such a Beauty I did grow,' by Mr. Herring. Equestrian Exercises by Miss Saunders. To conclude with a new Scotch Melo-Drama, called SIGISMORN, and the Danish Chieftain." *Times*, Monday, April 17, 1815, Issue 9497, E2.

102. A variety of wigs made of horsehair are part of courtroom attire in England. On ceremonial occasions, certain members of the court, judges, and those individuals who are King's Counsel (KC), Queen's Counsel (QC), or under a female monarch wore wigs (sometimes called "spaniel wigs") that extend to the shoulders. The longer wigs, which supposedly gave judges an owlish appearance, indicated both seniority and authority, which led to the popular expression, "The wisdom's in the wig." See Richard Shiel's *Sketches of the Irish Bar* (New York: Redfield, 1854), 174.

103. Harlequins were comic characters, derived from Italy's *Commedia dell'Arte*, often dressed in motley (multicolored clothing) and carrying a cane (or a sword), which functioned as a "slap-stick." In the production Ballard attends, the Harlequin shares the stage with a clown, which would be a more buffoonish character who amuses the audience, but, unlike Harlequin, has little wit or trickery. It is around this period when Harlequin and Clown, as characters, come to resemble each other, an evolution for which Joseph Grimaldi (1778–1837) is often considered responsible.

104. One hundred performances was considered a very long run for any theatrical event.

105. Whitehall Chapel was designed by the architect Inigo Jones (1673–1652) under the reign of James I.

106. Charles I was beheaded on January 30, 1649.

107. The term "mews" refers to a street or alleyway lined with stables. Later, these were often converted to dwellings, and the word is still a common street designation.

108. The presidential salary, until well after the Civil War, remained $25,000.

109. Kentish Town is on the north side of contemporary London, halfway between Regent's Park and Hampstead Heath.

110. The words to the Gloria Patri are as follows, "Glory be to the Father, and to the Son, and to the Holy Ghost: As it was in the beginning, is now, and ever shall be, world without end. Amen."

111. Edmund Kean (1787–1833) was celebrated for his Shakespearean roles, particularly Richard III. He premiered at Drury Lane in 1814.

Coleridge's assessment of Kean's skills was, to say the least, ambivalent. "To see him act," Coleridge wrote, "is like reading Shakespere [*sic*] by flashes of lightning . . . I do not think him thorough-bred gentleman enough to play Othello." Samuel Taylor Coleridge, *The Table Talk and Omnia of Samuel Taylor Coleridge* (Oxford: Oxford University Press, 1917), 44.

112. The afterpiece, implausibly titled *The Ninth Statue; or, The Irishman in Bagdad, A Musical Romance*, was by actor and playwright Thomas John Dibdin (1771–1841).

113. St. Paul's Cathedral was designed by Sir Christopher Wren (1632–1723) to replace "Old St. Paul's," which was destroyed in the Great Fire. It was completed in 1708 and remains one of the most prominent features of the skyline of central London.

114. The "Great Model" can still be seen in the crypt at St. Paul's.

115. Mutes, wearing sashes and carrying draped staffs (in either black or white fabric), were hired to lead funeral processions and appear mournful. When Oliver Twist is apprenticed to the undertaker Sowerberry, his "melancholy" expression prompts Mr. Sowerberry to observe to his wife that "he would make a delightful mute, my love." Charles Dickens. *Oliver Twist* (1846; Orchard Park: Broadview Press, 2005), 24.

116. The passage is from the poem "The Grave" by the Scottish poet Robert Blair (1699–1746). An 1808 (London: Cadell and Davies) edition of the poem was accompanied by twelve illustrations executed by William Blake (1757–1827).

117. The Monument, a 202-foot-tall tower, was designed by architect Sir Christopher Wren (1632–1723) and scientist Robert Hooke (1635–1703) to commemorate the Great Fire of London in 1666. The tower, which included a narrow stairwell and an observation platform, was completed in 1776. Unknown to most, the structure also functioned as a kind of "zenith telescope," which Hooke hoped to be able to use to make exact measurements from a cellar laboratory below the shaft of the Monument.

118. This critique of the Monument is from Alexander Pope's *Moral Essays* (Alexander Pope and Adolphus William Ward, *The Poetical Works of Alexander Pope* [London: MacMillan & Co., 1893], epistle iii, ll. 339, 1733–1734, 255). Pope, a Catholic, resented the imputation in one of the inscriptions formerly on the base of the Monument that Catholics were responsible for the fire, hence his reference to bullying and lying.

119. Some insight into the hospital at Greenwich, which was where many sailors retired, can be gleaned from Ackermann's *Microcosm of London* (3:248):

> The Hospital at Greenwich was established in 1694 on the site of a dilapidated palace southern bank of the Thames, just to the west

of London. The hospital, parts of which were designed by Christopher Wren, was used for disabled veterans of the Royal Navy. The pensioners are provided with clothes, diet, and lodging; and have an allowance, called tobacco money, which to the boatswains is two shillings and six-pence, to the boatswain-mates one shilling and sixpence, and to the seamen one shilling, per week. There are also one hundred and fifty nurses belonging to the hospital, who are widows of seamen.

The revenues of the Hospital arise from a duty of sixpence per month upon every mariner, whether in the king's or merchants' service; the profits of the North and South Foreland lighthouses; £6000 pounds out of the duty on coals; the forfeited estates of the Earl of Derwenter, and other inferior resources.

120. The Battle of the Nile (also known as the Battle of Aboukir Bay) occurred in 1798 and was one of Nelson's greatest triumphs.
121. Sir James Thornhill (1675/6–1734) was both an artist and a politician. The ceiling, painted between 1708 and 1725, depicts William and Mary, who reigned over England from 1689 through 1702, surrounded by the cardinal virtues (prudence, temperance, fortitude, and justice).
122. Richard Cumberland (1732–1811) wrote plays, poetry, fiction, criticism, and a memoir. *Wheel of Fortune*, written in 1795, was successful and helped contribute to his financial independence. His play *The Jew, or the Benevolent Hebrew* (1794) presented a central Jewish character in a positive light and an earlier work, *The West Indian* (1771), a study of prejudice, was performed frequently in many American cities, including Boston. Byron performed the role of Penruddock in amateur theatricals, and the play is featured in the poem "An Occasional Prologue, Delivered By The Author Previous To The Performance Of 'the Wheel Of Fortune' At A Private Theatre," published in *Hours of Idleness* (1807).
123. George Bartley (1782?–1858) was a comic actor who was well known for playing Falstaff.
124. George Colman (the younger; 1762–1836) was born in London, the son of a theater manager and playwright. Despite his father's interest in having him pursue law as a career, Colman followed in his father's footsteps and was immensely successful as a playwright. He managed the Haymarket Theatre but encountered enormous debts incurred by his father and struggled to repay his creditors. *Ways and Means*, a farce written in 1788, was surpassed in popularity perhaps only by his play *John Bull* (1803), which offered audiences a patriotic sense of self in response to the threat from Napoleon.
125. According to Feltham, "King Charles II authorized the construction of the Chelsea Hospital for old and injured soldiers. The building was designed by Christopher Wren. The present number amounts to 503;

and of out-pensioners to no less than 10,000. The former are provided with all necessaries; the latter have each 12*l.* *per annum.*" Feltham, *Picture of London for 1809*, 128.
126. St. James Park, which had a canal cut through its center, is situated between what is now Buckingham Palace and Whitehall Road.
127. Hyde Park, along with Kensington Gardens on its western edge, currently encompasses about 625 acres. Like St. James Park, it is one of the Royal Parks of London.
128. In the center of the bridge was a seven-story pagoda, which burned down in 1814 during the celebration of the end of the Napoleonic Wars.
129. This refers to the "Golden Jubilee," the celebration of George III's fiftieth year on the throne.
130. St. Mary Magdalen's Hospital was founded in 1758 and existed at the St. George's Fields location from 1772 to 1863. As Feltham explains, in *Picture of London for 1809* (159–61),

> the "object of the charity" is the relief and reformation of wretched outcasts from society; and the principle on which it is founded, gives it strong title to the countenance and favour of the public, and particularly of the female sex. No object can possible be more worthy of *their* care, than the rescuing from the deepest woe and distress, the most miserable of their fellow-creatures, leading them back from vice, to virtue and happiness, reconciling the deluded and betrayed daughter, to her offended mother, and restoring hundreds of unfortunate young women to industry, again to become useful members of the community.
>
> The hours of divine service are a quarter after eleven in the forenoon, and a quarter after six in the evening, and on account of the fascination of the singing, no place of worship in the metropolis is more worthy of the notice of a stranger.

131. Prince William Henry, Duke of Gloucester and Edinburgh (1743–1805), brother of George III, was secretly married in 1766 to Maria Walpole, the Dowager Countess of Waldegrave who was born an illegitimate child. Their marriage prompted the passing of the Royal Marriages Act of 1772, which made it illegal for a member of the royal family to marry before the age of twenty-five without the consent of the ruling monarch. George III invoked the act, which was rendered to invalidate George IV's secret marriage to Mrs. Fitzherbert in 1785.
132. This passage appears to be from a hymn or psalm used in the service. The following passage may also have the same source.
133. Handkerchiefs form an important part of Fagin's illicit inventory in *Oliver Twist.*

134. May Day, the first of May, is a traditional holiday with ancient roots and was considered a holiday for chimney sweeps.
135. Lady Mary Wortley Montagu (1689–1762) was a writer and an early advocate for the improved status of women. Her son, Edward Wortley Montagu (1713–1776), was something of an eccentric who frequently ran away from school and is said to have apprenticed himself to a chimney sweep.
136. The use of young boys who could fit inside chimneys and clean them from the inside made chimney sweeping one of the most notorious forms of child labor. Not only were the children, who were often orphans or simply sold into indentureship, abused by their masters, but they also experienced very dangerous working conditions that resulted in burns, physical deformity, a variety of cancers, and choking. The poet William Blake (1775–1827) empathizes with the poorly treated boys in two poems in his *Songs of Innocence and of Experience* (1794). Oliver Twist is almost apprenticed to a chimney sweep by the name of Gamfield, whose reputation, we are told, suffers under "the slight imputation of having bruised three or four boys to death already." In his his essay "The Praise of Chimney-Sweepers" (1822), collected in *Essays Of Elia* (London: J. M. Dent, 1941), Charles Lamb encourages his readers not merely to give young sweepers a penny, or "better to give him two-pence" (123). Charles Kingsley (1819–1875), novelist, cleric, and reformer, based his children's classic, *The Water Babies* (1862–63), on a fantasy based on Tom the chimney sweep, who is transformed into a clean and sprightly "water baby" after falling into a river and drowning.
137. Westminster Abbey, formerly a Benedictine monastery, existed on its present site from at least 1045 AD but was rebuilt between 1245 and 1517. It became a cathedral under Henry VIII, which saved the structure both destruction and dissolution by confiscating it entirely from the church for private use. The coronation of virtually every British monarch has taken place in the abbey, and it has served as a burial site for royalty and distinguished artists, writers, and politicians.
138. The old Westminster Bridge, completed in 1750, was an elegant structure built of stone and consisting of fifteen arches. It was replaced in 1862. Ballard was certainly told that the view from the bridge was considered particularly impressive, but he might well have come across Wordsworth's sonnet "Composed upon Westminster Bridge, September 3, 1802," extolling the view:

> Earth has not anything to show more fair:
> Dull would he be of soul who could pass by
> A sight so touching in its majesty:
> This City now doth, like a garment, wear

> The beauty of the morning; silent, bare,
> Ships, towers, domes, theatres, and temples lie
> Open unto the fields, and to the sky;
> All bright and glittering in the smokeless air.
> Never did sun more beautifully steep
> In his first splendour, valley, rock, or hill;
> Ne'er saw I, never felt, a calm so deep!
> The river glideth at his own sweet will:
> Dear God! the very houses seem asleep;
> And all that mighty heart is lying still!

See Wordsworth, *Poems*, vol. 1 (New York: Penguin, 1977), 574–75.

139. Sir Thomas Plomer was probably notable to Ballard, having been the victim of a swindle scheme by his fellow member of the House of Commons, Benjamin Walsh. Plomer asked Walsh to invest over £22,000 on his behalf, but Walsh invested it in American stocks under his own name instead. He was apprehended at the port city of Falmouth, presumably trying to escape England for the United States.

140. Poets' Corner, in the south transept of Westminster Abbey, is an area designated for the burial of significant literary figures or for memorials in their honor.

141. This tomb was sculpted by the popular artist Louis Francis Roubillac (1695–1762), who settled in England in the 1720s. His work, particularly this tomb of Sir Joseph and Lady Elizabeth Nightingale, was characterized by Horace Walpole as "more theatrical than sepulchral." See Augustus John Cuthbert Hare, *Walks in London* (London: Routledge, 1878), 318.

142. Wax funeral effigies of royalty and distinguished individuals, such as Nelson, were on display in Westminster Abbey. Although they were dressed in the appropriate attire, the clothing was often dirty and in bad repair. See Anthony and Richard Mortimer's *The Funeral Effigies of Westminster Abbey* (Woodbridge: Boydell, 1994).

143. The Stone of Scone (pronounced *skoon*), sometimes called the "Stone of Destiny," was used by ancient Scottish kings as part of the coronation ceremonies until it was captured by King Edward I in 1296. The stone was then installed as part of a coronation chair at Westminster Abbey. Last used in 1953 at the coronation of Queen Elizabeth II, it has since been returned (in 1996) to Scotland, where it will remain permanently except for future coronations.

144. Knights of the Garter date back to roughly 1348 when King Edward III established the chivalric honor. The motto "*Honi soit qui mal y pense*" ("Shame upon him who thinks evil of it") is attributed to King Edward, who, after retrieving the fallen garter of a woman of distinction, responded with the motto to insolent courtiers. The "companions"

of the garter include the sovereign, the Prince of Wales, and only twenty-four additional knights or ladies.
145. Charles Abbot (1757–1829), first Baron Colchester, was Speaker of the House of Commons from 1802 through 1817.
146. Robert Stewart (1739–1821), second Marquess of Londonderry, was generally known by the title Viscount Castlereagh. Born in Dublin, he was an active supporter of the Act of Union (1801) between Ireland and England as well as for the Catholic Emancipation (1829), which would permit Catholics to sit in Parliament. Castlereagh achieved some notoriety for the duel he fought with George Canning (1770–1827), his rival in the cabinet since 1809. Canning was injured and Castlereagh unharmed. He served as foreign secretary from 1812 through 1822 but finally succumbed to mental illness and took his own life in 1822.
147. Samuel Whitbread (1764–1815), who inherited his father's brewing fortune, was a vocal and eloquent reformer in Parliament. He was often a solitary voice for social reform, education, and support for the poor. He was also an advocate for peace with France and the United States. He committed suicide on July 6, 1815, perhaps due to illness or as a result of political and financial concerns.
148. William Draper Best (1767–1845), first Baron Wynford, was, at this time, solicitor-general for the Prince of Wales.
149. John William Ponsonby (1781–1847), fourth Earl of Bessborough, was from a Whig family with strong interests in Ireland. He was considered an important strategist but not a particularly strong speaker. His half-sister was Lady Caroline Lamb (1785–1828), an author who had a notorious affair with Byron in 1812. Ponsonby's aunt was Georgiana, Duchess of Devonshire. Ballard may also be referring to George Ponsonby (1755–1817), a cousin of John William Ponsonby who also served in Parliament and was Lord Chancellor of Ireland from 1806 through 1807.
150. Nicholas Vansittart (1766–1851), first Baron Bexley, was the longest-serving chancellor of the exchequer (essentially the minister of finance) in British history. He was a benefactor of Kenyon College in Ohio.
151. George Holme-Sumner (1760–1838) was elected to Parliament from Surrey and represented the borough from 1807 through 1826.
152. Alexander Baring (1774–1848), first Baron Ashburton, was born into a banking family that became known as Barings Bank until its collapse in 1995. Baring served in Parliament from 1806 through 1835 and was a strong opponent of restrictions against trade with the United States in 1812. He married Anne Louisa Bingham, the daughter of a Philadelphia banker.
153. George Tierney (1761–1830) was a Whig politician who served in parliament from 1796 through 1830, during which time he held posts as treasurer of the navy and master of the mint.

154. Sir Robert Peel (1788–1850), the son of a wealthy textile manufacturer and politician, was elected to Parliament (from a controlled district or "rotten borough") when he was twenty-one. Peel later became prime minister and is also remembered for his work in establishing the Metropolitan Police Force at Scotland Yard in 1829. In Peel's honor, police officers became known as "Bobbies" and "Peelers."
155. Samuel A. Otis (1789–1814), born in Massachusetts, served as a representative to the Continental Congress in 1787 and 1788 and was elected secretary of the United States Senate on April 8, 1789, a position he retained until his death.
156. Boston-born Samuel Dexter (1761–1816) served briefly in the House of Representatives and the Senate and served as secretary of war under John Adams.
157. Sir Francis Burdett (1770–1844), fifth baronet, was a strong opponent of Pitt and a popular reformer in Parliament. In 1810, Burdett opposed the arrest of a radical reformer and was arrested and sent to the Tower. He continued to speak out for universal male suffrage (voting by ballot) and Catholic emancipation. His vocal opposition to the Peterloo Massacre in Manchester led to the charge of seditious libel accompanied by a fine of £2000 and three months in the Marshalsea prison.
158. Parishes were civil (as opposed to religious) units of local government used to distinguish communities within districts or counties.
159. The practice of surveying the boundaries of one's parish probably reflected the need to establish, as a result of the Poor Laws, an awareness of who lived inside or outside the parish. The Poor Laws required that the parish need only take care of its own residents.
160. [Queen Charlotte Sophia, wife of George III.]
161. A levee was a reception that was often open to the public, at least as spectators.
162. Liveries were uniforms issued to servants, particularly coachmen, that were distinguishable from one aristocratic family to the next, not unlike contemporary silks worn by professional jockeys that distinguish the stable for which they ride.
163. Three ostrich feathers are a symbol of the Prince of Wales. The motto "*Ich Dien*" means "I serve."
164. Sedan chairs were enclosed boxes that held a single occupant and were carried by two servants who carried the boxes themselves on extended poles. Popular among the affluent classes in the eighteenth century, they were a rarity in the nineteenth century.
165. [The Prince Regent, later George IV, married Caroline Amelia Elizabeth of Brunswick in 1795, whom he neglected and later tried to divorce.]

166. Prince Edward Augustus (1767–1820), Duke of Kent and the fourth son of George III and brother of George IV, lived a military life and remained unmarried until the death of Prince Caroline, the heir to the throne. His rapid marriage in 1818 to Princess Victoria of Saxe-Coburg (1786–1861) resulted in the birth of a child, Princess Alexandrina Victoria of Kent (1819–1901) who, in 1837, became Queen Victoria. The Duke of Kent died in 1820.
167. John Philip Kemble (1757–1823) was celebrated as a great dramatic actor who was known for his intensity in a number of roles, including the title role of "the stranger" in Kotzebue's play. His sister was the great actress Sarah Siddons (1755–1831).
168. Elizabeth O'Neill (1791–1872) was the daughter of an Irish actor who was often compared to Sarah Siddons. Jane Austen was not particularly impressed when, in 1814, she saw her in *Isabella, or the Fatal Marriage: a Tragedy*, a play by Thomas Southerne (1660–1746) that was adapted by the actor and manager David Garrick (1717–1779). "We were all at the play last night to see Miss O'Neil in 'Isabella,'" Austen wrote to her friend Anna Lefroy on November 29, 1814. She continues, "I do not think she was quite equal to my expectations. I fancy I want something more than can be. I took two pocket-handkerchiefs, but had very little occasion for either. She is an elegant creature, however, and hugs Mr. Young delightfully." Deirdre Le Faye. *Jane Austen's Letters* (Oxford: Oxford University Press, 1995), 283.
169. Benjamin Thompson (1775/6–1816), playwright and translator, was so successful with his translation of August von Kotzebue's (1761–1819) *Menschenhass und Reue* (1790), which became *The Stranger*, he was often referred to as "Stranger Thompson." This version was revised by the playwright Richard Brinsley Sheridan (1751–1816).
170. The lengthy battle between the HMS *Endymion*, captained by Henry Hope, and the USS *President*, under the supervision of Commodore Stephen Decatur, actually took place on January 14–15, 1815, after the Treaty of Ghent had been signed but before both captains were aware of it. Ballard's cynicism here has to do with the fact that the *Endymion* was disabled in the complicated fight off the coast of Long Island, and the surrender of the *President* was the result of the intervention of two British frigates, the *Pomone* and the *Tenedos*.
171. Situated on St. Andrew's Street near Holborn Circus, this church was also rebuilt by Christopher Wren after the Great Fire. Thomas Coram (1668–1751), founder of the Foundling Hospital, is buried here, which explains the presence of the charity children.
172. This line, from Matthew 5:1, leads directly into the Sermon on the Mount.
173. Robert Lowth or Louth (1710–1787) was a biblical critic who served for a period as professor of poetry at Oxford. His clerical posts ranged

from archdeacon of Winchester to bishop of London. Lowth was also known for *A Short Introduction to English Grammar* (1762).

174. The foundling hospital was instituted in 1731 by the successful captain and merchant Captain Thomas Coram (1668–1751) and eventually moved to new structures in Bloomsbury (in the site now called Coram's Fields). The name "hospital" is meant to suggest a home offering hospitality for children, as Feltham explains in his 1809 guide to London:

> The Foundling Hospital was situated in Bloomsbury about a quarter of a mile from Holborn. It is in a direct line with the villages of Somer's-Town and Hampstead, and contiguous to the superb squares, Brunswick and Russel, the greater part of the former of which is erected on the lands belonging to the hospital.
>
> It is almost unnecessary to inform the reader, that the object of this institution is *to receive and maintain exposed and deserted children*; or, as the memorial presented to the king, when it was first incorporated, better expresses it, "*For preventing the frequent murders of poor miserable infants at their birth, and for suppressing the inhuman custom of exposing new-born infants to perish in the streets.*" It differs, however, from most of the foreign charities for foundlings in this, that on the continent all children are received indiscriminately, being left in a cradle or wheel, in a particular part f the building, without any questions being asked, whereas in our Foundling Hospital, even the reception of objects is regulated by a committee, who examine whether the case is such as to require the relief afforded by the institution or not. (Feltham, *Picture of London for 1809*, 155)

175. See John 11:35, when Jesus weeps after the death of Lazarus.
176. See Mark 10:14, when Christ rebukes the disciples for not allowing children to be brought to him to be touched.
177. The "Man of Sorrows" passage, from Isaiah 53:3, is taken by many Christians to be a prefiguration of Jesus Christ.
178. The British Museum was in a mansion called "Montagu House" located in Bloomsbury on Great Russell Street, the current site of the museum. The mansion was demolished in 1822 to allow for a larger structure designed by Sir Robert Smirke. Feltham records the contemporary details as follows:

> Persons who are desirous of seeing the Museum, must enter their names and address, and the time at which they wish to see it, in a book kept by the porter, and upon calling again on a future day, they will be supplied with printed tickets, free of expence, as all fees are positively prohibited. The tickets only serve for the specific day and hour specified; and if not called for the day before, are forfeited.

The Museum is kept open every day in the week, except Saturday, and the weeks which follow Christmas-day, Easter and Whitsunday. The hours are from nine till three, except on Monday and Friday, during the months of May, June, July, and August, when the hours are only from four till eight in the afternoon. (Feltham, *Picture of London for 1809*, 186–87)

179. Mary Linwood's (1755–1845) gallery of worsted, as it was sometimes called, was very popular. A catalog of the exhibit, originally published in 1798 remained in print until 1846. Feltham praises the exhibit lavishly:

> At Hanover Square. This exhibition consists of astonishing specimens of a new and fascinating branch of the arts, which has been created and brought to perfection by this lady, whose needle has become a most formidable rival to the pencil. In many respects her collection of worsted pictures is one of the great curiosities in the metropolis; and since its first appearance, the rooms have been a favourite morning lounge for the nobility, gentry, and foreigners of distinction. Some new valuable subjects are added every year; and no person ought to leave London without seeing this matchless exhibition. The admission is one shilling.

Ibid., 219.

180. Worsted is a two-ply yarn that is made from the longest fibers of a sheep's fleece to produce fine woolen fabric. It is also used, as in the case of Mary Linwood, for "crewel work" to create detailed embroidery.

181. In *David Copperfield* (1849–50; New York: W. W. Norton & Co., 1989), Dickens offers a contrasting perspective to Ballard's enthusiasm for Miss Linwood's needlework. Copperfield escorts Miss Peggotty to the gallery, an obligatory stop on their brief London tour, but his disdain for the exhibit is unequivocal. "I remember the gallery," Copperfield recounts, "as a Mausoleum of needlework" (402).

182. Sadler's Wells in Islington offered a wide variety of entertainment from legitimate theater to spectacular performances (with water effects). The great comedian Joseph Grimaldi (whose biography was written by Dickens) performed here, as did the so-called Patagonian Giant, Giovanni Belzoni. "It was a 'half-rural' place," Wordsworth wrote, where "giants and dwarfs/Clowns, conjurors, posture makers, harlequins,/Amid the uproar of the rabblement,/Perform their feats" (*The Prelude*, Book Seven [New York: W.W. Norton, 1979], ll. 271–74). The theater's proximity to the New River allowed for theatrical reproductions of naval battles and, as the *Microcosm of London* puts it, other "aquatic representations" (vol. 3, 41).

183. Somerset House, a large and stately structure on the banks of the Thames, was designed by Sir William Chambers (1723–1796). In

addition to housing the offices of the admiralty, the structure included space for a number of learned societies, including the scientific Royal Society and the Royal Academy of Art, an institution founded in 1768. Among the galleries was a large skylit room with paintings arranged from floor to ceiling.

184. *Gil Blas* (1715–1735) by Alain-René Lesage (1668–1747) was an immensely popular picaresque novel that was translated into English by the novelist Tobias Smollett (1721–1771). Smollett's fiction, including *Roderick Random* (1748) and *Peregrine Pickle* (1751), was influenced by Lesage, as were the novels of Henry Fielding (1707–1754), particularly his *History of Tom Jones, a Foundling* (1749).

185. The painting *Donna Mencia in the Robbers Cavern* (1815) is by the American artist Washington Allston (1779–1843) who studied with Benjamin West during a residence in London from 1801 through 1808.

186. [S. F. B. Morse, the inventor of the telegraph.] Morse's work on the telegraph began in 1837.

187. *Distraining for Rent* by Sir David Wilkie (1785–1841) shows a bailiff evicting a farmer and his family. Their property is listed before it is seized (the act of distraining), and friends try to intervene to prevent the eviction. The painting is in the National Gallery of Scotland in Edinburgh. The *Departure for London* is actually the *Departure to London* by Edward Bird (1772–1819). Recently sold at auction by Christie's (March 9, 2002, Lot 259), the painting offers a detailed vignette of cottage life in the country.

188. General Isaac Brock (1769–1812) was charged with defending the Canadian borders in and around what is now Ontario (then Upper Canada), Michigan, and New York from American military incursions. Brock was killed while leading his troops at the Battle of Queenston Heights, an area adjacent to the Niagara River. Notwithstanding his lack of affection for Canada, he has become a Canadian hero.

189. King's Bench, which primarily housed people convicted of debt or libel, gained some notoriety when five people were killed in 1768 in a riot that followed the imprisonment of the radical John Wilkes (1725–1797). King's Bench, as Feltham notes, was one of a number of prisons visited by London tourists:

> In most respects like the Fleet prison, but is larger, more airy, and more conveniently laid out. The rules, though more extensive, cost more to be obtained, and a prisoner in the inside, can only go out one day each term, or four days in a year, instead of the eighty or ninety days obtained in the Fleet. Being out of the town, the Bench, though more wholesome, is less in the way of friends who might call, which, to the chief part of prisoners, is a considerable disadvantage. There are nearly 300 rooms in this prison, but

the number of people confined is proportionally great, and decent accommodations are even more expensive than in the Fleet.

No stranger who visits London should omit to view these mansions of misery, and it would be an interesting employment to the opulent and humane, if they were occasionally to seek unfortunate objects in these prisons, upon which to bestow their superfluous wealth. It has occasionally happened, that a single twenty pounds, judiciously disposed, has set at liberty ten fathers of families. Even the trifle thrown in the poor's box [*sic*], from its being properly distributed, gladdens the hearts of hundreds of distressed men, women, and children.

Feltham, *Picture of London for 1809*, 176.

Located in the Borough of Southwark (pronounced "suthuk"), which is on the south bank of the Thames about one and a half miles from Charing Cross, the prison housed debtors and people accused, by the Court of King's Bench, of libel and similar crimes.

190. Racket was a game using a tennis racket played against one wall (or two) by individuals in debtor's prisons. In *Pickwick Papers* (Chapter 44), Sam Weller admires the talent of a couple of players while in the Fleet Prison.

191. [Charles R. de Berenger, an officer in the English army.] Charles Random de Berenger was a French officer who served in the Royal Navy under Lord Cochrane. De Berenger, a bankrupt, attempted a kind of stock fraud by counterfeiting letters that claimed Napoleon was dead and that a formal peace was close at hand for England and its allies. De Berenger and his coconspirators stood to make a great deal of money because their false information would increase the value of the funds they held.

192. [Thomas Cochrane, later tenth Earl of Dundonald, born 1775, died 1860. He was accused in 1814 of complicity in originating a fraudulent report of the entrance of the Allies into Paris and the death of Napoleon. Lord Cochrane claimed to be entirely innocent, he was imprisoned for a year, fined, and expelled from the House of Commons. His later career was very interesting for he was enrolled successively in the Chilean, the Brazilian, and the Greek navies, finally coming back to the British Navy, in which he achieved the rank of admiral from 1848 to 1854. He was exonerated in 1831 by William IV from all complicity in the so-called "Hoax" mentioned above, was restored to his rank and honors in 1847 by Queen Victoria, and in 1877 his heirs recovered a considerable sum as damages for his imprisonment and loss of pay.]

193. [Mary Anne Clarke, born, London, 1776, died, Boulogne, 1852. An English woman of obscure origin, mistress of the Duke of York and notorious from public scandals arising from this connection, she was

imprisoned in 1813 for a libelous publication, and after 1815 lived in Paris.] From about 1803 through 1806, Mary Anne Clarke was the Mistress of Frederick, Duke of York (1763–1827), who was then commander-in-chief of the army. Clarke offered to individuals who were willing to pay to include their names on the lists of commissions and special preferments regularly signed, but seldom reviewed, by the duke. After being acquitted for libel for publishing a pamphlet about York and his brother, she successfully managed to use her memoirs, which included letters from the Duke of York, to blackmail her way into a £7000 "award" as well as an annual annuity. Her downfall resulted from a subsequent publishing effort that resulted in her conviction for libel and a nine-month term in prison.

194. The old Bethlem Hospital "for the cure of lunatics" was on the south side of Moorfields. It housed about 260 inmates who "are admitted on petitions, signed by a governor with other formalities, to the committee of governors, who sit every Saturday at Bethlem Hospital. They remain till cured, or for twelve months, if not cured. In the last case they may be admitted again (and usually are) when there are hopes of recovery, or when the lunatic is absolutely incurable, and dangerous to society." Feltham, *Picture of London for 1809*, 151.

195. The Surrey Theatre, which in 1815 was known as "The Royal Circus," was rebuilt after a fire in 1805 and was under the management of the actor Robert Elliston (1774–1831). Although adapted for equestrian entertainment (like Astley's Amphiteatre), Elliston attempted (unsuccessfully) to obtain a patent to allow "legitimate" theater to be produced there. As a result, most dramatic productions were abbreviated adaptations of plays that were set to music.

196. St. Catherine's Church is probably St. Katharine Cree Church, an Anglican Church on Leadenhall Street near Leadenhall Market. One of the oldest churches in London, it was rebuilt around 1630 by Inigo Jones, although the bell tower dates back to 1504. "Cree" is probably derived from an abbreviation of "Christ Church."

197. Acts 10:34 suggests that God does not favor any one nation or individual over another and is commonly taken to be a rationalization for Christian missionary work. The passage reads as follows: "Then Peter opened his mouth, and said, 'Of a truth I perceive that God is no respecter of persons: But in every nation he that feareth him, and worketh righteousness, is accepted with him.'" Acts 10:34–35.

198. English authorities as well as missionaries, such as William Carey (1761–1834), were particularly concerned about female infanticide, which often occurred by drowning. Other Hindu practices, such as *suttee* (now against the law), in which widows cremated themselves on their husbands' funeral pyre were of enormous concern to missionaries. Attempts were also made to curtail murder and theft (*thuggee*

and *dacoity*). Much has been written about the colonial interactions inherent in British India, such as Satadru Sen's essay, "The Savage Family Colonialism and Female Infanticide in Nineteenth-Century India" (*J. Women's History* 14, no. 3 [2002]: 53–79), and it is well worth examining contemporary readings of these interactions.

199. The thirteenth century spire of St. Mary's Church in Stamford is 162 feet high.

200. Although an ancient bridge did exist at this site, Ballard must be referring to the bridge that replaced it in 1805.

201. Leeds was a major center for the production of cloth, but, as Aikin notes, there were at least two carpet manufacturers in 1792. See Aikin, *A Description*, 577.

202. William Hazlitt's (1778–1830) essay "The Indian Jugglers" begins with a description of their impressive skills. "Seeing the Indian Jugglers," Hazlitt writes, "makes me ashamed of myself. I ask what is there that I can do as well as this? Nothing." *Table Talk: Original Essays on Men and Manners* (1828; London: C. Templeman, 1857), 100–1.

203. The impressive ruins of the Cistercian monastery, Kirkstall Abbey, are just outside of Leeds on the River Aire. The abbey was founded in 1152.

204. Market days for cloth were on Tuesdays and Saturdays. Held at separate cloth halls, Tuesday was for white cloths only, while Saturday for mixed cloths, which, as Aikin explains, "are cloths made of dyed wool." Aikin, *A Description*, 572.

205. The Prince Regent's regiment was the Tenth Royal Hussars.

206. The Battle of Talavera in 1809 involved an uneasy alliance between England, under the leadership of General Arthur Wellesley (later the Duke of Wellington), and the Spanish General Garcia de la Cuesta. Pitted against French troops who were commanded by Joseph Bonaparte and Marshall Jourdan, the battle was particularly difficult with severe casualties. The French failed to advance, and victory, though hardly clear, was claimed by the English. Wellesley earned the titles Baron Douro and Viscount Wellington.

207. Cornelius the centurion is considered to be the first gentile to be converted. His conversion, by Simon Peter, marks an important moment in the history of Christianity by allowing the conversion of gentiles and removing the requirement of strict adherence to Jewish ceremonial laws.

208. Banns are announcements (often published) of intended marriages that provide an opportunity for possible objections to be expressed in advance. Three announcements are made over a period of three weeks. In Dickens's *Dombey and Son*, the character Toots cannot endure the third reading of the Banns that promise his beloved Florence Dombey away to her soul mate Walter Gay.

209. [This probably was the Rev. Laurence Sterne.] Sterne (1713–1768) is best known as the author of *The Life and Opinions of Tristram Shandy, Gentleman* (1759–1769).
210. [Some lines which I have seen which were written on Tintern Abbey are appropriate to thus building. They are as follows:

> "How many hearts have here grown cold,
> That sleep these mouldering stones among!
> How many beads have here been told!
> How many matins here been sung!
> On this rude stone, by time long broke,
> I think I see some pilgrim kneel,
> I think I see the censer smoke,
> I think I hear the solemn peal.
> But here no more soft music floats,
> No holy anthems chaunted now;
> All hush'd, except the ringdove's notes,
> Low murm'ring from yon beechen bough."]

The original source of this poem is unclear, although it continues to be cited throughout the nineteenth century. The earliest source for the poem seems to be George Nicholson's *The Cambrian Traveller's Guide: And Pocket Companion* (Stourport: Printed for George Nicholson, 1808), which might have been available to Ballard.
211. St. James's Church at 197 Piccadilly was designed by Sir Christopher Wren and consecrated in 1684.
212. Trinity Sunday, which celebrates the concept of the trinity, is the first Sunday after Pentecost (the fiftieth day after Easter). It is one of the principal feast days of the Anglican Church.
213. Ballard would never be able to take advantage of this invitation as John Kewley, whose church in New York was the Episcopal St. George's, converted to Catholicism and remained in Europe.
214. Doctor Franklin is Benjamin Franklin (1706–1790), who was still widely admired in England and Europe.
215. A turbot, pronounced either *tur-bo* or *tur-bit*, is a flatfish in the same family as the flounder.
216. Roque is a central character in George Colman's play *The Mountaineers* (1793).
217. Now a suburb of Manchester, Rochdale was a heavily industrialized town (producing mostly woolen and cotton products) in the early nineteenth century.
218. The Poor Laws provided financial relief to unemployed or poverty-stricken citizens.

219. The Corn Laws of 1815 stated that no flour or corn could be imported until the domestic price reached eighty shillings per quarter (a quarter was the equivalent of eight bushels or sixty-six gallons according to U.S. dry measure). In 1812, domestic corn, a term that encompasses all grains, was bringing in 126 shillings and sixpence, but by 1815, imports had forced the price down to sixty-five shillings sevenpence. This measure was intended to encourage farmers to continue growing their crops, but it had a severe impact on consumers who protested against the restriction of imports that consequently elevated the price of grain.

220. For a description of residences attacked by the mob and the measures taken to protect private and public property, see James Bonar's "The Disposition of Troops in London, March 1815," *English Historical Review* 16, no. 62 (April 1901): 348–54.

221. Samuel Solomon (1768/9–1819), a very successful quack doctor, published *A Guide to Health* in 1796 in which he advocated his own medicines. He operated a successful clinic in Liverpool where his dubious "medicines" were manufactured.

222. Buildings of significance in the United Kingdom generally had (and often still have) an individual, housed in a small office, who is responsible for custodial duties and other amenities needed by the occupants of the building.

223. Aside from the occasional accident, English stagecoach travel was very dependable, regular, and punctual, particularly when compared with European counterparts.

224. Liverpool's "Theatre Royal" was granted a Royal Patent in 1771 and opened in 1772. "The inhabitants of Liverpool," writes Aikin, "have at all times been liberal encouragers of dramatic entertainments." Aikin, *Description of the Country*, 343.

225. The "ten thousand wheels" of commerce is taken from William Cowper's (1731–1800) poem *The Task*. The passage, which comes from a section titled "The Garden," asks the reader to consider whether it is worth losing the beauties of pastoral landscapes for the attractions of the city:

> Cities then
> Attract us, and neglected nature pines,
> Abandon'd, as unworthy of our love.
> But are not wholesome airs, though unperfum'd
> By roses, and clear suns, though scarcely felt,
> And groves, if unharmonious, yet secure
> From clamour, and whose very silence charms,
> To be preferred to smoke, to the eclipse

> That Metropolitan volcanos make,
> Whose Stygian throats breathedarkness all day long.
> And to the stir of commerce, driving slow,
> And thund'ring loud, with his ten thousand wheels?

See Cowper, *The Task* (1785; Philadelphia: Bennet and Walton, 1811). ll. 729–40, 100.
226. This is an interesting political observation on Ballard's part.
227. This must have been a relatively common misconception, as Benjamin Silliman notes that he was asked a similar question.
228. The gardens were established in 1802 by Liverpool's intellectual and cultural patron William Roscoe (1753–1831).
229. Liverpool's Herculaneum pottery enjoyed a brief but spectacular existence. The newly refurbished pottery, which opened in 1796 (on the site of a small operation), grew very quickly, producing dinnerware of all kinds. Because of its location in the port city of Liverpool, much of the inventory was exported to Canada and the United States. Nevertheless, by 1840 the pottery shut down.
230. The Battle of New Orleans, which took place on January 8, 1815, actually took place after the War of 1812 was over. The American general Andrew Jackson (1767–1845) had been developing a defensive strategy to prevent the British, under Vice-Admiral Alexander Cochrane (1758–1832) and General Edward Pakenham (1778–1815), from taking New Orleans, an important port city. Jackson's fortifications were very sound, and the British received, both strategically and physically, a humiliating defeat that included close to three hundred soldiers killed and a total of about two thousand casualties.
231. General George Prévost (1767–1816), who served as governor of Canada (1811–1815), planned a southern invasion along Lake Champlain. The subsequent Battle of Plattsburgh was a huge embarrassment for Prévost, whose poor leadership resulted in the defeat of accompanying naval forces under Captain Downie, who died in the conflict. Prévost's defeat signaled the death blow for the British in the War of 1812.
232. Castine, a town in Penobscot Bay, was captured on September 3, 1814, by British troops under Sir John Sherbrooke (1764–1830). The advance resulted in full control of the Maine territory until it was ceded back to the United States as part of the Treaty of Ghent.
233. The "Fort of Castle William" is the site of Fort Independence, which protrudes into Boston Harbor.
234. Noddles Island is the name that was used for East Boston, where Logan Airport is currently situated.
235. Dissenters refer to Protestant denominations, such as Presbyterians, Baptists, and Quakers, that set themselves apart from the Church of

England, objecting to the conventions and practices of the church as well as the connection of church and state. The Act of Toleration of 1689 permitted dissenters to hold services in licensed meeting houses and to have their own preachers. Still, tolerance for dissenting groups was limited and certain laws, such as the Test Act (restricting dissenters from holding public office or from attending Oxford and Cambridge), effectively marginalized dissenters in British society.

236. Oatmeal cakes are a traditional Scottish recipe. They are essentially biscuits or cookies.

237. Ballard clearly means Northwich, rather than Northwick (in the south of England), which has long been the primary site for salt mining in England and is now home to a salt museum.

238. George Canning (1770–1827), an accomplished debater and orator, was a member of Parliament for the city of Liverpool at this time. Canning held many posts in the cabinet but was in ill health when, in 1827, he finally became prime minister and died after only 119 days in office. His rivalry with fellow Tory Castlereagh resulted in a duel between the two.

239. Chester, about forty miles south of Manchester, began as an important port and fortress established during the Roman occupation of Britain. It was occupied by the Normans in the early eleventh century and became the site for a castle constructed by William the Conqueror's nephew, Hugh the Wolf. One distinctive feature of the city are the "rows," double-decker streets that date back to the Medieval period. Chester (sometimes called "the walled city") is situated along the River Dee and is surrounded by a two-mile length of wall fragments, which date back to the Roman occupancy of Britain.

240. The term "gibbet" can simply refer to gallows, which were used for hanging in the execution of prisoners. Sometimes the bodies of these prisoners were suspended from a gibbet (occasionally in a cage) on the outskirts of a town to warn away highwaymen and other criminals. The last recorded use of a gibbet was in 1832. In William Wordsworth's poem *The Prelude*, he recalls the impact of seeing a body in a gibbet as a young boy:

> I led my horse, and stumbling on, at length
> Came to a bottom where in former times
> A man, the murderer of his wife, was hung
> In irons. Mouldered was the gibbet-mast;
> The bones were gone, the iron and the wood;
> Only a long green ridge of turf remained
> Whose shape was like a grave. (ll. 307–14)

241. The distant tower mentioned by Ballard is probably what is called the New Tower or Water Tower and stood in the river itself. Although

greatly modified in the eighteenth century, it still reflects its origins as a Norman stone motte and bailey fortress.
242. The race track forms a circle.
243. Convicted criminals, until 1829, could be branded on their hands (particularly on the thumb) to indicate that they had committed a crime. Often, the brand was a letter, such as "M" for malefactor.
244. The town went by both names until 1835 when the citizens officially discarded the name Bullock-Smithy, which they found embarrassing, for the more pleasant Hazel Grove.
245. This is almost certainly referring to Whaley Bridge, which is a small town about eighteen miles south of Manchester and leads into the Peak District.
246. This immense cavern in Derbyshire's Peak District was described as early as 1086. In Ben Jonson's (1572–1637) *The Devil is an Ass* (1616), Pug, the lesser devil, claims ancestral ownership of the cavern, calling it by its more familiar name "The Devil's Arse." The river that Ballard describes is aptly called the River Styx. Notwithstanding the river, the cavern was known for being a consistently dry space and was thus used for rope making.
247. As Ballard suggests, lead mining was not a successful enterprise here, but the entrance constructed by the miners opened up the impressive Speedwell Cavern to tourists. Benjamin Silliman also visited the mine on his tour of England.
248. Castleton is referred to as "the gem of the peaks" in contemporary tourist guides.
249. Micah Hall, an "attorney-at-law," died in 1804. His epitaph (partially in Latin) is widely noted in travel narratives. In *All the Year Round*, Dickens writes of attending church in Castleton and notes that Hall's epitaph "taught me as much as the sermon." See "A Sunday in Peakland," in *All the Year Round* (London: F. M. Evans & Co., 1895), 275. The Latin inscription reads, "*Quid eram, nescitis; Quid sum, nescitis; Ubi abii, nescitis; Valete.*" William Andrews, *Curious Epitaphs* (London: William Andrews & Co., 1899), 216.
250. The natural springs at Buxton have been visited since Roman times, and the city consequently became something of a resort. The mineral water is still bottled and sold in England under the Buxton name.
251. Bare-fisted boxing, perhaps because of its brutality, was very popular in England. Ballard is almost certainly referring to the second of two matches (in 1810 and 1811) between the British fighter Tom Cribb (1781–1848) and Thomas Molineaux (1784–1818), a freed slave from the United States. Molineaux, whose jaw was broken in the 1811 fight, was the first American to compete for the British championship. Both boxers were immortalized in popular Staffordshire figurines marketed around that time.

252. Robert Lewin (1739–1825) was a controversial Presbyterian minister in Liverpool who supported the American cause in the War of 1812.
253. Abbot Lawrence (1792–1855) became a significant figure in the textile industry in Massachusetts. He later served as a congressman and as ambassador to Britain. Both Dennie and Barnes appear to have been merchants as well.
254. Staffordshire brought together ideal resources, coal and clay, for the production of pottery. The towns of Burslem, Hanley, and Stoke-on-Trent were broadly known as centers for ceramics. The most famous of the potteries in this area was Josiah Wedgwood's factory that opened in 1769, which he named Etruria. The construction of the Trent and Mersey Canal in 1777 facilitated the transport of the fragile earthenware.
255. Mary was imprisoned in a number of houses and castles, including Tutbury Castle in 1569 and 1585, before she was beheaded at Fotheringhay Castle in 1587. Ballard may have known about John Ballard (d. 1586), a priest who conspired with Mary and others to execute Elizabeth I.
256. Eleanor of Castile (1241–1290) died on the way to Lincoln, the site of a cathedral in Lincolnshire. Edward I (1239–1307), who was devoted to her, accompanied her body to its burial in Westminster Abbey and had twelve memorial crosses placed at each of the locations that the cortège rested overnight. The last of these crosses, "Charing Cross," originally stood at the northernmost end of Whitehall.
257. Ballard associates lace making with William Cowper's lament in his poem "Truth" for the lace makers in the village of Olney in Buckinghmshire, where he lived for almost two decades:

> Yon cottager, who weaves at her own door,
> Pillow and bobbins all her little store;
> Content though mean, and cheerful if not gay,
> Shuffling her threads about the livelong day,
> Just earns a scanty pittance, and at night
> Lies down secure, her heart and pocket light;
> She, for her humble sphere by nature fit,
> Has little understanding and no wit.

See Cowper and Benham, *The Poetical Works of William Cowper* (London: MacMillan, 1889), ll. 317–24. 82.

258. The Mansion House, completed in 1752, is the official residence of the Lord Mayor of London.
259. Samuel Birch, who was sheriff of London in 1811 and Lord Mayor in 1815, had a pastry and confectionery shop, established by his father, at

15 Cornhill. He was also known as an orator, a dramatist, and a poet. See *The Antiquary*, vol. 43 (1907), 297.
260. The amateur actor Richard "Romeo" Coates (1772–1848) was a notorious dandy who made a name for himself in the role of Shakespeare's Romeo. His outlandish performances included spreading a handkerchief on the stage so that when the performance called for a death scene, he would have a place to put his hat without soiling it. Byron, having attended the Haymarket Theatre to see Coates portraying Lothario in Nicholas Rowe's (1674–1718) *The Fair Penitent*, wrote that Coates, "performed Lothario in a *damned* and damnable manner." See Thomas Moore's *Letters and Journal's of Lord Byron* (Paris: A. & W. Galignani, 1830), 111). Coates adopted the motto "while I live, I crow" and often hired pages to announce the arrival of his curricle by shouting "Cock-a-doodle-doo," leading to yet another nickname, "Cock-a-doodle Coates."
261. The Boar's Head Tavern, Falstaff's favorite haunt, first appears in *Henry IV Part 1* (2, 4). Falstaff asks for a cup of "sack," which was a sweet wine that was fortified with brandy. In *Henry IV Part 2*, Shakespeare introduced the character Mistress Quickly, who is the proprietor of the Boar's Head.
262. "Seventy-Fours" were two-deck battleships that carried seventy-four guns.
263. The Royal Opera House on Bow Street in Covent Garden reopened after a fire in 1809. The following excerpts from Feltham's *Picture of London for 1809* (199) provide a brief overview of the opera:

> Formerly, the opera performers were not only all Italians, (or nearly so) but consisted of the best that Italy could furnish. Latterly, however, dancing has so greatly prevailed as to have threatened to triumph over the more refined and noble art of music. To allow time for the performance of ballets, operas which originally consisted of three acts, have been reduced to two; and a ballet is now often extended to a greater length than an act of an opera.
>
> The scenery is, in general, rich and brilliant; but the space behind the curtain is by no means equal to that which the Opera machinists enjoyed before the conflagration. The audience part of the house is however, built on a scale of great magnitude. There are five tiers of elegantly-ornamented boxes, a spacious pit, and a most amply gallery. The opera generally opens for the season in December, and continues its representations on the Tuesday and Saturday of every week till June or July. The price of admission to the boxes or pit is half-a-guinea, and to the gallery five shillings. The doors open a quarter before six, and the performance begins at seven. Persons may walk from the pit or boxes behind the scenes during the performance.

NOTES TO PP. 57-109   185

264. These are very expensive prices that were affordable to only the wealthiest patrons.
265. The opera on this evening was the recently premiered "*Barseni, Regina di Lidia*" by the Portuguese composer Marcos Antônio da Fonseca Portugal (1762–1830), sometimes called *Il Portogallo*.
266. Ballard may be referring here to the French dancer (sometimes called "*le dieu de la danse*") Auguste Vestris (1760–1842), who was celebrated for an expressive and athletic style of dance that was considered highly innovative. Vestris's son, Armand (1787–1825), was also a dancer. The celebrated singer, actress, and manager Eliza Lucy Vestris was briefly married to Armand but struck out on her own after he abandoned her. She later married the manager and comic actor Charles James Mathews (1802–1878), son of Charles Matthews (the elder).
267. The highly fashionable Bond Street, in London's exclusive Mayfair District, was home to elegant shops catering, in particular, to the dandies of the time. These dandies, sometimes known as "Bond Street Loungers," perfected a style of walking called "the Bond Street Shuffle" in which they could saunter up and down the street while putting themselves on display as well as ogling women and each other.
268. A quizzing glass was a monocle fitted with a magnifying glass. It was used as a fashionable (and often suggestive) affectation by the dandies of the day.
269. Princess Charlotte (1796–1817) was the only daughter of the Prince Regent (George IV), and Queen Caroline.
270. A pelisse is a long dress or cloak (frequently fur-lined) that opens at the front (often toward the hemline).
271. Romans 14:7 states, "For none of us liveth to himself, and no man dieth to himself."
272. *The Grecian Daughter* (1772) was written by the Irish poet, playwright, politician, and lawyer Arthur Murphy (1727–1805).
273. Charles Mayne Young (1777–1856) was a well-respected tragedian in London. He was often compared to both Kean and Kemble, two of the leading actors of the age.
274. George Colman's *Ali Baba; or, The Forty Thieves, Destroyed by Morgiana, a Slave*, with music by Thomas Kelly (1762–1826), was first performed at the Theatre Royal on Drury Lane in 1806.
275. Benjamin West (1738–1820), born in Springfield, Pennsylvania, was a celebrated artist in both the United States and Britain. West moved to England in 1763 and was greatly admired by George III, who commissioned many paintings from him. Among his best-known paintings is *The Death of General Wolfe* (1770), which can be found in the National Gallery of Canada. One of the founders of the Royal Academy (established in 1768), West died in England and was buried at St. Paul's Cathedral.

276. Princess Charlotte Augusta (1796–1817), as the only daughter of George IV (who, at that time, was the Prince of Wales) and Caroline of Brunswick (1768–1821), was the only legitimate heir to the throne. Caught between her feuding parents, she was eventually kept relatively isolated in Warwick House until she married Prince Leopold of Saxe-Coburg (1790–1865) in 1816. Notwithstanding the general loathing for the Royal Family among the public, Charlotte was both loved and admired, much to the chagrin of her despised father. Thus her death in childbirth, in 1817, after fifty hours of labor and a stillborn son, was a very serious national tragedy.

277. George Tierney (1761–1830) was an active Whig and supporter of Queen Caroline. Ballard's irony here is exactly the response that Tierney wanted to elicit (among the British citizenry) by drawing attention to the Prince Regent's staggering debts for public inspection.

278. As a rising young merchant, Ballard can only be thinking optimistically about his own prospects.

279. The battle of Waterloo, in which Napoleon was defeated, took place on June 18, 1815. Napoleon then returned to Paris and was abdicated on June 22. He was apprehended by the British on July 15, 1815, and exiled to St. Helena, an island off the coast of Africa, where he died in 1821.

280. The Mansion House is the official residence of the Lord Mayor of London and is used for a variety of ceremonial functions. It was designed by George Dance (the elder; 1695–1768) and was completed in 1752.

281. Weepers were lengths of black crape fabric that were tied around a mourner's hat.

282. "Squibs and crackers" are fireworks.

283. [Johanna Southcott died at London, 1814. A religious fanatic, founder of a sect (still in existence in England) at one time numbering 100,000 followers. She wrote prophecies in doggerel verse, and, professing to be the inspired woman of the Apocalypse, announced in 1314 that she was about to give birth to the Shiloh. Ten days after making this announcement she died of the dropsy.] Joanna Southcott was born in 1750 and represented herself as the woman mentioned in Revelations 12:1–6 who is supposed to give birth to a "man child" (the "Shiloh" of Genesis 49:10) who would, according to Revelations, "rule all nations with a rod of iron."

284. The British Institution for the Encouragement of Fine Arts was essentially a gallery established in 1806 by London art connoisseurs to display the artwork of contemporary and past artists.

285. William Bullock (1780–1843) maintained a collection of curiosities in the Egyptian Hall, which was located at 22 Piccadilly.

286. Charles Willson Peale (1741–1827), the American artist and collector of natural history artifacts, established a museum in Philadelphia in 1786. The museum is visible in Peale's famous self-portrait, *The Artist in his Museum* (1822), which can be found at the Pennsylvania Academy of Fine Arts.
287. Snuff was very finely ground tobacco that was inhaled. Snuff boxes, though relatively small, could be very elegant and expensive.
288. The sale of the snuff boxes may have been to help repay debts owed by Sir Gregory Osborne Page Turner (1785–1843), who, according to the *Times of London* (Saturday, November 11, 1815) was attempting to defend himself, in the Court of Chancery, from "the Commission of lunacy that had been issued against him."
289. Admission to Vauxhall was one shilling "but on nights of unusual splendour in the illuminations, &c. it is more." [3*s.* 6*d.*] The splendors, as described in Feltham's *Picture of London for 1809*, were many:

> These gardens are beautiful and extensive, and contain a variety of walks, brilliantly illuminated with variegated coloured lamps, terminated with transparent paintings; and disposed with so much taste, that they produce an enchanting effect upon entering the garden. Facing the west door is a large and superb orchestra, decorated with a profusion of lights of various colours; and on the left, at a small distance, is a spacious and elegant room, in which the band performs when the weather is unfavourable. Although the entertainments are more varied than formerly, the vocal department still forms a prominent attraction: it is always *miscellaneous*, generally supported by respectable performers. The present singers are, Mrs. Bland, Mrs. Franklin, Miss Tyrrell, Miss Daniels; Messrs. Dignum, Gibbon, and Denman.—Leader of the band, Mr. Brookes. At ten o'clock, a bell announces the opening of a beautiful cascade, which, exhibiting some rural and comic scenery, delights and surprises. Fire-works of the most ingenious kind, have lately been introduced to heighten the attractions of this charming place:—nor are those the only allurements for the senses; in a great number of recesses, parties take suppers and other refreshments, provided with the utmost attention, and charged according to a bill of fare, with the prices annexed. From 5,000 to 15,000 well-dressed persons are occasionally present. The gardens open about the middle of May, and close about the end of August. The doors are opened at seven o'clock, and the concert begins at eight. (208–9)

290. "Mr. Bland" may refer to either James Bland (1798–1861) or, less likely given his age, his brother Charles Bland (1802–in or after 1834). Both were children of the mezzo-soprano Maria Theresa Bland

(1769–1838), who was featured at Vauxhall Gardens and who was a regular performer at Drury Lane for decades.

291. See Frances Terpak, "Free Time, Free Spirit: Popular Entertainments in Gainsborough's Era," *Huntington Library Quarterly* 70, no. 2 (June 2007): 209–28.

292. Astronomy, along with the sciences in general, had become very popular in England.

293. *Wild Oats* (1789) was the most popular comedy by the Irish-born John O'Keefe (1747–1833).

294. Though renowned for his stage presence as a comic actor, Robert William Elliston (1774–1831) found much greater success in managing theaters, including Drury Lane (in 1819). Elliston acquired theaters throughout England, helping to advance regional theater. Elliston was a significant figure in the opposition of the Royal Patent, which mandated (until 1843) that only theaters with a Royal Patent (Drury Lane, Covent Garden and summer performances at the Haymarket in London) could present stage dramatic productions, as opposed to pantomime or rhymed musical comedies.

295. William Dowton (1764–1851) was primarily a comic actor and was known particularly for his Falstaff.

296. Joseph Shepherd Munden (1758–1832) was celebrated by Charles Lamb, Leigh Hunt, and the critic Sir Thomas Talfourd for being one of the greatest comic performers of his time, both for his physical humor and his ability to add comic meaning to the most trivial expressions.

297. Thomas Knight (d. 1820) was renowned for his role as Sim, the devoted but simple-minded son of Farmer Gammon in *Wild Oats*. Knight was also well-known for comic roles in Shakespeare's works, such as Sir Andrew Aguecheek (*Twelfth Night*) and Touchstone (*As You Like It*). Knight also wrote plays in which he performed, including *The Turnpike Gate* (1799).

298. When Princess Solms-Braunfels married Prince Ernest Augustus, Duke of Cumberland, on May 29, 1815, in Neustrelitz, Germany, and subsequently on August 29, 1815, at Carlton House, she had already been married twice. She became Queen of Hanover when Ernest Augustus succeeded to the Hanoverian throne on June 20, 1837. Why Ballard uses the name "Salm Salms" is not clear.

299. Dolly's Chop-House on Paternoster Row near St. Paul's Cathedral was established in the 1740s and was frequented by Samuel Johnson, David Garrick, and Oliver Goldsmith. It was demolished in the 1880s.

300. Ballard may have overlooked a day here given that the performance of *Alexina the Exile of Siberia* by Frederic Reynolds (1764–1861) is only advertised as having taken place on Thursday, July 6.

301. Charles James Mathews was appearing in the role of Sir Fretful Plagiary in Richard Brinsley Sheridan's *The Critic, or, Tragedy Rehearsed* (1779).
302. Catherine (Kitty) Stephens (1794–1882), a London-born actress who debuted at Covent Garden in 1813, was noted for her operatic voice, and she frequently performed solo concerts. After retiring in 1835, she married George Capel-Coningsby, fifth earl of Essex (1757–1839).
303. The Glass-Working Exhibition of one Mr. Finn is described in Leigh's *New Picture of London* (1824–25). Located at 161 the Strand, the miniature items that were demonstrated and sold included "pens, ornamental ships, fancy figures of various descriptions, birds crosses quadrupeds, baskets, &c" (385).
304. The "Great Synagogue" (Bet ha'Knesset ha'Gedolah), which had been rebuilt in the 1790s, was on Duke Street near Aldgate. The synagogue was home to an Ashkenazi congregation of German origin. Sephardic Jews (of Spanish and Portuguese origin) established a congregation in the area of Bevis Marks (on Heneage Lane), which remains the oldest synagogue in London. It was one of six synagogues in London.
305. "Shylock" is the central figure in Shakespeare's *The Merchant of Venice*. Ballard's hostility toward Jews and Jewish practices, expressed here and later when he discusses rag fairs, seems somewhat out of place given his democratic sentiments. Still, hostility toward Jews was prevalent on both sides of the Atlantic. Having been expelled from England in 1290 (the area called "old Jewry" dates back to that time), they were allowed to return (for complex reasons) in 1656 under Oliver Cromwell's Protectorate.
William Combe, in *The Microcosm of London*, is more sympathetic to London's Jews. "Notwithstanding the frequent bloody and destructive persecutions which they have successively suffered," Combe writes, "some of which were so unsparing, as to threaten them with annihilation; though they have continually had to encounter the outrage and extreme hatred, as it were, of all human kind, they have still continued to exist; and, more or less, even in their outcast state, to prosper and flourish." Ackermann, *Microcosm of London* vol. 3, 161.
306. "Din most horrible" is a quote from Johann Wolfgang Goethe's *Wilhelm Meister's Travels* (London: George Bell & Sons, 1885), 52.
307. William Dodd (1729–1777) was a clergyman and author. In 1777, he forged the name of Lord Chesterfield, his former pupil, to a bond for £4200, and in spite of the efforts of Dr. Johnson and other influential people to save him, he was executed at London.
308. In addition to serving as a livestock market for over eight hundred years, Smithfield served as the site for Bartholomew Fair, held every August 24. Set up to be on the outskirts of London, it was considered, as Feltham notes, to be too much in the heart of London by the early

nineteenth century. In 1852 the market was relocated northward to a site in Islington now called Caledonian Park.

Smithfield market, situated in the very centre of the metropolis, is a disgrace to the police, and to the corporation of London. Besides the nuisance of herds of cattle being exposed to sale in the heart of the town, scarcely a market-day passes on which more than one unfortunate person is not gored to death by the over-driven and ill-treated animals. What is still more disgraceful, slaughter-houses are permitted in every part of the metropolis; so that it is impossible for any one to avoid the danger to their persons and the offence to their feelings, resulting from a public market for cattle existing in the centre of such a city as London; and from the brutalized practices of the brutes in the shape of men who drive the animals to the slaughter-house. (Feltham, *Picture of London for 1809*, 260)

309. The "Strand Bridge," designed by the engineer John Rennie (1761–1821), was opened as "the Waterloo Bridge" on June 18, 1817, the second anniversary of the Battle of Waterloo. The bridge, which did require a toll, was eventually replaced in 1945.
310. "Viz." is a contraction of the Latin word "*videlicet*" and can be read as "namely" or "that is to say."
311. Proroguing is the ceremonial process of concluding the sessions in both houses of Parliament.
312. Barker's Panorama was a large structure in Leicester Square. A variety of panoramic scenes, particularly battles and cityscapes, were exhibited there. The price of admission was a shilling.
313. [Samuel Whitbread (1758–1815) was an able advocate of parliamentary reform, religions and civil liberty, the abolition of slavery, and similar liberal causes and a strong opponent of Pitt's war policy.] Whitbread, who inherited the brewing company started by his father, was troubled with depression, which was exacerbated by business troubles and critical treatment of him by the press and caricaturists. He cut his throat with a razor.
314. James Lackington's (1746–1815) bookstore at 32 Finsbury Place was one of the largest in London and all of England, hence the store's name (which Lackington exploited), "The Temple of the Muses." Lackington pioneered the idea of "remaindering" books, which was particularly important in an era when print materials were so expensive.
315. Ballard is quoting from James Beattie's (1735–1803) *The Minstrel; or The Progress of Genius* (1771), stanza 50. Beattie was a poet and professor of moral philosophy at the University of Aberdeen.
316. Ballard is drawing on James Thomson's (1700–1748) remarkably popular poem, *The Seasons* (1730). See *The Poetical Works of James Thomson* (New York: Appleton, 1854), 80. It may be worth noting

that Feltham also cites this passage in his equally lavish description of Richmond Hill: "Who has not heard of Richmond Hill?—And who ever saw it, and was not enchanted with the rich landscape which it presents? Windsor, Harrow, Hampton-Court, Twickenham, Petersham, and a whole country filled with villas, turrets, woods, and richly cultivated woods, ravish the eye of the spectator. The prospect, cannot be described in more correct language, than in that of Thomson, who resided many years at the house in Kew Foot Lane now called Rossdale House." Feltham, *Picture of London for 1809*, 289–90.

317. The combination of "pipe and tabor," a simple flute and a small drum, goes back to medieval times. The instruments were often used to accompany Morris Dancing, an English folk tradition that Ballard may be alluding to when he notes that people were "footing" to the music.

318. [Thomson, James, 1700–1748. A poet and writer of plays, one of which, "Sophonisba," written in 1730, contained the famous line (which killed the piece) "O Sophonisba! Sophonisba O!" parodied by every one as "O Jemmy Thomson, Jemmy Thomson O!" Also wrote the famous song "Rule Britannia."]

319. Milton Hill is now part of Quincy and can be located at the intersection of Centre Street and Adams. It was a fashionable area, particularly for summer homes in the late eighteenth century.

320. This is taken from Thomson's *Seasons*, section I, ll. 1407–8: "Here let us sweep/The boundless landscape."

321. Bunhill Fields is located not too far from City Road and was a cemetery for dissenters and nonconformists.

322. This passage is taken from Samuel Owen's *The Thames: Or, Graphic Illustrations of Seats, Villas, Public Buildings and Picturesque Scenery* (London: Vernor, Hood, and Sharpe, 1811).

323. The "patent" of the Haymarket, run by George Colman, allowed it to open from May 15 to September 15, but because Drury Lane and Covent Garden theaters did not close until the end of June, the "operations" of the Haymarket did not begin until then. Feltham writes, "The performances are highly respectable, and various new pieces are generally produced here in the course of each season." Feltham continues, "This theater contains three tiers of boxes, a pit, and two galleries. The price of admission to the boxes is five shillings; to the pit three shillings; to the first gallery two shillings; and to the second gallery one shilling. The doors open at six o'clock and the performance begins at seven. Half-price is not taken at this theater." Feltham, *Picture of London for 1809*, 202.

324. Ballard is referring to the comic actor Charles Mathews (1776–1835). In addition to the *Bee-Hive, A Musical Farce in Two Acts* (1811) by the surgeon John Gideon Millingen (1782–1849), Ballard saw Robert

Jameson's *Love and Gout* (1814) and George Colman's *The Blue Devils* (1798), which were also performed that evening.
325. Col. Tuttle possibly refers to John Leighton Tuttle, born in Littleton Massachusetts, who died in the battle at Sacket's Harbor in 1813.
326. Highgate is a well-to-do suburb north of London and adjacent to Hampstead Heath.
327. The "causeway" Ballard describes has a long history, which Dickens describes in "Chronicles of English Counties" published in *All the Year Round* (April 3, 1886, 159): "In the days when the highway over Highgate Hill was a mere track through the forest, an anchorite, it is said, established his hermitage close by, and for long afterwards the cell was never without an occupant. One of these hermits, of a more industrious temper than the generality of the brotherhood, is said to have devoted all the time he could spare from his devotions, to building a causeway to Islington, filling up the muddy pools with stones, and bridging over the Slough of Despond with faggots and trunks of trees."
328. The Barouche, a four-wheel carriage with two inside seats facing each other, was considered a very elegant form of transportation; a folding roof could be brought forward either for inclement weather or privacy, or it could be retracted. Chariots were generally pulled by four horses and could accommodate four passengers sitting on two seats facing forward while the driver sat on a separate box.
329. John Quincy Adams (1767–1848) took up the office of Envoy Extraordinary and Minister Plenipotentiary at the Court of Great Britain on May 26, 1815. His lodgings were at 67 Harley Street, not too far from Cavendish Square.
330. Washington Allston (1779–1843) was an American poet and painter, born in South Carolina and educated at Harvard. Charles Robert Leslie (1794–1859), though born in London to American parents, was raised in Philadelphia prior to returning to England in 1811. Leslie's most notable paintings were of scenes taken from literature. Samuel F. B. Morse (1791–1872) was born in Charlestown, Massachusetts, in a strongly Calvinist and Federalist family. He attended Yale College where he attended lectures on electricity given by Benjamin Silliman, but his work in painting had also gained the notice of Washington Allston. Morse visited England in 1811 with his mentor, Allston, and returned to the United States on August 21, 1815. Morse distinguished himself as a portrait painter but also gained fame for his work on the telegraph and the development of Morse code.
331. The term "cheapening" means that the woman was trying to bargain down the price of the shoes.
332. Ballard is quoting from Shakespeare's *Hamlet* (1.3), drawing on Ophelia's response to cautionary advice from her brother Laertes:

> Do not, as some ungracious pastors do,
> Show me the steep and thorny way to heaven;
> Whiles, like a puff'd and reckless libertine,
> Himself the primrose path of dalliance treads,
> And recks not his own rede.

333. East India House, the headquarters of the East India Company, was in Leadenhall Street. A large and impressive structure, it was demolished in 1929.
334. Tipu Sahib (1749–1799) was the sultan of Mysore, the southern part of what is now India. Throughout his life, he was engaged in a series of wars with the British until he was finally killed defending Srirangapatna, his capital.
335. Hafiz was a Persian poet from the fourteenth century who wrote mystical verses in the Sufi tradition. Among the many legends associated with him is his apologetic encounter with the invader and conqueror Tamerlane (1336–1405), who was offended by a poetic reference to his native Samarkand.
336. This automaton, now in the Victoria and Albert Museum, represents the death of the soldier Hugh Munro, who was fatally attacked by a tiger. Sultan Tippoo had the device made to commemorate the attack, which he considered a positive omen, given that the victim was the son of Sir Hector Munro (1726–1805), one of the British generals in the Anglo-Mysore wars. "Tippo's Tiger," as the object came to be called, was brought back to England in 1799 and put on display at East India House. It was also widely reproduced as a figurine by the Staffordshire potteries.
337. Thomas Bolton & Sons Limited was a well respected and significant manufacturer in copper and brass.
338. Hyde Park, one of the largest and most significant parks in central London (near Mayfair), was part of the grounds of Kensington Palace (on the western edge of the park), which includes Kensington Gardens.
339. John Quincy Adams (1767–1848) was appointed by James Madison to serve as minister to Great Britain in 1815. He held the position until the end of Madison's presidency in 1817 and did much to restore strong Anglo-American ties.
340. According to the *Journal of Travels in England, Holland, and Scotland* (New Haven: Converse, 1820) by Benjamin Silliman, the American scientist who visited England in 1805, the alien office was "of recent establishment and was instituted in consequence of the abuse of the almost unrestrained liberty which foreigners had, till then enjoyed in England. It is said that some French emissaries were detected in surveying the principal ports, and in other machinations against the safety

of the country. In consequence of this, foreigners of every description are now registered at the alien office in Crown-street, Westminster, and the government possesses a history of them from the moment of their arrival till their departure out of the kingdom" (196).

341. Henry Addington, Lord Sidmouth (1757–1844) had been a member of the House of Commons and, briefly, prime minister. In 1812, he was appointed home secretary and thus would have been the authorizing individual for Ballard's departure back to United States. Sidmouth developed a reputation, while home secretary, for being authoritarian and insensitive because of his role in suspending habeas corpus (1817) in Peterloo (1819) and in the implementation of the restrictive Six Acts, also in 1819.

342. By "douce," which is from the French for gentle, soft, or sweet, Ballard's friend is simply suggesting a bribe, hence the four shillings that Ballard slips to the clerk.

343. The HMS *Bellorophon* saw duty in the Battles of the Nile and Trafalgar (among others) and was captained by Frederick Maitland (1777–1839) when Napoleon surrendered to him. Napoleon, who never stepped on English soil, spent three weeks on the *Bellerophon*, which was made off-limits to visitors. He was then transferred to the HMS *Northumberland*, which, in August 1815, escorted him to St. Helena.

344. Camberwell was a pleasant, almost rural, suburb about three miles south of the center of London.

345. Less than ten miles to the West of London, Kew Palace was then a relatively new structure (in the Gothic style). Queen Charlotte resided in a structure on Kew Green, called "The Dutch House" (now refereed to as Kew Palace), and died there in 1818. The castle was razed in 1828, and the current site, Kew Gardens, houses the Royal Botanic Gardens.

346. Ballard is probably referring to the village of Hammersmith (now a large suburb of London), which is about five miles west of London's city center. Slough is about seven miles farther west and near Windsor Castle.

347. Established in 1456, Magdalen College (pronounced "maud-lin"), situated on High Street, was one of the first colleges at Oxford to teach science.

348. Trinity College, Oxford was founded in 1555 by Sir Thomas Pope. The chapel, consecrated in 1694, was apparently designed by Henry Aldrich (1648–1710), dean of Christ Church College, Oxford.

349. New College, Oxford was founded in 1379 by William of Wykeham, and, in spite of its name, it is one of the oldest colleges at Oxford.

350. William of Wykeham (1320–1404) was a cleric, a statesman, and an architect. He served as bishop of Winchester, held office as chancellor of England, and contributed to the design of Windsor Castle.

351. This ceiling, a depiction of the Ascension, was painted by the same Sir James Thornhill (1675/6–1734), responsible for the ceiling at the Greenwich Hospital.
352. In June 1814, in order to celebrate the defeat of Napoleon (and his exile to Elba), the Duke of Clarence hosted the emperor of Russia and the king of Prussia as well as generals and diplomats allied in the victory. In addition to festivities in London, the "Allied Sovereigns" visited Oxford for a reception.
353. The gift of Sir Thomas Bodley (1545–1613), the Bodleian Library is the main research library of Oxford. Bodley not only donated his extensive collection, but also provided funds to restore the old library. He arranged with the "Stationer's Company" that the library would receive a copy of every work registered with them in London and encouraged donations to the library from friends.
354. Hertford College, on Cattle Street just opposite the Bodleian, was originally found in 1282 as Hart Hall and had been attended by John Donne, Jonathan Swift, and Thomas Hobbes. The college suffered serious financial reverses in the late eighteenth and early nineteenth centuries when, in 1822, only seven years after Ballard's visit, it was taken over by a separate college. It did not reemerge as Hertford College until 1874, when it was supported by Sir Thomas Baring.
355. Fox (1749–1806) was a prominent Whig reformer. As a supporter of the American and the French Revolutions, as well as other "radical" causes, he was a constant irritant to George III and William Pitt. The town of Foxborough, Massachusetts, is named in his honor.
356. Designed by James Gibbs (1682–1754) and a gift of the royal physician John Radcliffe (1652–1714), the Radcliffe Camera ("camera" simply means chamber or room) served as Oxford's Science Library.
357. Blenheim, which is located in the town Woodstock, Oxfordshire, was originally a gift to John Churchill (1650–1722), the first Duke of Marlborough, for his role in the defeat of the French in several battles, including the Battle of Blindheim (Blenheim). The manor at Woodstock was expanded to a palace with funds from Queen Anne and the Duke of Marlborough himself. The magnificent structure was designed by Nicholas Hawksmoor (1661–1736) and Sir John Vanbrugh (1624–1726) with the intention of being a monument to the defeat of the armies of Louis XIV (1638–1715; called "The Sun King") in the "Wars of Spanish Succession" (1701–1714). The extensive grounds of Blenheim were designed by England's most prominent landscape architect, Lancelot "Capability" Brown (1716–1783). Sir Winston Churchill (1874–1965) was born at Blenheim and is buried in a churchyard adjacent to the grounds.
358. The coachman, in declaring himself a freeholder, is indicating with justifiable pride that he actually owns property and thus has the right to vote.

359. The linstock is a device used to hold a match at a distance in order to kindle a fire or set off a charge.
360. Sir Edward Thomason (1769–1849) produced a wide variety of objects in metal, such as buttons, medallions (for which he was very well known), corkscrews, and similar inventions.
361. English fascination with the ruins of the village of Herculaneum and the city of Pompeii, destroyed by the eruption of Vesuvius on August 24, 79 AD, was intensified by the work of Sir William Hamilton (1730–1803), who was Britain's ambassador to Naples from 1764 through 1800. A collector of antiquities, he sold much of what he owned to the British Museum in the 1770s. His books did much to stimulate interest as well. They include *Observations on Mount Vesuvius, Mount Etna, and other Volcanoes of the two Sicilies*, which was published in London in 1772 and the well-illustrated *Campi Phlegraei, Observations on the Volcanoes of the two Sicilies, as they have been communicated to the Royal Society of London, by Sir William Hamilton*, published in Naples in 1776. Hamilton's wife, Lady Emma Hamilton, had an extended affair with Lord Nelson, thus intensifying public interest in their lives.
362. The restriction of the American visitor to factories may be an instance of concern on the part of British manufacturers about Americans "stealing" techniques for their own use.
363. Bathing machines, which could be found at seaside resorts, were essentially cabanas on wheels drawn by a horse or donkey. They were backed into the water at a depth that would allow bathers, particularly women, to leave the cabana through a back door and discreetly enter the water for a swim away from the gaze of onlookers and often in an area designated for one gender only. Invented in the mid-eighteenth century, they remained popular until the late nineteenth century.
364. A gig is a small carriage drawn by one horse.
365. Francis Egerton, third Duke of Bridgewater (1736–1803), commissioned the engineer James Brindley (1716–1762) to design a canal (opened in 1761) to connect the town of Worsley (the site of his coal mines) to Manchester and beyond. The canal extended along the River Mersey to Runcorn where it connected with Trent and Mersey Canal (opened in 1777 and also developed by Brindley). The creation of these canals signaled the beginning of an era of extensive canal development in England.
366. Although once the site of a priory and subsequently an abbey, by 1815, the older structures had been incorporated into a Georgian mansion. The Priory was owned by a succession of Sir Richard Brookes from about the seventeenth century.
367. The passage is from British poet Lucy Aikin's (1781–1864) *Ode to Ludlow Castle*:

> From yon high tower the archer drew
> With steady hand the twanging yew,
> While, fierce in martial state,
> The mailed host in long array,
> With crested helms and banners gay,
> Burst from the thund'ring gate. (ll. 13–18)

368. Runcorn, though still a health resort on the River Mersey in Ballard's time, very shortly became a cargo port and a site for the manufacture of soap and chemicals.
369. Improvements in the development of steam engines, particularly by James Watt and Matthew Boulton, accelerated the development of steamboats, which were eliciting attention as a legitimate form of travel in the late eighteenth century. The commercial success of steamboats owes much to the work of American inventors, including the gunsmith William Henry (1729–1786), John Fitch (1743–1798), and, of course, Robert Fulton (1765–1815).
370. A "wake" could refer to a parish festival held annually to commemorate the dedication of a church.
371. Bear baiting was permitted in England until 1835 when parliament passed the "Cruelty to Animals Act."
372. Ballard may be recalling a story that was frequently told about an encounter between Voltaire and Benjamin Franklin who simply shook hands when they met. Onlookers were very disappointed and encouraged the two men to embrace by exclaiming, "*Il faut s'embrasser, à la Françoise.*" Charles Moulton describes the occasion in his *Library of Literary Criticism* (Buffalo, NY: Moulton, 1902), 81. It is also worth mentioning the current fashion in dining for serving food "*à la française*," that is, placing all the main dishes at the center of the table and allowing diners to serve themselves.
373. George Morland (1763–1804) was an English painter whose work depicted animals and rustic scenes.
374. The church Ballard visits here is St. Oswald's Church, which possibly dates back well before the oldest parts of the structure from the thirteenth century. Legend has it that the "Winwick Pig" was a frequent visitor to the original construction site of the church and, every night, moved stones from the original site to where the church is now located.
375. Warrington was, indeed, well known for its files, which were supposedly well tempered to withstand rough usage.
376. Properly called "Eaton Hall," this was the traditional home of the Grosvenor family since the fifteenth century. Under the second Earl Grosvenor (1767–1845), the structure was rebuilt in the Gothic style by the architect William Porden (1755–1822).

377. The elder Sir Stephen Richard Glynne (1780–1815; also spelled *Glynn*) was father of Sir Stephen Richard Glynne (1807–1874) and Catherine Glynn who, in 1839, married William Ewart Gladstone (1809–1898). Gladstone, a liberal, was one of England's most influential leaders and served as prime minister over the following periods: 1868 through 1874, 1880 through 1885, 1886, and 1892 through 1894.

378. According to Welsh legend, Winifred (*Gwenfrewi* or *Winefride*), the daughter of Prince Tewyth, took a vow of chastity and refused the advances of the chieftain Caradoc of Hawarden. Caradoc cut off her head, but she was restored to life after her uncle, St. Beuno (d. 660), placed it back on her body. The well supposedly emerged on the site where she was revived, and it has become a shrine for pilgrims who are attracted to its healing powers. The structure around the present pool dates back to the fifteenth century and may have been built at the request of Margaret Beaufort (1443–1509), the mother of Henry VII.

379. The mountainside from which Ballard views the shore is probably Halkyn Mountain, the site of Roman lead mines. The geology of Wales, or Cumbria, led to the definition of the geological period that we call "the Cambrian Period," which began 542 million years ago.

380. This "River Dee," as distinguished from other rivers by the same name, is about seventy miles long and forms the border between Wales and England. The river originates in Snowdonia (the region around Mt. Snowdon) and flows into the Irish Sea.

381. An "understrapper" is a subordinate or an underling.

382. Washington Irving's (1783–1859) collection of observational essays, *Salmagundi Papers*, derived its name from a seventeenth century salad that included meat, seafood, vegetable, fruit, nuts, flowers, and a spiced dressing. The essay that Ballard is referring to is "Memorandums for a Tour to be entitled, 'The Stranger in New Jersey; or, Cockney Travelling.' By Jeremy Cockloft, the Younger." In the town of Brunswick, New Jersey (probably New Brunswick, the site of Rutgers University), a "slew-eyed" (cross-eyed) taverner by the name of Vernon is mentioned, and the narrator notes, "people of Brunswick, of course, all squint." See Washington Irving, *The Complete Works: Salmagundi*, ed. Bruce I. Granger and Martha Hartzog (Boston: Twayne, 1977), 104.

383. Here, Ballard, whose native Massachusetts was a stronghold of Federalism, is asserting a poignant, if not controversial, opinion critical of Federalism in general. That view, even after the War of 1812, would surely have irritated many potential readers had this memoir been published in his lifetime.

384. The "loyalist" notion of England as "the mother country" was purely a phenomenon in the northeastern part of the United States, particularly Massachusetts and farther north. Loyalists, who opposed independence altogether, generally made their way to upper and lower Canada (now Ontario and Québec).
385. A Jacobin was a supporter of revolution and republican-style democracy.
386. The *Milo*, another sailing packet, left Boston on March 12, 1815, the same day as the *Liverpool Packet*, but arrived on April 3, 1815 (at least a day before the *Liverpool Packet*), making it the first American ship to arrive in the United Kingdom after the peace. The two ships seem to have departed Liverpool simultaneously as well.
387. The Tuskar Lighthouse, just off the southwest coast of Ireland, had just been completed in June 1815.
388. The "caboose" refers to a structure on deck where the cooking is done, essentially, what we now call the "galley."
389. The ship, at this point (assuming Ballard's rough numbers are correct), is still about 2,600 miles from Boston and about seven hundred miles west of the Azores.
390. The Atlantic flying fish (*Cypselurus heterurus*), which is also called the "four wing flying fish," sails (rather than flies) through the air after breaking the surface at speeds of up to thirty miles per hour. It can be found in the more tropical waters of the north and south Atlantic.
391. Cape Ann is the rocky peninsula at the northern edge of Massachusetts Bay.

Appendix A–G

1. Readers of Tom Stoppard's play *Arcadia* (London: Faber and Faber, 1992) will recall that when Lady Croom complains to her architect, Noakes, that the "new" hermitage on her ground will be unoccupied, he offers to "advertise" for one. Her response is abrupt, immediate, and logical: "But surely a hermit who takes a newspaper is not a hermit in whom one can have complete confidence" (86).
2. W. S. Scott, *Green Retreats: The Story of Vauxhall Gardens, 1661-1859* (London: Odhams Press, 1955), 54.
3. William Makepeace Thackeray, *Vanity Fair* (Boston: Houghton Mifflin, 1963).
4. The popular song "Boney on the Isle of St. Helena" captures the feeling of triumph experienced by the British. It was most recently recorded by the group "Uncle Earl" on Rounder Records (ASIN: B000MTPAE0).
5. John Ashton, *Modern Street Ballads* (New York: Benjamin Blom, 1968), 343–345.

6. "Volks" is Cockney dialect for folks.
7. Count Matvei Platov (1751–1818), who headed Russian Cossack cavalry, was responsible for the enormous difficulties faced by Napoleon's troops on their retreat from Moscow.
8. The Serpentine is the river in Hyde Park.
9. "Cock boats" were small rowboats belonging to larger ships.
10. The Golden Cross was the most important coaching inn on London's West Side.

Bibliography

Ackermann, Rudolph, W. H. Pyne, William Combe, Augustus Pugin, and Tjomas Rowlandon. *The Microcosm of London*. London: R. Ackermann, 1808–1811.
Aikin, John. *A Description of the Country from Thirty to Forty Miles Round Manchester*. 1795. Reprint, New York: Augustus M. Kelley, 1968.
———. *Annals of the Reign of George III*. Vol. 2. Stroud: Nonsuch, 2006.
Albert, William. *The Turnpike Road System in England 1663–1840*. Cambridge: Cambridge University Press, 1972.
Allen, Thomas, and J. Rogers. *The Panorama of London, and Visitor's Pocket Companion, in a Tour through the Metropolis*. London: Whittaker, Treacher, 1830.
Altick, Richard. *The Shows of London*. Cambridge, MA: Harvard University Press, 1978.
Andrews, William. *Curious Epitaphs*. London: William Andrews, 1899.
Anon. *A Modern Sabbath; or, a Sunday ramble and Sabbath-day journey . . . in and about the cities of London and Westminster, and borough of Southwark, etc. 1775–76?*. Reprint, London: B. Crosby, 1794.
Appleby, Joyce Oldham. *Inheriting the Revolution: The First Generation of Americans*. Cambridge, MA: Belknap, 2000.
Ashton, John. *Modern Street Ballads*. New York: Benjamin Blom, 1968.
———. *Social England Under the Regency*. 1890. Reprint, New York: Gale Group, 1968.
Austen, Jane, and Deirdre Le Faye. *Jane Austen's Letters*. Oxford: Oxford University Press, 1995.
Bagster, Samuel. *Samuel Bagster of London, 1772–1851: An Autobiography*. London: Bagster, 1972.
Banner Jr., James M. *To the Hartford Convention: The Federalists and the Origins of Party Politics in Massachusetts, 1789–1815*. New York: Knopf, 1969.
Barbauld, Anna Letitia, Elizabeth Kraft, and William McCarthy. *Selected Poetry and Prose*. Peterborough, ON: Broadview, 2002.
Bartlett, D. W. *What I Saw in London Or, Men and Things in the Great Metropolis*. Auburn, NY: Derby and Miller, 1852.

Bigelow, Andrew. *Leaves from a Journal; or Sketches of Rambles in North Britain and Ireland*. Boston: Wells & Lilly, 1821.
Blair, Robert. *The Grave*. London: Cadell and Davies, 1808.
Bonar, James. "The Disposition of Troops in London, March 1815." *English Historical Review* 16, no. 62 (April 1901): 348–54.
Borneman, Walter R. *1812: The War that Forged a Nation*. New York: Harper Perennial, 2004.
Bridgeman, Harriet, and Elizabeth Drury. *The British Eccentric*. New York: C. N. Potter, 1976.
Brooks, Ann, and Bryan Haworth. *Boomtown Manchester, 1800–1850: The Portico Connection*. Manchester: Portico Library, 1993.
Brown, Richard D. *Knowledge Is Power: The Diffusion of Information in Early America, 1700–1865*. New York: Oxford University Press, 1989.
———. *The Strength of a People: The Idea of an Informed Citizenry in America, 1650–1870*. Chapel Hill: University of North Carolina Press, 1996.
Burke, Edmund. *The Annual Register,: Or, A View of the History, Politics, and Literature for the Year 1815*. London: J. Dodsley, 1759.
Byron, George Gordon, and Thomas Moore. *Letters and Journal's of Lord Byron*. Paris: A. & W. Galignani, 1830.
Chandler, James. *England in 1819. The Politics of Literary Culture and the Case of Romantic Historicism*. Chicago: University of Chicago Press, 1998.
Coleridge, Samuel Taylor, and Coventry Patmore. *The Table Talk and Omnia of Samuel Taylor Coleridge*. Oxford: Oxford University Press, 1917.
Colton, Calvin. *Four Years in Great Britain: 1831–1835*. New York: Harper & Bros., 1835.
Commager, Henry Steele. *Britain Through American Eyes*. New York: McGraw Hill, 1974.
Cooper, James Fenimore. *Gleanings in Europe: England*. Edited by James P. Elliott, R. D. Madison, Donald A. Ringe, and Kenneth W. Staggs. 1828. Reprint, Albany: State University of New York Press, 1982.
Cowper, William. *The Task*. 1785. Reprint, Philadelphia: Bennet and Walton, 1811.
———. and Thomas Benham. *The Poetical Works of William Cowper*. London: MacMillan, 1889.
Croker, John Wilson, and Bernard Poole. *The Croker Papers, 1808–1857*. New York: Barnes & Noble, 1967.
Davis, Jim. "'They Shew Me Off in Every Form and Way': The Iconography of English Comic Acting in the Late Eighteenth and Early Nineteenth Centuries." *Theatre Research International* 26, no. 3: 243–56.
David, Saul. *Prince of Pleasure: The Prince of Wales and the Making of the Regency*. New York: Atlantic Monthly, 1998.
Denlinger, Elizabeth Campbell. *Before Victoria: Extraordinary Women of the British Romantic Era*. New York: New York Public Library, 2005.

Defoe, Daniel. *A Tour Through the Whole Island of Great Britain.* 1724–1726. Reprint, Harmondsworth: Penguin, 1975.
d'Haussez, Baron. *Great Britain in 1833.* Philadelphia: E. C. Mielke, 1833.
Dickens, Charles. *All the Year Round.* London: F. M. Evans, 1895.
———. *David Copperfield.* New York: W. W. Norton, 1989.
———. *Memoirs of Joseph Grimaldi.* 1838. Reprint, New York: Stein and Day, 1968.
———. *Oliver Twist.* 1846. Reprint, Orchard Park: Broadview, 2005.
———. and Mark Wormald. *The Pickwick Papers: The Posthumous Papers of the Pickwick Club.* 1836–1837. Reprint, New York: Penguin, 2000.
Dillenberger, John. *Benjamin West. The Context of His Life's Work.* San Antonio: Trinity University Press, 1977.
Doyle, Richard. *Richard Doyle's Journal, 1840.* Edinburgh: J. Bartholomew in association with British Museum Publications, 1980.
Eaton, Clement. "Winifred and Joseph Gales, Liberals in the Old South." *Journal of Southern History* 10, no. 4 (1944): 461–74.
Egan, Pierce. *Life in London: or, the Day and Night Scenes of Jerry Hawthorn, Esq. and Corinthian Tom.* 1821. Reprint, London: Cassell, 1900.
Erickson, Carolly. *Our Tempestuous Day: A History of Regency England.* New York: Morrow, 1986.
Evans, Eric J. *The Forging of the Modern State: Early Industrial Britain, 1783–1870.* Foundations of Modern Britain. London: Longman, 1983.
Feltham, John. *The Picture of London for 1809, Being a Correct Guide to All the Curiosities, Amusements, Exhibitions, Public Establishments, and Remarkable Objects, in and Near London.* London: W. Lewis, 1809.
———. *A Tour of the Isle of Mann in 1797–1798.* Bath: C. Dilly, 1798.
Fox, Celina. *London—World City, 1800–1840.* New Haven: Yale University Press in association with the Museum of London, 1992.
Fraser, Flora. *The Unruly Queen: The Life of Queen Caroline.* New York: Knopf, 1996.
Galperin, William H. *The Historical Austen.* Philadelphia: University of Pennsylvania Press, 2003.
Goethe, Johann Wolfgang. *Wilhelm Meister's Travels.* London: George Bell & Sons, 1885.
Gronow, R. H., and C. J. Summerville. *Regency Recollections Captain Gronow's Guide to Life in London and Paris.* 1862. Reprint, Welwyn Garden City, UK: Ravenhall, 2006.
Halévy, Elie. *A History of the English People in 1815.* London: Ark Paperbacks, 1987.
Hare, Augustus John Cuthbert. *Walks in London.* London: Routledge, 1878.
Harvey, A. D. *Sex in Georgian England: Attitudes and Prejudices from the 1720s to the 1820s.* New York: St. Martin's, 1994.

Harvey, Anthony, and Richard Mortimer. *The Funeral Effigies of Westminster Abbey.* Woodbridge: Boydell, 1994.
Hazlitt, William, A. R. Waller, and Arnold Glover. *The Collected Works of William Hazlitt.* Vol. 8. London: J. M. Dent, 1903
Hilton, Boyd. *A Mad, Bad, and Dangerous People?: England, 1783–1846.* The New Oxford History of England. Oxford: Oxford University Press, 2006.
Hoare, Richard Colt, and M. W. Thompson. *The Journeys of Sir Richard Colt Hoare Through Wales and England, 1793–1810.* Gloucester [Gloucestershire]: A. Sutton, 1983.
Hobsbawm, E. J. *The Age of Revolution, 1789–1848.* Cleveland: World, 1962.
Hunt, Leigh. *The Autobiography.* London: Constable, 1903.
Ippel, Henry. "British Sermons and the American Revolution." *Journal of Religious History* 12, no. 2 (1982): 191–205.
Irving, H. B. *A Book of Remarkable Criminals.* London: Cassell, 1918.
Irving, Washington. *The Complete Works: Salmagundi.* Edited by Bruce I. Granger and Martha Hartzog. Boston: Twayne, 1977.
———. *The Sketch-book of Geoffrey Crayon, Gent.* New York: Maynard, Merrill, 1906,
Jackman, William T. *Development of Transportation in Modern England.* Cambridge: Cambridge University Press, 1916.
Johnson, Paul. *The Birth of the Modern: World Society, 1815–1830.* New York: HarperCollins, 1992.
Jones, Colin, and Dror Wahrman, eds. *The Age of Cultural Revolutions: Britain and France, 1750–1820.* Berkeley: University of California Press, 2002.
Kaye, Thomas. *The Stranger in Liverpool, Or, An Historical and Descriptive View of the Town of Liverpool.* Liverpool: Thomas Kaye, 1812.
Kelly, Ian. *Beau Brummell: The Ultimate Man of Style.* New York: Free Press, 2006.
Knight, Charles. *Pictorial Half-Hours of London Topography.* London: Charles Knight, 1851.
Lamb, Charles. *Essays of Elia/by Charles Lamb; Edited & Selected by Athelstan Ridgway.* London: J. M. Dent, 1921.
Leigh, Samuel. *Leigh's New Picture of London: or . . . a Brief and Luminous Guide to the Stranger, On All Subjects Connected with General Information, Business, or Amusement.* London: Leigh, 1819.
Lockwood, Allison. *Passionate Pilgrims: The American Traveler in Great Britain, 1800–1914.* New York: Cornwall, 1981.
Low, Donald A. *The Regency Underworld.* Thrupp: Sutton, 1999.
McCullough, David. *John Adams.* New York: Free Press, 2002.
Mingay, G. E. *The Gentry: The Rise and Fall of a Ruling Class.* Themes in British Social History. London: Longman, 1976.

Mitton, G. E. *Jane Austen and Her Times*. London: Methuen, 1905.
Moss, William, and David Brazendale. *Georgian Liverpool: A Guide to the City in 1797*. Lancaster: Palatine, 2007.
Moulton, Charles. *Library of Literary Criticism*. Buffalo, NY: Moulton, 1902.
Murray, Venetia. *High Society: A Social History of the Regency Period, 1788–1830*. London: Viking, 1998.
Nardinelli, Clark. *Child Labor and the Industrial Revolution*. Bloomington: Indiana University Press, 1990.
Nash, John. *Views of the Royal Pavilion*. 1826. Reprint, London: Pavilion, 1991.
Nichols, R. H., and F. A. Wray. *The History of the Foundling Hospital*. London: Oxford University Press, 1935.
Nicholson, George. *The Cambrian Traveller's Guide: And Pocket Companion*. Stourport: George Nicholson, 1808,
Nodal, J. H., and George Milner. *A Glossary of the Lancashire Dialect*. Manchester: Alexander Ireland, 1875.
Owen, Robert. *A New View of Society*. London: Privately Printed, 1813.
Owen, Samuel. *The Thames: Or, Graphic Illustrations of Seats, Villas, Public Buildings and Picturesque Scenery*. London: Vernor, Hood, and Sharpe, 1811.
Parissien, Steven. *Regency Style*. London: Phaidon, 1992.
———. *George IV: Inspiration of the Regency*. New York: St. Martin's, 2002.
Phillips, George L. *England's Climbing-boys; A History of the Long Struggle to Abolish Child Labor in Chimney-Sweeping*. Boston: Baker Library, Harvard Graduate School of Business Administration, 1949.
Phillips, Richard. *A Morning's Walk from London to Kew*. London: 1817.
Plowright, John. *Regency England: The Age of Lord Liverpool*. Lancaster pamphlets. London: Routledge, 1996.
Poovey, Mary. *A History of the Modern Fact: Problems of Knowledge in the Sciences of Wealth and Society*. Chicago: University of Chicago Press, 1998.
Pope, Alexander, and Adolphus William Ward. *The Poetical Works of Alexander Pope*. London: MacMillan, 1893
Porter, Roy. *London, a Social History*. Cambridge, MA: Harvard University Press, 1995.
Priestley, J. B. *The Prince of Pleasure and His Regency, 1811–20*. New York: Harper & Row, 1969.
Pückler-Muskau, Hermann. *A Regency Visitor; The English Tour of Prince Pückler-Muskau Described in His Letters, 1826–1828*. New York: Dutton, 1958.
Rauch, Alan. *Useful Knowledge: The Victorians, Morality, and the March of Intellect*. Durham: Duke University Press, 2001.

Raumer, Friedrich von. *England in 1835; A Series of Letters Written to Friends in Germany During a Residence in London and Excursions into the Provinces.* 1836. Reprint, Shannon: Irish University Press, 1971.

Robins, Jane. *The Trial of Queen Caroline: The Scandalous Affair That Nearly Ended a Monarchy.* New York: Free Press, 2006.

Rush, Richard. *A Residence at the Court of London.* 1833. Reprint, London: Century, 1987.

Scott, W. S. *Green Retreats: The Story of Vauxhall Gardens.* London: Odhams, 1955.

Scharf, George, and Peter Jackson. *George Scharf's London Sketches and Watercolours of a Changing City, 1820–50.* London: J. Murray, 1987.

Schkolne, Myrna. *People, Passions, Pastimes, and Pleasure: Staffordshire Figures, 1810–1835.* Winston Salem: Hot Lane, 2006.

Sen, Satadru. "The Savage Family Colonialism and Female Infanticide in Nineteenth-Century India." *J. Women's History* 14, no. 3 (2002): 53–79.

Shepherd, Thomas. *Metropolitan Improvements or London in the Nineteenth Century.* 1827–31. Reprint, New York: Benjamin Blom, 1968.

Shiel, Richard. *Sketches of the Irish Bar.* New York: Redfield, 1854.

Silliman, Benjamin. *Journal of Travels in England, Holland, and Scotland.* New Haven: Converse, 1820.

Simond, Louis, and Christopher Hibbert. *An American in Regency England: The Journal of a Tour in 1810–1811.* 1815. Reprint, London: Robert Maxwell, 1968.

Skinner, John. *Journal of a Somerset Rector, 1803–1834.* Edited by Howard and Peter Coombs. Bath: Kingsmead, 1971.

Smith, E. A. *George IV.* New Haven, CT: Yale University Press, 1999.

Smith, John Thomas. *Lives of Famous London Beggars, with Forty Portraits of the Most Remarkable.* 1818. Reprint, Diprose and Bateman, 1900.

———. *The Streets of London: Anecdotes of Their More Celebrated Residents.* London: Bentley, 1861.

Southey, Robert. *Letters from England.* 1807. Reprint, London: Cresset, 1951.

Speck, W. A. *Robert Southey: Man of Letters.* New Haven, CT: Yale University Press, 2006.

Sperling, Diana, and G. E. Mingay. *Mrs. Hurst Dancing, and Other Scenes from Regency Life, 1812–1823.* London: Gollancz, 1981.

St. Clair, William. *The Reading Nation in the Romantic Period.* Cambridge: Cambridge University Press, 2007.

Terpak, Frances "Free Time, Free Spirit: Popular Entertainments in Gainsborough's Era." *Huntington Library Quarterly* 70, no. 2 (June 2007): 209–28

Thackeray, William Makepeace. *Vanity Fair.* Boston: Houghton Mifflin, 1963.

Thomis, Malcolm. *The Luddites: Machine-Breaking in Regency England*. New York: Schocken, 1972.

Thompson, F. M. L. *Gentrification and the Enterprise Culture: Britain, 1780–1980*. The Ford Lectures, 1994. Oxford: Oxford University Press, 2001.

Thomson, James. *The Poetical Works of James Thomson*. New York: Appleton, 1854.

Thornbury, Walter. *Old and New London: A Narrative of its History, its People, and its Places*. London: Cassell and Company, 1897.

Tomalin, Claire. *Jane Austen: A Life*. New York: Knopf, 1997.

———. *Mrs. Jordan's Profession: The Actress and the Prince*. New York: Knopf, 1995.

Tyler, Royall, and Cynthia A. Kierner. *The Contrast Manners, Morals, and Authority in the Early American Republic*. New York: New York University Press, 2007.

Uglow, Jenny. *The Lunar Men*. New York: Farrar, Straus, and Giroux, 2002.

Vale, Edmund, and Thomas Hasker. *The Mail-Coach Men of the Late Eighteenth Century*. Newton Abbot: David & Charles, 1967.

Van der Kiste, John. *George III's Children*. Far Thrupp: A. Sutton, 1992.

Walker, George. *The Costume of Yorkshire*. Leeds: Robinson & Son, 1814.

Wardroper, John. *Wicked Ernest: The Truth About the Man Who Was Almost Britain's King*. London: Shelfmark, 2002.

Weeton, Ellen, and Edward Hall. *Journal of a Governess*. London: Oxford University Press, 1936.

White, R. J. *Life in Regency England*. New York: Putnam, 1963.

Williams, Raymond. *The Country and the City*. New York: Oxford University Press, 1973.

Wilson, Ben. *The Laughter of Triumph William Hone and the Fight for the Free Press*. London: Faber and Faber, 2005.

———. *The Making of Victorian Values: Decency and Dissent in Britain, 1789–1837*. New York: Penguin, 2007.

Wilson, Harriette. *Harriette Wilson's Memoirs*. Edited by Leslie Blanch. 1825. Reprint, London: Century, 1985.

Wood, Gordon S. *The Americanization of Benjamin Franklin*. New York: Penguin, 2004.

Wordsworth, William, and John O. Hayden. *The Poems*. Vol. 1. New York: Penguin, 1977.

———. *The Prelude: 1799, 1805, 1850*. New York: W. W. Norton, 1979.

Young, Arthur. *A Six Weeks Tour, through the Southern Counties of England and Wales*. London: W. Nicoll, 1768.

INDEX

Ackermann, Rudolf, 180–81n235
Act of Toleration (1689), 9
Act of Union (1801), 8, 18, 142n, 169n146
Adams, John, 25, 141, 143n28, 147n4, 170n156
Adams, John Quincy, 92, 94, 111(A), 192n329, 193n339
Adolphus, Duke of Cambridge, 19
advertising: street, 39, 98, 135E
Aikin, Lucy (writer), 100, 196n367
Alexander I, Czar, 54, 111
alien office, 94, 193–94n340; bribery, 94, 194n342
Allston, Washington (artist), 14, 47, 57, 92, 174n185, 192n330
America: American identity, viii; American Revolution, 9–10, 18; Anglo-American (wartime relationship), 29, 149n20; Do all Americans speak English?, 66, 180n227; English attitudes, 35; gardening contrasted, 68–69; ignorance of the British about, 66, 67; ignorance reduced in Liverpool, 75; "John Bull swallows," 55; lifestyles contrasted, 105–6; Navy (American) manned by Englishmen, 61; New England audiences (indecency), 41; print of the "Capture of Washington" with "President's Palace," 76; Republican pride/lack of taxes, 44; Republican response to class elitism, 61–62; treatment of Revolutionary War veterans, 51
architectural style, 102–3
art. *See* Allston, Washington; Bird, Edward; British Institution for the Fine Arts; Leslie, Charles Robert; Linwood, Mary; Morse, Samuel F. B.; Somerset House; Thornhill, James; West, Benjamin; Wilkie, Sir David
Astley's amphitheatre, 44, 162–63n101
astronomy, 84, 188n292
Athenaeum, Liverpool: books, 29, 74
Austen, Jane: on Elizabeth O'Neill, 171n168; *Northanger Abbey*, 5, 17, 133E, 143n18, 152n38

ballad singers/vendors, 68
Ballard, Joseph: biographical detail, 25–26; estimate of, 2–3, 23–24; style, 2, 3
Balm of Gilead, 65
Bank of England, 37, 158n72
banns, 62, 177n208
Barbauld, Anna Lætitia, 16, 151n34
Baring, Alexander, 53, 169n152
Barret, George Rogers, 115
Bartholomew Fair, 189–90n308
Bartley, George (actor), 51, 165n123
Bath, city of, 5
bathing machines, 99–100, 196n363

Bayard, James (American politician), 111
Beadles, 37, 38 Fig. 2, 158n73
bear-baiting, 101, 197n371
Beattie, James (poet), 89, 190n315
Beckford, William (Lord Mayor), 37, 159n78
beggars: ballad singers/chapmen, 68; blind, 30 Fig. 1; techniques of, 92; tumbling boys, 31; Rochdale, begging a penny in, 64
Belzoni, Giovanni (explorer), 173n182
Bernard, John (American actor), 37, 78, 158n71
Bethlehem Hopital (Bedlam), 58, 176n194
Birch, Samuel (Lord Mayor), 183–84n259
Bird, Edward (artist), 174n187
Birmingham, 12; "preferable to Manchester," 99
Black, Joseph (chemist), 154n51
Blair, Robert (poet), 164n116
Blake, William (poet), 164n116, 167n136
Blenheim, 97, 195n357
Blenkinsop, John (engineer), 155n58
blind, the, 29–31, 149n27; asylum, 150n28–29
Bodleian Library (Oxford), 97, 195n353
Bolton & Sons (metalworkers), 94, 193n337
books and book-sellers, 85; Lackington's, 88, 190n314
boots (servant), 152n43
Boston, 68, 89; Common or Mall, 85; Milton Hill, 90, 190–91n319; return voyage to, 109
Boulton, Matthew (engineer), 22, 197n369
boxing, 74, 182n251, 182n250

Bradford, village of, 63
Bragg, Billy (musician), 151n35
Braille, 149n27
bribery and tipping, 94–95, 102, 104, 106
Bridgewater, Duke of (Francis Egerton), 196n365
Brighton Pavilion, 20
brig of war, 148n12, 149n19
Brindley, James (engineer), 196n365
"Britannia rules the waves," 55
British culture: from American perspective, 45, 79
British Institution for the Fine Arts, 80, 186n284
British Museum (Montagu House), 56, 172–73n178
Brock, General Isaac, 57, 174n188
Brontë, Charlotte, 152n38, 154n52
Brown, Lancelot "Capability" (landscape architect), 195n357
Brummell, Beau (dandy), 5, 143n17
Budworth, village of, 69
Bullock's Museum, 80–81, 186n285
Bunyan, John (author), 90
Burdett, Sir Francis (radical politician), 43, 161n94, 170n157
Burke, Edmund (author, politician), 15
Burney, Fanny (author), 17
Burns, Robert (poet), 154n51
Burslem, village of, 75
butcher shops, 86, 182n250
Buxton, village of, 74, 182n250, 184n260
Byron, George Gordon, Lord, 14, 154n51, 165n122

cabs and hackneys, 50, 133–34E, 147n2
Camberwell Grove, 85, 87, 93, 95, 194n344
Canada, 57, 174n188, 180n231, 199n384

Index

canals, 100, 181n238, 196n365
Canning, George (politician), 21, 169n146
cant, 6
"Capture of Washington," 76
caricature and satire, 13, 128D, 130D. *See also* Cruikshank, George; Gillray, James; Hone, William; Rowlandson, Thomas
Carlton House, 78, 79
Carlyle, Thomas (author), 17
Caroline of Brunswick, Princess, 18–19, 127–28, 146n59
carriages, 92
Castine, Maine (battle of), 67, 180n232
Castlereagh, Viscount (Robert Stewart), 21, 85, 169n146, 182n248–49
Castleton, village of, 72, 73, 182n248
Catholic Emancipation, 169n146
Chandler, James, 3
Chapel Royal, St. James, 77, 185n269
Charing Cross, 183n256
Charles I, King, 45
Charlotte, Princess, 77, 186n276
Charlotte of Mecklenburg, Queen: levee, 54, 170n160
Chelsea Hospital, 51, 165–66n125, 181n239
Chester: city of, 70, 102, 181n239
child labor: in Birmingham, 121C, 151n36; in Leeds, 60; picking up dung, 35; sent north from London, 32; woolen mills, 6:00 a.m to 7:00 p.m.: they pass "a quick but miserable existence" or become "vicious members of society," 36
chimney sweeps, 52, 166–67n134–36
Christie's auction house, 161n88
Churchill, Sir Winston, 195n357

Clarence, Duke of (William IV), 19, 195n352
Clarke, Mary Anne (mistress), 20, 58, 175–76n193
Clay, Henry (American politician), 111
clergy: Anglican, misbehavior of, 33, 152n38; a "living," 152n38–40; St. Paul's service: "chanting prayers in a lazy and ridiculous manner," 46. *See also* dissenters
cloth hall (Leeds), 62, 177n204
clowns and harlequins, 44, 163n103
clubs in London, 5
coach travel, 35, 36, 49; barouche, 92, 192n328; changing horses, 59, 75; chronometers (locked) to time "stages," 65; fares, 133–34 E, 150n32; gig, 100, 196n364; Golden Crown Inn, 200n10; Manchester to Liverpool (fare = 6 shillings), 66; riding outside, 95, 150n31; size, weight capacity, 31, 150n31–32; speed of, 60, 76; woman sleeping in, 60
coal, 22, 37, 75, 184n260; Leeds, 36, 60, 155n58, 155n60
Coates, Romeo (actor), 76, 184n260
Cochrane, Lord Thomas (swindler), 58, 85, 175n192
Cochrane, Sir Alexander (Admiral), 180n230
cock boat, 138, 200n9
coffee houses, 78, 157n65
Coleridge, Samuel Taylor (poet), 14, 163–64n111, 185n274
Colman, George (the younger), 153n48, 165n124, 190–91n324
commerce: cloth hall (Leeds), 177n201; decline of England (projected), 106; commerce:

cloth hall (Leeds), (*continued*) entrepreneurial sense in the English, 81, 84; exchange rate (£1 = $2.00), 44; general, 8, 12–13; jeweller's shops on the Strand, 81; Liverpool shipping, 66; manufacturers averse to American visitors, 99, 106; merchants claim link to royalty, 47; shop windows, endless variety, 44; stock fraud, 175n191; street merchants, 44; tipping: porters/chambermaids/innkeepers, 65, 102
Congress of Vienna, 21, 46
Cooke, George Frederick (actor), 160n83
Cooper, James Fennimore (author), 7
Cora (English brig): newspapers and food exchanged, 108
Coram, Thomas, 171–72n174
corn laws, 21, 64–65, 146n63, 179n219
Covent Garden (theatre), 11, 39, 42 Fig. 6, 86, 159–60n81; guarded by soldiers for order, 39
Cowper, William (poet): *The Task*, 179–80n225; "Truth," 183n257
Cribb, Tom (boxer), 182n251
Crocker, Joseph Ballard, 2, 3
Cromwell, Oliver, 59, 100, 189n305
Crown Jewels, 43, 161n93
Cruikshank, George (cartoonist), 13, 82 Fig. 10, 128D, 130D
Cumberland, Duke: stipend for marriage, 85. *See also* Ernest Augustus, Duke of Cumberland
Cumberland, Richard, 165n122

currency, 12; abbreviations of, 162n96; explanation of British, 139G
custom house (Liverpool): inspector bribed, 106; and inspectors, 104, 106

dairy production, 69
Dalton, Joseph (chemist), 22
Dance, George (architect), 22, 186n280
dandies, 5, 129 Fig. A3; "Bond Street Loungers," 77, 185n267–68; "imitators of the Prince," 79
Darley, Ellen Westray (American actress), 37, 78, 158n69
Darwin, Charles (scientist), 21
Darwin, Erasmus (poet/physician), 4
Davy, Humphry (chemist), 4, 22
De Berenger, Charles Random, 58, 175n191
debt: national, 146n64
Dee, River, 102, 104, 198n380
Defoe, Daniel (author), 8, 143n34
Delicate Investigation, The, 146n59
Derby, Earl of (Edward Smith Stanley), 33, 151n33
Derbyshire, 71
Detroit, Battle of: banner from, 45
Dexter, Samuel (American politician), 53, 170n156
d'Haussez, Baron Vharles Lemercier de Longpré, 9, 145n43
Dickens, Charles: *All the Year Round*, 182n249, 192n327; *David Copperfield*, 173n181; *Dombey and Son*, 177n208; *Life of Grimaldi*, 11, 145n47; *Oliver Twist*, 164n116, 166n132, 167n136; *Pickwick Papers*, 8, 23, 175n190; *Sketches by Boz*, 134E

INDEX   213

dissenters, 68, 180–81n235; dissenting clergy, affinity with American clergy, 66; dissenting clergy "an honor to their profession," 33, 180–81n235; Presbyterian, 74
Dodd, William (cleric/forger), 87, 189n207
Dolly's Chop-House, 85, 188n299
Dorchester, village of, 96
Dowton, William (actor), 84, 188n295
drunkenness among laborers, 32, 67, 102
Drury Lane Theatre, 11, 37, 41, 157n66, 157–58n67; Kean as Penruddock in "The Wheel of Fortune," 51; Kean in Richard III, 46; "Wild Oats," 84; "The Woodman's Hut" After-Piece, 37
Duke of Gloucester: William Henry, 166n131
Duke of Kent: Edward Augustus, 54, 170–71n166

Eastcheap, 76
East India Company, 143n45; "richest collection of eastern curiosities in the world," 93–94, 193n333; Tipu's Tiger (automaton), 93, 193n334, 193n336
Eaton House, 102, 197n376
Edgeworth, Maria, 16
Edgeworth, Richard Lovell, 16
education: children deprived of, 36, 60; children undeserving of, 61; factory fund for instruction, 67; mothers reading to children, 81
Edward I: crosses for Eleanor of Castile, 75, 183n256
Egan, Pierce (writer), 9, 143n29
Egypt (style and influence), 6

election: handbills, 98
Elizabeth I, Queen (effigy), 43
Elliston, Robery William (theatre manager), 84, 188n294
Endymion, H.M.S.: battle with "The President," 55, 171n170
Engels, Friedrich, 121C
engineering and technology, 12, 121C; file manufacture (Warrington "of exquisite fineness"), 102, 197n375; packing press (32 tons of power), 60; pin manufactory, 99; roads, English superior, 101; scissors from Sheffield, 36; steamboats, English ("far behind" American steamboats), 101, 197n369; steam-powered coal wagons (100 tons), 60, 155n58
England: Ballard's views about, 105
England in 1815 (Ballard): Provenance, 5
Ernest Augustus, Duke of Cumberland, 20, 85, 188n298

farming: dairy, 69
Farren, Elizabeth, 32, 151n33
federalism, 10, 105, 198n383
Feltham, John, 8
Fielding, Henry, 35, 154n54, 174n184
Fiennes, Celia, 8
figurines, 145n52; Cribb and Molineaux, boxers, 182n251
fire (in London), 86
fishmongers, 86
Fitch, John (engineer), 197n369
Fitzherbert, Maria (mistress of George IV), 18, 143n16
flying fish, 108, 199n390
food and dining, 145n52; breakfast, British vs American, 105; breakfast hour, 80; dining food

food and dining (*continued*)
(Chelsea pensioner's Sunday
meal), 51; dinner and supper,
105; fish (turbot), 64,
178n215; fishmongers and
butchers, 86; oatmeal bread,
180–81n236; pork, 36
Foundling Hospital, 55, 59, 77,
171n174
Fourth of July, 85–86
Fox, Charles James (politician), 97,
195n355
Franklin, Benjamin, 63, 178n214
Frederick, Duke of York and Albany,
19–20, 175–76n193
freeholder, 195n358
French Revolution, 1, 6, 18
frigates, 148n14
Fulton, Robert, 197n369
funeral service: of American, British
customs of, 78–79; child of
Mr. C, 90; procession led by
mutes, 47, 164n116; weepers,
186n281

Gales, Joseph, Jr., 156n62
Gallatin, Albert (American
diplomat), 111
Galperin, William, 17
Gambier, Admiral James (English
treaty negotiator), 111
gaming (gambling), 5
gardening, 69
gaslight, 41, 161n88
gentry, 146n57
geology, 146n65, 66
George III, King: death of, 1;
Golden Jubilee, 51, 166n129;
madness (porphyria), 2, 5;
residence at Windsor, 95
Georgian era, viii
gibbet, 70, 181n240
Gillray, James (cartoonist), 13

Gladstone, William Ewart
(politician), 198n377
glass works, 33, 86, 189n303
Glynne, Sir Stephen Richard,
198n377
Godwin, William (author), 15
Goethe, Johann von Wolfgang
(author), 4, 189n306
Gog and Magog, 37, 159n79
gold, 29, 149n24
Golden Jubilee, 166n126
Goulburn, Henry (English
politician), 111
Greenwich Hospital, 164–65n119;
veterans (disabled) at
Greenwich Hospital, 47, 49, 50
Fig. 8
Grimaldi, Joseph (actor/clown), 57,
163n103, 173n182
Guildhall, 37, 39 Fig. 3, 158–
59n74, 159n79; Gog and
Magog, 37, 159n79
gunpowder: used in mines, 70, 72
Guy's Hospital, 43, 162n96

Halévy, Elie: England in 1815, 3
Halifax, village of, 63
Halton Castle, 100
Hamilton, Sir William and Lady
Emma, 196n361
Hammersmith, village of, 194n346
Hanley, village of, 75
Hanover, House of, 4
Hartford Convention, 10, 28,
149n17
Hawarden, village of, 103
Haymarket Theatre, 11, 91,
190–91n323
Hazlitt, William (author/critic),
157–58n67, 160n87, 177n202
hermits and hermitages, 199n1
Highgate, village of, 91, 192n326
Hilton, Boyd, 3
Hindus, 176–77n198

INDEX 215

Hoare, Richard Colt (author), 8
Holywell, village of, 103, 104
Hone, William (satirist), 13, 130–31D
Hood, Thomas (author), 79, 84
horse racing, 79
hotels and lodging: cost, 65, 99
Houghton Mifflin, 3, 142n
Hounslow Heath, 96
House of Commons: inelegant, oratory/mediocrity, 53
Hunt, Leigh (critic and editor), 160n87
Hunter, Robert (anatomist), 21
Hutton, James (geologist), 154n51
Hyde Park, 51, 94, 166n127, 193n338; Serpentine River, 200n8

iceberg, 27
Independence Day: celebrated in London, 86
India, 59, 93–94
Indian jugglers, 60, 177n202
Indian Trader (ship): newspapers and potatoes exchanged, 107
Industrial Revolution, 4, 12, 142n14, 64
Irving, Washington, 105, 141n6, 198n382
Islington, 37

Jackson, Andrew, 180n230
Jacobin, 199n385
Jefferson, Thomas, 10
Jeffrey, Francis (editor), 157n63
Jenkinson, Robert Banks (Lord Liverpool), 20–21
Jenner, Edward, 21
Jewish merchants: buying gold, 13, 29; "rag fair": cast-off clothes, 92–93; synagogue services, 86–87

Jews, 86, 189n305; mock dialect, 92–93
Joao (John) of Portugal, Regent, 151n37
"John Bull," 55, 153n50
Jonson, Ben, 182n246; play by Colman, 165n124
Jordan, Dorothy (actress), 19

Kean, Edmund (actor), 11, 46, 51, 160n83, 163–64n111
Kemble, John Philip (actor), 54, 171n167
Kensington Gardens, 94
Kent, Duke of, 19, 54
Kentish Town, 45
Kewley, Rev. John, 63, 178n213
Kew Palace and Green (gardens), 89, 95, 194n345
King's Bench Prison, 57, 174n189
Kingsley, Charles (cleric/author), 167n136
King's Mews, 45
Kirkstall Abbey (Leeds), 61, 63, 177n203
Knight, Thomas (actor), 84, 188n297

labor, 102, 121–25C, 183n257
lace-making, 75–76
Lackington's Bookstore, 88, 190n314
Lamb, Charles (author): *Essays of Elia*, 167n136
Landor, Walter Savage (author), 142n12
La Pique (frigate), 28, 148n16
law: branding prisoners, 182n243; bribery customs, 106; Chester Prison, 71; embezzlement, 168n139, 189n306; forgery, 87, 189n307; gibbeted bodies outside Chester, 70, 181n240;

law: branding prisoners (*continued*)
King's Bench Prison, 57, 174n189
Lawrence, Abbot (American politician and merchant), 75, 183n253
Lawrence, William (physician), 21
lawyers, 44, 52–53, 163n102
Leeds, 60, 177n201; Leeds Library, 35, 154n52; woolens/clothhall, 8, 35, 62, 177n204
Leicester, town of: known for stockings, 75
Lesage, Alain-René (author), 174n184
Leslie, Charles Robert (artist), 14, 92, 192n330
Lewin, Robert (Presbyterian minister), 183n252
Linwood, Mary (needlework artist), 14, 56, 173n179–81
Liston, John (actor), 41, 160n87
Liverpool, 1, 2, 29, 64, 104; Americans in, 75; Botanic Garden, 66, 180n228; Herculaneum pottery, 67, 180n229; St. James' Walk, 66
Liverpool Athenæum, 74, 149n26
Liverpool Packet, 1, 27, 104, 106, 141n
Liverpool Theatre. *See* Theatre Royal: Liverpool
London, 37, 167–68n138, 145n52; buskers (handbills), 47; cabs, 49; Finsbury Square (tuppence to view through a telescope), 83–84; Hyde Park and St. James Parks, 51; Hyde Park woods, 94; Kensington Gardens, 94; New England Coffee House ("the general resort of Yankees"), 37, 157n65; traffic, right-hand side, 47; traffic statistics on London Bridges, 87
London Bridge, 47, 57

Lord Mayor: procession and coach, 47
Louth, Robert (scholar/poet), 55, 171n173
Luddites, 12, 121C
Lunar Society, 143n15

Madison, James, 10, 45, 106, 193n339
Magdalen College, Oxford, 194n347
Magdalen Hospital for penitent prostitutes, 51–52, 166n130
Maine, territory of, 180n232
Manchester, 64, 74, "dull, smoky, rainy hole," 74; infirmary, 64; Portico Library, 34, 153n45
Mansion House, 39, 76, 183n258, 186n280
Marlborough, Duke of (George Spencer), 46, 97–98. *See also* Blenheim
Mary, Queen of Scots, 75, 97, 183n255
Massachussetts State Legislature, 54
Mathews, Charles (actor), 75, 185n266, 91, 189n301, 191–92n324
May Day, 52, 166–67n134
McAdam, John Loudon (engineer), 23
medicine: Guy's Hospital, 43, 162n96; immense number of patients, 43; quack cures, 47, 65
Mersey River, 100
Milo (packet), 107, 199n386
mining: Lord Grosvenor's lead mines, 104; salt mines, 70, 181n237; Speedwell mine (lead), 72
monarchy, 4–5, 45, 127–32, 182n251
Montagu, Lady Mary Wortley (author), 52, 167n135

Montgomery, James (poet), 36, 157n63
monument, 47, 48 Fig. 7, 164n117–18
Moore, Margaret (thief), 43, 161n93
Morland, George (artist), 101, 197n373
Morse, Samuel F. B. (artist), 14, 26, 57, 92, 174n186, 192n330
mother country, viii, 10, 199n384
Munden, Joseph Shepherd (actor), 84, 158n70, 188n294
Murphy, Arthur (playwright), 185n272
Murray, Matthew (engineer), 155n58
muslin, 6, 143n20
Musquito, H. M. S. 28, 148n11

Napoleon: apartments fitted up in the tower, 95; "Bony on the Isle of St. Helena" (song), 199n4; confined to Bellerophon, 95, 194n343; defeated at Waterloo/Celebration, 79–80; escape from Elba, 1, 149n18; poem celebrating victory over, 137–38F; Scotsman's support of, 35; wanted poster (hoax), 42
Nash, John, 6, 20, 146n62
natural history, 21–22, 81, 186n285, 187n286
Needle's Eye, 36, 155n59
negroes, 86. *See also* slave trade
Nelson, Lord Horatio, 31, 150n30, 49, 159n77, 165n120, 196n361
Newark, village of, 59
New College, Oxford, 96, 194n349
New Orleans, Battle of, 28, 67, 180n230
New York: Hellgate, 89
Nile, Battle of (Aboukir Bay), 49, 165n120

Northampton, 75
Northwick (Northwich): salt mines, 69, 181n237
Norton Priory, 100

oat-cakes (Havers), 36, 155n56
O'Keefe, John (playwright), 188n293
Old Bailey, 42, 161n89
O'Neill, Eliza (actress), 39, 54, 78, 160n82, 171n168, 184–85n265–66
Opera (Royal Opera House), 76, 184n263
Order of the Garter, 53, 168n144
Orders in Council (1807), 20
Otis, Samuel (American politician), 53, 170n155
Owen, Robert (industrialist), 12, 121–25C, 151n36
Oxford, 95, 96–97, 194–95n347–56

packing press, 60
Paine, Thomas, 15
Pakenham, General Edward, 180n230
Paley, William, 21
panoramas, 13, 88, 190n312
parishes, 54, 170n158–59
Parliament, 87
passport, 92, 182n245–48
Paternoster Row, 85
Peak District, 71; "Devil's Arse" cavern, 72–73, 182n246
Peale, Charles Willson (American artist): museum, 81, 187n286
Peel, Sir Robert (politician), 169–70n154
pensioners, military, 49, 50 Fig. 8, 51
Perceval, Spencer (politician): assasination of, 20
Peterloo, 15, 170n157, 194n341
pickpockets, 52

pin manufactory, 99
Pitt, William (the elder), Earl of Chatham (politician), 159n75
Pitt, William (the younger) (politician), 143n16, 159n75–76
Platow, Count Matvei (Russian General), 200n7
Plattsburgh, Battle of, 67, 180n231
Plomer, Sir Thomas (judge), 52–53, 168n139
pollution/smoke: buildings in London injured by, 37; London, 39; Manchester, "smoke hangs perpetually over the city," 34, 64, 74
Pompeii and Herculaneum, 99, 196n361
Ponsonby, John William (politician), 53, 169n149
Poor Laws, 64, 155–56n61, 170n159, 178n218
Pope, Alexander (poet), 47, 164n118
porters, 179n222
poverty: children earn 67¢ per week, 32; cleaning dung, 1 shilling per day, 35; drinking wages, 102; hovel owned by a servant of the Duke of Bedford, 68; Rochdale, 64; Sheffield laborers poorer than "inhabitants of American back settlements," 36
Presbyterians, 74
President, USS, 55, 171n170
Prévost, General George (governor of Canada), 67, 180n231
pricing: cost of food, 44; excessive taxes, 44; stagecoach (1 added shilling per stage), 65
Priestley, Joseph (chemist/author/radical), 4, 21, 151n34
Prince Regent, 127–31; appearance of, 87–88, 127 Fig. A2, 129 Fig. A3; carriage of, 88; debts, 79; marriage to Caroline, 170n165; Prorogues Houses of Parliament ("his countentenace exhibits the marks of intemperate habits"), 87; succession to throne, 4; symbol of (ostrich feathers), 170n163; trouble with the public, 54
Princess Charlotte Augusta, 77, 186n276
Prisons: Chester, 71; Fleet, 174n189; King's Bench, 57, 174n189; Tower of London, 43, 95
prostitution ("women of the town"): at Covent Garden, 41
Pückler, Muskau, Prince Hermann, 145n44
punishment: hand burning, 71, 182n243; hanging/gibbet, 70, 181n240; imprisonment for debt, 174n189

Queenstown (Heights), Battle of, 45
Quincy (Mass.), 190–91n319

racket (Tennis), 57, 175n190
Radcliffe Camera, 97, 195n356
rag fair, 92–93
Ranelagh Gardens, 116
reading and literacy, 81, 145n53
Regency, the: overview, 4–5, 127–31; Regency style, 5–6, 143n21
religious services: Camberwell Grove (Dr. Dodd's nephew preaching), 87; Camberwell Grove (preacher on "path of dalliance"), 93; Episcopalian form, 80; Johanna Southcott (prophetess), 80, 186n283; Leeds service ("preacher was tolerable"), 62; Magdalen

Hospital, 51–52, 166n130; preacher "insensible to the importance of his subject," 55; Presbyterian Church, Dr. Lewin, 74, 183n252; small congregation (due to dissenters), 68; St. Catherine's, aid for infants sacrificed in India, 59, 176n196; St. James (Leeds), 74; St. Paul's "ridiculous," 46; synagogue ("disgusted with the little reverence" of "these Shylocks"), 86, 189n304; Whitehall Chapel, 45, 163n105
Rennie, John (engineer), 190n309
rent and taxes, 69
Repton, Humphry (landscape architect), 6
Reynolds, Sir Joshua (artist), 96
Ricardo, David (economist), 12–13
Richard III, 43, 162n95
Richardson, Samuel (author), 154n54–55
Richmond Hill, 89, 91, 190–91n316
roads, 23; driving/walking side, 47
roasting jacks, 44, 162n99
Rochdale, village of, 64, 178n217
Rowlandson, Thomas (cartoonist), 8, 13, 145n51
Royal Exchange, 37, 40 Fig. 4, 76, 159n80; diversity of people, 76
Royal Institution, 14
Royal Marriages Act, 18, 166n131
Runcorn, village of, 100, 197n368
Rush, Richard (politician), 7, 143n29

Sadler's Wells, 57, 173n182
salt mines, 69–70
Scott, Sir Walter, 14–15, 154n51, 157n63
Scottish Enlightenment, 154n51
seasickness, 27, 107

sedan chairs, 54, 170n164
self-interest: governs countries and individuals, 106
servants, appearance of, 28; excessive attention, 61
seventy-fours (gunships), 76, 170n162, 184n262
Shakespeare, 11; birthplace (a hovel), 98; *Hamlet*, 192–93n332; *Henry IV, Pt. I*, 76, 184n261; *Henry IV, Pt. II*, 76; *Macbeth*, 32; *Merchant of Venice*, 189n305; *Richard III*, 46; Stratford, 98–99; *Romeo and Juliet*, 39
Sheffield, 36, 155n60
Shelley, Mary (author), 15
Shelley, Percy Bysshe (poet), 16–17, 146n55
Sheridan, Richard Brinsley (playwright), 171n169
shipping, 66
shipwreck and flotsam, 108
Siddons, Sarah, 11, 54, 171n167–68
Sidmouth, Lord (Henry Addington) (politician), 94, 194n341
Silliman, Benjamin (American scientist), 6, 29, 68, 117–20, 143n22, 149n23, 180n227, 192n330, 193–94n340
Simond, Louis (American/French author), 6
Six Acts (1819), 194n341
slave trade, 111, 114
Slough, village of, 95
Smirke, Robert (architect), 6, 159–60n81, 172–73n178
Smith, Adam (economist), 154n51
Smith, Standfast (merchant), 147n5
Smith, William (geologist), 22
Smithfield Market, 87, 189–90n308
Smollett, Tobias (novelist), 174n184
snuff boxes, 81, 187n287–88
Soane, John (architect), 6

Somerset House, 57, 58 Fig. 9, 173n183, 186n283
Southcott, Joanna (religious visionary), 80, 186n283
Southey, Robert (poet), 183n254
Spode, Josiah (potter), 14
Staffordshire, 7, 14, 75, 147–48n9, 157n63
St. Alban's, 37, 157n64
Stamford, village of, 59
St. Andrew's Church, 55, 89, 171n171
St. Catherine's Church, 59, 176n196
steam baths, 92
steamboat: British vs. American, 101, 197n369
steam engine, 60, 155n58
Stephens, Catherine (actress), 86, 189n302
Stephenson, George, 22
Sterne, Laurence (author), 62, 178n209
St. James Church, 63, 178n211
St. James Park, 51, 166n126
St. Mary's Church (Stamford), 59, 177n199
St. Monday (holiday), 32, 151n35
Stockport, town of, 71
Stone of Scone, 53
Stoppard, Tom (playwright): *Arcadia*, 199n1
St. Paul's Cathedral, 41 Fig. 5, 46, 164n113–14
Strand Bridge, 87, 190n309
Stratford-upon-Avon, 98
St. Thomas's Hospital, 44, 162n98
St. Winifred's Well, 103; legend of, 104, 198n378
Surrey Theatre, 58, 176n195
synagogue, 86, 189n304

Talavera, 62, 177n206
taxes and duties, 45; salt, 70; window, 34, 152n44. *See also* corn laws

tea, 105
telescope vendor, 83–84 Fig. 11, 188n292
Telford, Thomas (engineer), 23
Thackeray, William Makepeace (author), 17, 116, 128–30. 142n12, 199n3
Thames, The, 41 Fig. 5, 89
theatre and entertainments: Astley's amphitheatre, 44, 162–63n101; bathing machines, Liverpool, 99–100, 196n363; books, 85, 88, 190n314; bear baiting, 101, 197n371; boxing: "scientific fighters," 74, 182n250, 182n251; itish Institution (art gallery), 80, 186n284; British Museum, Bullock's, 56, 80, 172–73n178, 186n285; Covent Garden, 11, 39, 42 Fig. 6, 159–60n81, 86; Drury Lane, 11, 37, 41, 46, 51, 84, 157n66, 157–58n67; Haymarket Theatre, 11, 91, 190–91n323; Indian jugglers/sword swallowers (Leeds), 60, 177n202; Miss Linwood's Needlework Gallery, 14, 56, 173n179–81; opera, 76, 184n263; panoramas, Robert Barker's, 13, 88, 190n312; Sadler's Well (Islington), 57, 173n182; Somerset House (art gallery), 57, 58 Fig. 9, 173n183, 186n283; street performers: ballad singers/telescope vendor, 68, 83–84, 188n292; Surrey Theatre, 58, 176n195; Tower of London, displays, 42–43; Vauxhall, 12, 82–83, 115–20, 115 Fig. A1, 116 B, 117–20 B. *See also* Theatre Royal
Theatre Royal: Liverpool, 65, 179n224; Manchester, 47, 153n47

Index

Thompson, Benjamin (playwright), 171n169
Thompson, F. M. L., 17
Thomson, James (poet), 89, 90, 91, 190n316, 191n318, 191n320
Thornhill, James (artist), 49, 97, 165n121, 186n277, 195n351
Tierney, George (politician), 79, 169n153
Tintern Abbey, 8, 178n210
tipping and gratuities, 65, 102
tobacco, 49, 50 Fig. 8
Tower Hill, 43
Tower of London: Crown Jewels: attempted theft of, 42, 43, 161n91–93; tedious tour guides, 43
Treaty of Ghent, 1, 10, 28, 111–14, 147n6, 171n170
Trinity College, Oxford, 95, 194n348
Trinity Sunday, 63, 178n212
Turbot, 64, 178n215
Tuscar Light, 107, 199n387
Tutbury, 75

Union Jack (flag), 18

Vansittart, Nicholas (politician), 53, 169n150
Vauxhall, 12, 82–83, 115 Fig. A1, 115–20; four thousand people in an evening, 83; hermit, 116B; Silliman's description of, 117–20B
Vauxhall Bridge, 87
Vestris, Eliza (singer, dancer), 77, 185n266
Victoria, Priness (later Queen), 19, 170–71n166

Wakefield, Priscilla (writer), 16
Wales: Halkyn Mountain, 198n379; St. Winifred's Well, 37, 198n378
Walsh, Benjamin (swindler), 168n139
War of 1812, viii, 10; English generally opposed to it, 18, 106; stain on national character, 76
Warrington, town of, 31, 32, 67, 69, 102, 151n34, 197n375
Warwick Castle, 97
Warwick House, 79, 186n276
Washington, capture of, 76
Waterloo victory, 2, 79; celebrations, 79–80; collection for veterans, 89
Watt, James (engineer), 22, 154n51, 197n369
Webster, J. W. (American professor/murderer), 27, 37, 43, 147n7
Wedgwood, Josiah (potter), 14
Wellington, Duke of, 79, 177n206, 185n275
West, Benjamin (artist), 12, 49, 56, 78, 92
Westminster Abbey, 52, 90–91, 167n137; funeral effigies, 168n142; Poet's Corner, 53, 168n140; Stone of Scone, 168n143
Westminster Bridge, 44, 52, 167n138
Westminster Hall, 52
Whalley-Bride, 71
Whitbread, Samuel, 88, 169n147, 190n313
Whitehall Chapel, 45, 163n105
wigs, 44, 163n102
Wilkie, Sir David (artist), 57, 174n187
Wilks, John (radical), 174–75n189
window tax, 34, 152n44
Windsor Castle, 95–96
Winwick, village of: fair, 101; Winwick Pig, 101, 197n374
Wollstonecraft, Mary, 15
women: fashions, 81; labor/exploitation, 67; mothers

women: fashions, (*continued*)
    instructing children at Bullock's
    Museum, 81; servers, 85
Woodstock, village of, 97–98
Wordsworth, William, 116B,
    145n52; "Lines Composed
    upon Westminster Bridge,"
    167–68n138; *Lyrical Ballads*,
    4; *The Prelude*, 181n240; on
    Sadler's Wells, 173n182
workhouses, 155–56n61
Wren, Christopher (architect), 46,
    165n124, 171n171, 178n211
Wykeham, William of, 96,
    194–95n350

yeomen of the guard, 42, 161n92
Young, Charles Mayne (actor), 78,
    185n273